the complete
Mushroom Hunter

This edition published in 2015 by
CRESTLINE
an imprint of Book Sales
a division of Quarto Publishing Group USA Inc.
142 West 36th Street, 4th Floor
New York, New York 10018
USA

Printed with permission of and by arrangement with Quarry Books, a member of Quarto Publishing Group USA Inc.

First published in the United States of America by
Quarry Books, a member of
Quarto Publishing Group USA Inc.
100 Cummings Center
Suite 406-L
Beverly, Massachusetts 01915-6101
Telephone: (978) 282-9590
Fax: (978) 283-2742
www.quarrybooks.com

Library of Congress Cataloging-in-Publication Data
Lincoff, Gary.
The complete mushroom hunter : an illustrated guide to finding, harvesting, and enjoying wild mushrooms / Gary Lincoff.
p. cm.
Includes index.
ISBN-13: 978-0-7858-3315-4
1. Mushrooms—Identification. I. Title.
QK617.L5245 2010
579.6'163—dc22

2010003957

10 9 8 7 6 5 4 3 2

Cover Design: Rockport Publishers
Design: bradhamdesign.com
Layout: Sylvia McArdle
Cover Images: clockwise from top left, David Work, Gary Lincoff,
        Nancy Ward, David Work

Printed in China

the complete
Mushroom Hunter
An **Illustrated Guide** to **Finding, Harvesting,** and **Enjoying Wild Mushrooms**

Deadly cort

Choice morel

Poison panther

Gary Lincoff

CONTENTS

CHAPTER 4:
Medicinal Mushrooms

CHAPTER 5:
Bringing Home the Harvest: Mushroom Recipes

APPENDIX I:
Mushroom Arts & Crafts

APPENDIX II:
Essential Guide to Major Posionous Mushrooms, Symptoms of Poisoning, and Treatment

Russula xerampelina

INTRODUCTION

ot long ago, it was possible to believe that the only edible mushroom came in a can. The common cultivated mushroom was something that was, essentially, a condiment. It could be put on pizza, served in a sauce over steak, or added with bacon bits to a spinach salad. It was a novelty food, a side dish, something for occasional use, but of no nutritional value (or so it was believed). It held no interest at all as an entrée, and was most frequently seen on dinner tables in that ubiquitous can of cream of mushroom soup.

As for medicinal mushrooms, there was penicillin: end of story. Mushrooms, even today, are still not widely accepted as useful medicinals. Although worldwide mushrooms are held in high regard, they still suffer from an undeserved image problem.

More than 1,000 kinds of wild mushrooms are sold as edible mushrooms around the world. Some markets in Italy offer more than 200 different fresh wild mushrooms. More than 100 kinds of mushrooms are now being cultivated. More than 400 kinds are medicinal and are being used by people in almost every country.

The average mushroom consumption in Japan is said to be about 3 ounces (85 g) per person per day. At a per capita consumption of mushrooms in the United States of 4 pounds (1.8 kg) per year, that's what the average Japanese person consumes in just three weeks, eating primarily cultivated mushrooms. People picking wild mushrooms can consume more than 4 pounds (1.8 kg) a week during the season.

Why Should I Gather My Own Mushrooms?

Many people who buy their own groceries need to see, feel, and smell the produce before they buy it. Buying wild mushrooms in the market offers you more variety than just buying the white button mushroom, but it can't compare with the colors and fragrances of these mushrooms in the wild. Following the guidelines outlined in this book, gathering your own mushrooms in the wild is not a risky venture threatening you or your family's health. Rather, it offers a way to enhance the flavors and textures of the meals you now make, allowing you to incorporate a number of choice edible wild mushrooms.

Mushrooms' Nutritional Benefits

Wherever we are living, we are becoming more and more concerned about what we are eating and how our food is produced and marketed. Mushroom consumption will increase as we become more aware of its benefits. What many once believed was of no food value has become central to a new lifestyle that involves choosing foods that are good for us, not just foods that taste good.

Mushrooms, whether wild or cultivated, contain medicinally beneficial polysaccharides in addition to amino acid complexes that are high in lysine. Lysine is an essential amino acid notably absent in food staples, including wheat, rice, corn, and barley. Eating mushrooms with bread or in pasta or with rice or polenta, or in a mushroom-barley soup, which is how mushrooms are eaten in much of the world, is the surest way to get the most nutritional benefit from them. In addition, mushrooms are rich in vitamins and minerals and low in fat and calories (depending on how you cook them). Besides, mushrooms are not injected with hormones or raised on bonemeal. And hunting wild mushrooms has all the advantages of being in the great outdoors, the only caveat being a little care in selecting choice edible kinds.

If you take this book along with you, a walk in the park or the local woods will no longer be simple exercise or a way to pass time. It will be an opening into a world beneath your feet and over your head that has always been there, unobserved.

Perhaps you have seen mushrooms in your neighborhood and wondered what they were, but knew no way to distinguish the edible ones from the poisonous. This book helps you recognize some of the best edible mushrooms and reliably distinguish them from any poisonous look-alikes.

Collecting chanterelles

CHAPTER 1:

Mushrooms: The What and the Who

Mushroom hunting is an activity that comes to us out of prehistoric times. The "Iceman," the man dubbed "Ötzi" whose body was found frozen in a glacier near the Austrian-Italian border, has been dated as being 5,000 years old, and he was carrying two mushrooms in a pouch. One was the birch polypore (*Piptoporus betulinus*), a common bracket fungus found on birch trees, which is believed to have been used by him medicinally against intestinal parasites or as a styptic or compress to stanch bleeding. The other, the tinder fungus (*Fomes fomentarius*), also a common bracket fungus on birch, was used as a source of tinder for lighting or maintaining a fire. Whatever other mushrooms his people might have used, that he was traveling with these two indicates a considerable knowledge of mushrooms and their uses.

Our knowledge of the use of mushrooms goes back in China more than 12,000 years, but written records go back only about 2,000 years. The Romans relished wild mushrooms and wrote about how they used them in their feasts as well as the occasions on which the reputed poisoning of emperors occurred, such as Claudius in 54 CE. Today, in Paris, Prague, and Moscow, and any number of European cities in between, during the mushroom season, many of those who drive out to the country on weekends are going to hunt mushrooms. Some leave Moscow Friday night and sleep in their cars near entrances to their favorite hunting sites to be the first ones in the woods when dawn breaks on Saturday morning. Some landowners outside of Paris have been known to slash the tires of cars with Parisian license plates parked near wooded areas: people everywhere become possessive of the mushrooms they consider their own. While it might be seen by tourists as a curious cultural activity in Prague, to the citizens of the Czech Republic, mushroom hunting is the national sport, and people flock to the summer and early autumn woods to fill baskets with wild mushrooms. It has been estimated that 40 percent of the Finnish population heads out into the woods to collect mushrooms during their short summer season.

Fly agaric (*Amanita muscaria*)

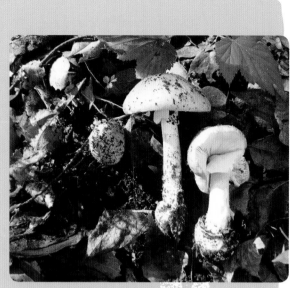

Death cap (*Amanita phalloides*)

Mushroom Poisoning and Health Hazards

In France, mushroom hunting is so popular that hospitals recognize a syndrome dubbed *les ramasseurs de Dimanche*, "the Sunday pickers." These are the people who pick mushrooms over the weekend and show up at the emergency rooms on Monday morning. Worldwide there are thousands of cases of mushroom poisoning every year, but all but a few of these are stomach upsets from eating a mushroom that is a gastrointestinal irritant, or eating a mushroom that is partially decomposed or infested with larvae, or eating too much of a good thing, or drinking too much alcohol along with a celebratory meal after a successful hunt. Every country where mushrooms are collected in the wild usually reports at least one fatality a year. With mushrooms, it could be said—with the caveat that you need to exercise caution and be attentive to details—that the only thing you have to fear is fear itself.

From time to time we read about mass poisonings, where large numbers of people eating a common meal all die from mushroom poisoning. This is almost always where people are deprived of their regular food by war or dislocation and poisonous mushrooms misidentified by the victims are consumed in large quantities and, especially, where good and timely medical care is not available. This happened not long ago in Turkey, where migrants harvesting a crop found, cooked, and consumed the death cap (*Amanita phalloides*). In another instance, a group of Czechs on vacation in the former Yugoslavia found and ate a large amount of what they took to be chanterelles. These twenty-five Czech tourists were poisoned by the jack-o'-lantern mushroom (*Omphalotus olearius*), a look-alike for the chanterelle and something that they never saw in their homeland or ever read about. They were all hospitalized for a few days because the mushroom they ate isn't deadly, just a violent gastrointestinal irritant, but they were terrified to be sickened by something they didn't know and hospitalized in a country where they couldn't speak the language.

More recently, Nicholas Evans, author of *The Horse Whisperer*, and his family, while vacationing in Scotland, picked and ate a deadly mushroom, something called *Cortinarius speciossisimus*, which they mistook for something edible, presumably chanterelles. All four suffered some degree of kidney failure and were given dialysis treatments in a local hospital.

Although there are a number of poisonous, even deadly, mushrooms in the woods, and though it is true that a single mushroom can prove to be a deadly meal, mushroom field guides, if used as intended, serve to alert and inform mushroom hunters of the dangers of mistaking poisonous look-alikes for choice edible mushrooms.

Double Standards

It wasn't so long ago that the British wouldn't eat tomatoes because they were in the same family as deadly nightshade. Carrots are in the same family as poison hemlock, and peas and cherries are in families that can cause serious human illness. We learn what we can eat and how to eat it. In much of the world there is an irrational fear that mushrooms are different, that people can't learn to tell the difference between the edible and the poisonous, and that the best defense is to reject all wild mushrooms.

There are no signs where mushrooms are sold alerting shoppers to cook their mushrooms, and most or nearly all shoppers assume that all mushrooms can be eaten raw, just like the white button mushroom. Even so, even the white button mushroom should be cooked, just as all market mushrooms should be cooked to make them all more digestible as well as to break down any toxins that heat can remove. Morels and chanterelles, for example, are somewhat poisonous raw and need to be cooked to render them safe to eat.

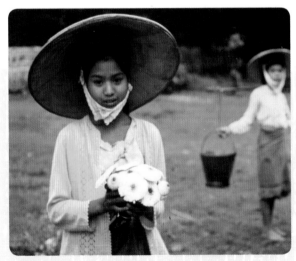

Children are not inherently afraid of mushrooms. This one is pleased to be holding an edible mushroom. Mycophobia is a cultural overreaction.

Mycophilia and Mycophobia

Some years ago, an American banker named R. Gordon Wasson and his Russian bride, Valentina Pavlovna, discovered that they differed fundamentally in how they approached something so seemingly innocuous as mushrooms. She adored them, talked to them as if they were children, and collected them for dinner. He stood back in fear and disgust at his new bride's open display of affection for wild mushrooms on their honeymoon. They researched this difference and discovered that not just individuals but whole peoples could be classified in one of two groups, the *mycophiles*, or those who love mushrooms, and the *mycophobes*, those who are fearful of them or reject them as something too poisonous to even touch. (Sometimes these two groups are referred to as *fungophiles* and *fungophobes*.) This research so intrigued Wasson and Pavlovna that they made a career of studying how different cultures use mushrooms.

Wearing gloves, disposing of mushrooms in doubled plastic bags, or disposing of any mushrooms is overkill. Warning adults is sufficient, and keeping children and pets from eating wild mushrooms is a matter of supervision.

In general, the citizens of Continental Europe are called mycophiles, while the peoples in English-speaking countries are called mycophobes. Asian countries, including China, Japan, and South Korea, are mycophilic, while countries such as India, or wherever England had colonies, are mycophobic. French Canada is mycophilic; English Canada is mycophobic. In the United States, immigrant communities of European backgrounds, such as the Italians and the Poles, are mycophilic, while the general population is mycophobic. In Mexico, where mushrooms are gathered and sold in the markets, it would seem that the people are

A General Guide to Mycophilia and Mycophobia

Mycophobic	Mycophilic
United Kingdom and Ireland	Most of Continental Europe
India, Pakistan, and other former British colonies, such as Australia and the United States	Asian countries such as China, Japan, North Korea, and South Korea, and Australian aborigines
English Canada	French Canada
General Spanish population	Catalans and Basques
Hispanic Mexico	Native peoples in Mexico
South America Spanish background	South America: Some native peoples
Africa: Most of the continent	Africa: Scattered peoples in West and East Africa

mycophiles, but that only applies to people of Indian heritage; Mexicans of Spanish heritage are mycophobic. We might think that Spain as a whole is mycophilic, as it is in Continental Europe, but Spain is really a composite of different peoples living within a nation-state. The Catalans of Barcelona and the Basques of northeastern Spain are mycophiles, while much of the rest of Spain are mycophobes.

It can appear complicated, because it's not as cut-and-dried as this dichotomy implies. Moreover, in nontraditional cultures, people are more open to change and can incorporate things such as mushrooms into their diets, things that their parents would never dream of eating. Even in traditional societies, a sudden dietary change can occur when people discover something good to eat that had long been ignored by their ancestors.

Even among mycophiles, those who love mushrooms don't love the same mushrooms. It might be an ancient saying that there's no disputing taste, but when it comes to preferences, not only is there wide disagreement among countries of mycophiles, but also within countries there is a

wide range of preferences. Some people love mushrooms that have a more meaty texture; others prefer mushrooms that are reminiscent of okra. In the same mountain forest, two groups of mycophiles could collect mushrooms side by side, though one would collect only the strongly fragrant matsutake, the other the slimy capped bolete genus *Suillus*. Neither may care for the other's mushrooms.

Are They Edible, or Are They Magic?

Of all the questions asked by people who see you picking mushrooms, after the seemingly obligatory "are they edible?" question, perhaps the most common is "Are those magic mushrooms?" There is a widespread awareness that some mushrooms (some species of *Psilocybe*) can cause hallucinations, and people who don't know one mushroom from another are curious about whether you have found magic mushrooms. Most people who love to eat mushrooms, who scour the woods for edibles, also know nothing about magic mushrooms. Those who do know about magic mushrooms have usually only read about them, and wouldn't know them if they tripped over them.

People who use magic mushrooms in traditional cultures, such as the shamans or spiritual healers in Oaxaca, Mexico, see and use them differently than do urban dwellers, who use them as a recreational drug. The shamans use them to contact a spiritual world, to connect with a power that can speak through shamans who have been "be-mushroomed." The shamans can connect people who have come to them for help with something they need, which they intuit through the mushrooms. Both groups, then, urban dwellers and shamans, use the same mushroom for very different purposes.

RUSSIAN MUSHROOM USE

In the Russian Far East, in the Kamchatka peninsula, both ethnic minorities and Russians hunt for mushrooms. The Russians are looking for edible mushrooms; the Koryaks are only looking for the fly agaric (*Amanita muscaria*). The Russians consider the fly agaric to be very poisonous. The Koryaks ignore the edible mushrooms collected by the Russians and pick, dry, barter, or buy only the fly agaric. This mushroom is the spiritual mushroom non plus ultra of all the different minority peoples of the Kamchatka peninsula. It is eaten for the powers, both physical and spiritual, that it is believed able to confer on those who consume it. Siberian shamans use the fly agaric in a poultice applied externally to wounds or infections, and internally to enable them to leave the body and "fly" over the earth, up into the heavens and down below ground, to meet long-dead ancestors. Both the Russians and the ethnic minorities, then, are mycophilic, but they differ in just about every other way.

In the Russian Far East but west and across the water from Kamchatka, there is an ethnic minority called the Nanai. They hunt mushrooms in the forest and, like the Russians, collect boletes and chanterelles, and a variety of good edibles. Unlike just about everyone else, however, they perform ritual dramas in the forest where they act out the search for mushrooms and the anxious lookout for bears. The performance concludes with leaving baskets of choice edible mushrooms placed on colorful cloths on the ground for the protective spirits in the forest.

Tatiana, Koryak shaman

Fly agaric (*Amanita muscaria*)

Nanai mushroom ceremony

Caesar's mushroom (*Amanita caesarea* group) is spread out on mats and sold alongside squash flowers.

Lobster mushroom (*Hypomyces lactifluorum*)

World Markets

If you travel and explore world markets it's hard not to notice the mushrooms for sale. In Mexico City or Veracruz, in Paris or Rome, in Tokyo or Kyoto, in Chinese cities such as Kunming and Canton (Guangzhou), mushroom displays are remarkable not just for their quantities and variety, but also for how each country or region has a distinct and different set of mushrooms for sale.

Mexico

The main produce market in Mexico City, for example, has a 20-foot (6 m)-long table piled with corn smut (*Ustilago maydis*), a fungus we only associate with diseased corn. In Mexico, and now in a few other countries, it is a delicacy, worth more than the corn itself. One way this gray to blackish growth on corn is enjoyed is stuffed in a dough wrapper and cooked as an empanada. The Caesar's mushroom (*Amanita caesarea* group) is spread out on mats and sold alongside squash flowers. Another *Amanita*, the blusher (*A. rubescens*) is also sold here. A variety of boletes (species of *Boletus*) and large coral fungi (species of *Ramaria*) are displayed, as well as the orange milk and indigo blue milk caps (*Lactarius deliciosus* and *L. indigo* groups). The lobster mushroom (*Hypomyces lactifluorum*), a parasite on another mushroom that actually improves the flavor and texture of the host, is popular in Mexican markets. It has now migrated north to a few upscale markets in the United States. More than 100 different wild mushrooms can be found in one Mexican market or another throughout the growing season. A few are even mushrooms that aren't considered edible elsewhere, including what we call poison pie (*Hebeloma*), and what is considered indigestible, the scaly vase chanterelle (*Gomphus floccosus*).

Porcini (*Boletus edulis*)

Yellow-leg chanterelle
(*C. lutescens*)

Sweet tooth or hedgehog
(*Hydnum repandum*)

Western Europe

By contrast, a market in Paris or Rome has the
cepe or porcini (*Boletus edulis*), the chanterelle
(*Cantharellus cibarius*), and, later in the season, the
yellow-leg chanterelle (*C. lutescens*), the trompette
de la mort (also called the black trumpet, *Craterellus cornucopioides*), pied de mouton (also called
sweet tooth or hedgehog, *Hydnum repandum*),
and in-season truffles. White truffles (*Tuber magnatum*), black truffles (*Tuber melanosporum*), and
summer truffles (*Tuber aestivum*) are the three
common ones in the markets, the latter being
the much cheaper and least flavorful of the three.
Then, among the differences, Paris has tons of
"champignon de Paris" (or the common cultivated
mushroom, *Agaricus bisporus*), and Rome has the
choice ovuli, the unopened buttons or egg stage of
Caesar's mushroom, *Amanita caesarea*. Many other
mushrooms are sold throughout Europe at farmers' markets and elsewhere, but these are the half
dozen or so best known and loved.

The marketing of wild mushrooms in Europe is
carefully controlled. Local mushroom inspectors
are trained and certified to be able to identify the
mushrooms that can be sold in the marketplace.
Each locality has a somewhat different list and number of wild mushrooms that it allows to be sold. The
collecting of these mushrooms in European forests
is also tightly regulated so that people are only allowed to pick on certain days of the week and only
a limited amount at any one time.

Caveat Emptor

When shopping for mushrooms in the marketplace, a little caution is in order. The mushrooms should be in good condition, that is,
not broken or flattened, or wet or smelly, but
dry and firm and robust. And, the mushrooms
cannot be eaten raw like celery or carrots,
but must be cooked to be safe to eat. Raw
or undercooked morels or chanterelles, for
example, can cause vomiting.

The mushroom names used in the marketplace are often market names that don't
reflect relationships. For example, white trumpets are really oyster mushrooms (*Pleurotus ostreatus*), not a white relative of black trumpets.
The violet chanterelle (*Gomphus clavatus*) is
not a purple relative of the yellow chanterelle
(*Cantharellus cibarius*).

Sometimes mushrooms are sold that can cause
some people a mild to severe GI upset, for
example, the Manzanita bolete (*Leccinum man-
zanitae*). Sometimes wild mushrooms are sold
and labeled as cultivated. Misidentified wild
mushrooms have also been sold in the market,
for example, blue-colored *Cortinarius* have
appeared in bins labeled "blewits." There's
always the possibility that a poisonous species
can be sold by mistake for an edible kind. If
what you buy is included in this book, use it to
compare description and photo with product.

Dongu (shiitake, *Lentinula edodes*)

Ling-zhi (reishi, *Ganoderma lucidum*)

White jelly (*Tremella fuciformis*)

China

In China, a visible difference is apparent at once. In Canton (Guangzhou), the big three market mushrooms are the wood-ear (*Auricularia polytricha*), the dongu (shiitake, *Lentinula edodes*), and the paddy straw (*Volvariella volvacea*); none of these is traditional in Mexican or European markets. Dried mushrooms that are used primarily as medicinal foods include the ling-zhi (reishi, *Ganoderma lucidum*), the white jelly (*Tremella fuciformis*), and the Caterpillar fungus (*Cordyceps sinensis*). In the restaurants in Canton and Hong Kong an odorless stinkhorn, the bamboo fungus (*Phallus rubrovolvata*), is considered a delicacy, as expensive as lobster. The Chinese even went so far as to develop and cultivate this mushroom. It is so highly esteemed that it was served to U.S. President Richard Nixon and to British Prime Minister Margaret Thatcher on the occasion of their state visits to China.

In southwestern China, in Kunming, in Yunnan province, giant termite mushrooms (*Termitomyces robustus*) are sold by the roadside, as they are in Burma (Myanmar) and elsewhere in Southeast Asia. Five other choice edible roadside market mushrooms include oysters (*Pleurotus ostreatus*), porcini (*Boletus edulis*), bloody milk caps (*Lactarius sanguifluus*), green russulas (*Russula virescens*), and a mushroom unknown in the rest of the world, a leathery-tough, clustered fan-shaped fungus called ganba-jun (*Thelephora ganba-jun*). This last is sliced sliver-thin and cooked and served like a pasta, and it is just as tender.

Japan

Of all the mushrooms available in China, only the shiitake, the reishi, and the oyster are in markets in Japan. Instead, the Japanese, who mostly consider as food only items that are understood to be medicinal, prefer the highly aromatic matsutake (*Tricholoma matsutake*); the shimeji (white or brown beech mushrooms, *Hypsizygus marmoreus*); the enoki (*Flammulina velutipes*), a mushroom lacking almost all flavor and texture; and the nameko (*Pholiota nameko*), a tiny, slimy-capped mushroom that is served in a traditional autumn season clear soup. In Japan, mushrooms are steamed, stewed, or grilled, and served with dipping sauces, ways that favor their choice edibles. When compared with what people prefer in other parts of the world, the Japanese seem to prefer gilled mushrooms to nongilled mushrooms.

Matsutake (*Tricholoma magnivelare*)

Chaga (*Inonotus obliquus*)

Caterpillar mushroom (*Cordyceps sinensis*)

United States

The U.S. marketplace is a mushroom desert in comparison to most of Europe and Asia. Only one mushroom can be found in all but a few markets, and that is the common cultivated mushroom (*Agaricus bisporus*), which comes in at least four forms: the white button mushroom, the brown button mushroom, the cremini, and the portobello. This is the same mushroom that years ago was only found in the United States sold in cans. Other mushrooms sold in U.S. markets are either sold in specialty shops or upscale groceries.

Altogether, there are more than two dozen mushrooms sold in U.S. markets, some more familiar than others. At iconic or upscale markets in the major cities, there are, in season, fresh wild morels (species of *Morchella*) as well as cultivated ones. In addition to the usual suspects—the common cultivated mushroom, cremini, and portobello—there are fresh porcini (*Boletus edulis* group), chanterelles (*Cantharellus cibarius*), hedgehogs (*Hydnum repandum*), oyster mushrooms in different colors—salmon-pink, yellow, white to gray (species of *Pleurotus*)—blue-foot (*Lepista personata*), enoki, shiitake, and beech mushrooms. Italian white and black truffles come into American markets in late autumn and early winter.

Medicinal Mushrooms

Three medicinal mushrooms that are high-end items on the world market, at least in parts of Asia, though ignored by all but a few in the rest of the world, are mushrooms that are not used as foods. These are the turkey-tail polypore (*Trametes versicolor*), the chaga (*Inonotus obliquus*), and the caterpillar mushroom (*Cordyceps sinensis*). The turkey-tail is a common decomposer on fences and wood in urban and suburban areas. Chaga is fairly common on white and yellow birch trees, and caterpillar mushrooms (species of *Cordyceps*) occur wherever there are insects: they infect the overwintering larval stage, eat through the body cavity, and when the nutrients run out, send up a spore-bearing fruiting body. The market value of these mushrooms, outside of specialty shops and online sellers, mushrooms that in China or Siberia can be more costly than truffles, is less than the cost of a candy bar.

Blue-foot (*Lepista personata*)

Nameko (*Pholiota nameko*)

Large bouquetlike mushrooms, such as maitake (hen-of-the-woods), are often found sold in the autumn in farmers' markets, as are the chicken mushroom (*Laetiporus sulphureus*) and the cauliflower mushroom (*Sparassis spathulata*). For eye-catching color, three beautiful wild mushrooms sold in some markets are the purple-capped blewits (*Lepista nuda*), the bright red to orange lobster mushroom (*Hypomyces lactifluorum*), and the almost indigo blue chanterelle (*Polyozellus multiplex*).

Mushroom Markets in Immigrant Communities

Matsutake is sold in Japanese markets. Djon-djon, a species of *Psathyrella*, used to blacken and flavor rice, is sold in Haitian markets. Every city that has a "Chinatown" has markets that sell the same half dozen mushrooms essential to the Chinese diet and health: the wood-ear, dongu (shiitake), white jelly fungus, ling-zhi (reishi), and caterpillar fungus. Some sell dried bamboo fungus (*Phallus*, a stinkhorn) or monkey head (bear's head, *Hericium*). A mushroom hunt in ethnic markets can produce a basketful of exotic edibles.

Some of these can only be collected in the wild, and there is a thriving worldwide business in the marketing of desirable mushrooms. The Italians want porcini, the Japanese want matsutake, and the Chinese want caterpillar fungus (*Cordyceps*); these are purchased abroad to sell in local markets. The Japanese purchase matsutakes from the Pacific Northwest, the Atlas Mountains in Morocco, and South Korea, all to meet local demand because their local production has declined disastrously from a century ago. Porcini and chanterelles are imported by European countries from Africa and Asia, where these mushrooms are abundant, and morels are shipped from India and Pakistan to Europe and the United States.

Because there is so much money involved, and because so few people are expert in recognizing the real McCoy, inferior species of truffles, nonporcini boletes, and fragrant but tasteless matsutakes get into our markets and restaurants. The same kind of problem exists if you are trying to recognize the difference between wild salmon and the much less expensive farm-raised salmon, or between real diamonds and fake. (Incidentally, this book shows you how to recognize the real McCoy and, once you have it, what to do with it.)

Almost all of the mushrooms seen in the world marketplace can be found in one form or another in the wild—that is, in your front yard, your backyard, your local park, or your woods. A few can even be found inside your house, in a potted plant or in a damp basement. Just as you learn your way around a market so that you can find what you want, so too can you learn to "read" your outdoor markets, your property, your parks, and your woods.

Mushroom Hunting Regions of the World

Now that we have discussed the various mushroom markets in the world, we will focus on the mushroom growing and hunting regions of the world. I highlight the following nine major regions of the world when discussing seasonal availability, especially as featured on the charts on pages 54–55, 106–107, and 128–129. Each region has unique climates, precipitation, and other factors that affect its particular mushroom season.

Region	Seasonal Availability
1. Eastern and Central North America from Canada to Mexico and through Central America (NA)	Eastern Canada south through the United States, Mexico, and Central America and west to the 100th Meridian (approximately eastern Kansas) represents a distinctive floral community of plants and mushrooms. The main variations are when the mushrooms occur (i.e. earlier in warmer climates), and how long they last.
2. Rocky Mountains of North America (RM)	The Rocky Mountains of North America is an integrated mountainous area with a summer mushroom flora.
3. California and the Pacific Northwest of North America (CAPNW)	The entire west coast of North America has a single mushroom season that goes north with the spring and south with the fall and winter. California in particular has a fall-winter season and a spring season, while the Pacific Northwest has a spring season and a fall season. (In both subregions, the summer is dry.)
4. South America (SA)	Because South America extends from the northern hemisphere into the southern, the dates for mushrooms vary widely north to south. Many of the same mushrooms occur in both places.
5. Europe (including western, central, and eastern Europe) (EUR)	Europe, from the U.K. to Russia, has a distinctive spring season and fall season.
6. Mediterranean (including southern Europe, North Africa, and parts of the Middle East) (MED)	Southern Europe, North Africa, and countries bordering on the Mediterranean Sea have a characteristic mushroom season that comes with the fall rains, and can last from October through February. Some of the mushrooms in the Mediterranean region also occur in the Mediterranean climate of southern California.
7. Southern Africa (AFR)	Southern Africa includes South Africa and all bordering countries. This region has a distinctive May to June mushroom season (same as the rainy season).
8. Asia (from India to Japan) (ASIA)	A vast area, to be sure, but many of the mushrooms in the Himalayas also occur across northern Asia to Japan. Many of the mushrooms in Southeast Asia are similar to those that occur in both Japan and eastern North America.
9. Australia and New Zealand (ANZ)	Australia and New Zealand share latitude, seasonal rains, and some similar trees and mushrooms. The mushroom season comes with the rains a month or two after New Year's and runs through April and May.

The author discussing mushrooms

CHAPTER 2:

Mushroom Hunting

From searching out mushrooms in grocery stores and farmers' markets to finding exotic kinds listed on menus in restaurants and sampling the diversity of flavors and textures available in many world cuisines, it's a small but significant step to noticing them on your front lawn and in your backyard. Once your curiosity is aroused, there's no turning back. It's on to your local parks to see what treasures can be found there. With a grocery list of what to look for, with a friend or two in tow, or along with a local mushroom club, the big move is into the deep, dark woods to bag the big game, to find morels, chanterelles, and porcini, and to come home with choice edible wild mushrooms to cook for that incredible meal that will be fondly remembered forever.

No matter where you are in any urban or suburban locale on the planet, from Fairbanks, Alaska, to Buenos Aires, Argentina, from London to Hong Kong, from Kyoto, Japan, to Christchurch, New Zealand, the mushrooms of the lawns and backyards and parks are much the same, with a few local differences. The mushrooms that inhabit lawns and wood chip mulch are cosmopolitan decomposers: any lawn anywhere is much the same as any other.

Woodland mushrooms that are decomposers are often cosmopolitan, too. Many woodland mushrooms, however, are mycorrhizal; that is, they develop a symbiotic relationship with particular trees, giving the trees needed micro-nutrients, such as nitrogen, phosphorus, and potassium, in exchange for the sugars that tree leaves make during photosynthesis. This means that as the tree diversity changes from place to place, country to country, continent to continent, so do the mushrooms that are symbiotic with those particular trees.

The New York Mycological Society on a hunt in New York City's Central Park

Lawns

A beautiful lawn is a thing homeowners have long been taught to cherish. But even in a lawn free of weeds and other imperfections, come spring lawn fungi pop up here and there. Given rainfall and mild weather, a community of lawn fungi appears throughout the temperate zones of the Northern and Southern hemispheres. A lawn in Chicago or Buenos Aires or Cape Town, will present much the same scene. There is a spring lawn flora followed by a different one in the summer, and again in the autumn. There are individual differences here and there, but there is a core of species that occurs everywhere in lawns in their season.

Early Season

By spring, the lawn mower's mushroom (*Panaeolina foenisecii*) pops up in lawns and grassy areas. Where white clover is abundant the mushrooms can be hard to see, but in pure lawn they stick up straight. Almost all the spring mushrooms in lawns are mushrooms with gills that have dark spores. The same holds for mushrooms that grow up out of horse or cow dung. Because lawns are sometimes fertilized with manure, the mushrooms that appear in pastures can pop up in some lawns. These include small inky caps (species of *Coprinus*), the dung-loving genus *Panaeolus*, and magic mushrooms (species of *Psilocybe*). (These mushrooms are mostly inedible.)

The first mushroom of summer is the dunce's cap (*Conocybe lactea*), a white-capped mushroom with a conical shape and cinnamon-colored gills, and so fragile that before noon the mushroom collapses into the grass. Along with it is a small, yellow circular-capped mushroom with brown gills, the shield agrocybe (*Agrocybe pediades*). These three mushrooms (the lawn mower's, the dunce's cap, and the shield agrocybe) are the standard-bearers of lawns just about everywhere in early spring. (These mushrooms are not edible.)

Dunce's cap (*Conocybe lactea*)

Shaggy mane (*Coprinus comatus*)

The first choice edible that appears in lawns is the shaggy mane (*Coprinus comatus*), perhaps the most cosmopolitan mushroom on the planet. Its tall cylindrical white and scaly cap with gills that turn inky black and dissolve on maturity is so distinctive in lawns that people know it everywhere. It comes up both spring and autumn, sometimes in countless numbers in the autumn, and is an example of a mushroom that fruits twice a year, just not during hot summers.

Summertime

Summer lawns often sport the fairy ring mushroom (*Marasmius oreades*), another choice edible. Some lawns show arcs and circles that are darker green than the grass around them. These are the sites where the fairy ring mushroom will fruit every summer. Year after year the ring gets larger, and rings 20 feet (6 mm) in diameter are not uncommon, with mushrooms growing all along the periphery. Sometimes there are two or more intersecting rings. The only concern for a mushroom hunter is to identify the mushroom correctly. There are several common mushrooms that produce fairy rings in grass, and at least one (the sweating mushroom, *Clitocybe dealbata*) is a poisonous look-alike for *Marasmius oreades*, and can be found growing with it in intersecting fairy rings!

Another choice edible that occurs in fairy rings or scattered in summer lawns is the pink bottom (*Agaricus campestris*), a close relative of the common cultivated mushroom (*Agaricus bisporus*). More people know the pink bottom than most other wild mushrooms because it's in lawns in front of them, and it has a white cap, a short stalk, and distinctly pink-colored gills that eventually mature and turn chocolate brown.

Fairy ring (*Marasmius oreades*)

Pink bottom (*Agaricus campestris*)

Chlorophyllum molybdites

Late Summer and Autumn

Late summer and autumn lawns and grassy areas are host to a number of mushrooms, some good edibles and some quite poisonous. Puffballs are common in lawns, and the true puffballs that produce a hole at the top of the "ball" through which spores are ejected are readily recognized. The eating stage for them, though, is when they are white and closed. Then, the true puffball, when cut in half, reveals a context that is white and unmarked. As it ages, it becomes a yellowish green inside, but the common look-alikes for puffballs will show the outline of a mushroom (in the case of a destroying angel, *Amanita virosa*), a blackish context (false puffball, *Scleroderma citrinum*), or layers of green or red colors (stinkhorn eggs, genus *Phallus* or *Mutinus*). The giant puffballs (*Calvatia gigantea* and *C. booniana*) are so large that the only thing that could be confused with them is a soccer ball. One giant puffball in good condition (firm and white throughout when cut in half) is enough to serve a crowd and have them come back asking for seconds.

A common poisonous mushroom of lawns and grassy areas in late summer and early autumn, especially after hot summers, is the green-spored lepiota (*Chlorophyllum molybdites*). It looks like a parasol or shaggy parasol mushroom (*Macrolepiota procera* or *M. rachodes*) or even like an *Agaricus*, with its white somewhat scaly cap, its straight stalk with a ring, and its gills that are white when young. As it ages the gills turn a gray-green, and the spore print is greenish. Because of the often large size of its white cap, and its conspicuous appearance in an otherwise totally green lawn, it is the most commonly seen mushroom in lawns in subtropical regions, but it can occur in fairy rings farther north. Although it is said to be safe to eat if boiled first, when it is just sautéed, as most people prepare mushrooms, it causes severe stomach upset.

The best of the autumn lawn and grassy area mushrooms is the horse mushroom (*Agaricus arvensis*). It often occurs in fairy rings, and it has large white caps, brown gills, and a stalk with a ring on it, and the odor of the gills is distinctly fragrant, like anise or almond extract. The odor is an essential component of its identification because there are other species of *Agaricus* that could be mistaken for it, but they have either no distinctive odor or a smell of iodine or creosote. The cut base of the stalk of the poisonous ones is bright yellow.

Common Psathyrella (*Psathyrella candolleana*)

Mica cap (*Coprinus micaceus*)

Backyards

Backyards, whether groomed or not, usually have trees and shrubs, and there's often wood chip mulch placed around the trees and shrubs to keep down weed growth. Wood, whether as a tree, a stump, or mulch, is a great substrate for all those mushrooms that feast by decomposing wood. Even before the first mushroom comes up in a lawn, stumps and the base of trees sport clusters of inky cap mushrooms like *Coprinus micaceus*. These often dense masses of light brown conical caps quickly turn into an inky mess and disappear, but they are often the first of the year's mushrooms.

Unless the oyster mushroom (*Pleurotus ostreatus*) appears first. The oyster is a year-round mushroom and is resiliant in climate extremes. It can fruit during thaws in January and reappear every month if conditions support it. The oyster grows on trees, fallen logs, and stumps. It's the same mushroom that is sold in the markets and, if fresh and firm, can be the equal of any wild or cultivated mushroom.

Oyster mushroom (*Pleurotus ostreatus*)

Spring Agrocybe (*Agrocybe dura* complex)

Deadly galerina on wood (*Galerina autumnalist*)

Wine cap (*Stropharia rugoso-annulata*)

Wood Chip Mulch

The three most common spring mushrooms in wood chip mulch are the ever-present spring Agrocybe (*Agrocybe dura* complex), the ubiquitous and fragile *Psathyrella candolleana*, and the tasty edible, wine cap (*Stropharia rugoso-annulata*). Gathered young, when the caps have barely opened, wine caps are a good spring edible. The wine cap is grown commercially in France. Look in wood chip mulch for these distinctively large, burgundy to pale tan, cracked caps, with gray-purple gills and a cog wheel–like ring on the thick stalks. It's possible to harvest 10 to 30 pounds (4.5 to 13.6 kg) of wine caps in a cool, wet spring.

One mushroom that cannot go unnoticed in spring wood mulch is a stinkhorn (*Phallus rubicundus*). If the breeze is blowing your way, you know it's there before you see it: its odor is unmistakable, unless it's mistaken for a different stinkhorn. This orange- to reddish-capped, phallic-shaped mushroom is so common in wood mulch, and so picturesque, that its appearance in city parks stops tourists in their tracks.

As spring turns to summer, and summer to autumn, wood chip mulch shows changes that reflect the seasons, but nothing compares with the appearance of the magic mushrooms in the autumn. The

Stinky squid stinkhorn
(*Pseudocolus fusiformis*)

Wine cap
(*Stropharia rugoso-annulata*)

Deadly galerina (*Galerina autumnalist*) on wood

Bird's nest (*Crucibulum leave*)

Stinkhorn (*Phallus rubicundus*)

Deadly galerina (*Galerina autumnalist*) on wood

common blue-staining *Psilocybe* (*Psilocybe cyanescens*) seems to be omnipresent in autumn to late autumn mulch sites, the cooler weather often prompting a bumper crop.

Fall is also the time that the deadly galerina starts appearing on wood—in backyards, in urban and suburban parks, and in woods, wherever there are decaying logs—throughout the northern hemisphere, from North America and across Europe and Asia. In mountainous country, where fall can mean heavy snow, the deadly galerina appears in the summer. In places where there's a Mediterranean climate, with late fall rains, the deadly galerina appears after these rains, often well into winter. It can even be seen, despite its scientific name, *Galerina autumnalis*, during morel hunts in the spring.

Whenever and wherever it appears, it is the poster child of the LBM (little brown mushroom), and this is the best reason why dark-spored gilled mushrooms should not be eaten, especially by beginners.

Chicken (*Laetiporus sulphureus*)

White chicken (*Laetiporus cincinnatus*)

Maitake (hen-of-the-woods, *Grifola frondosa*)

Backyard Trees

Backyard hardwood trees from spring into the autumn can produce shelves of the choice chicken mushroom (*Laetiporus sulphureus*) and clusters of the white chicken mushroom (*Laetiporus cincinnatus*) at the base of trees. At the base of oaks in some autumn woods, giant bouquets of maitake mushrooms (hen-of-the-woods, *Grifola frondosa*) can be harvested year after year from the same tree. Some years people who look just for this mushroom, often retired people who walk about city and suburban parks with a stick in one hand and a large paper bag in the other, can find dozens of "hens," or "sheep heads," as they are called in some places. These mushrooms can be so large that the excess must be preserved, and people will freeze some, or dry it for winter soups and stews, or pickle the caps for appetizers.

Summer and autumn fruitings of the jack-o'-lantern mushroom (*Omphalotus illudens*) are common, and lead to one of the cited causes of mushroom poisoning. The jack-o'-lantern is often mistaken for the choice edible chanterelle. Because the jack-o'-lantern is so conspicuous, so orange, and growing in often large clusters on wood, at the base of trees, or in grass on buried wood, it is collected by people who don't know how to tell a chanterelle except by its color, and even here they're not the same. Like other gastrointestinal irritants, the jack-o'-lantern causes a one- to two-day bout of cramps, vomiting, and diarrhea, something that is more than enough to turn even die-hard mushroom lovers off mushrooms for life.

The autumn mushroom that is Public Enemy Number One among tree arborists is the honey mushroom (*Armillaria mellea*). It's the mushroom that causes more damage than any other to people's trees, and there's hardly a yard that does not have honey mushroom growing in it. The honey mushroom grows as a clone and can put up genetically identical fruitings over a wide area, even where buildings and roadways come in between. That not every tree in your front or backyard sports fruitings of the honey mushroom doesn't mean it isn't present vegetatively. Also, not every fruiting is from a clone that is necessarily parasitic; some behave like saprophytes, decomposing dead wood rather than infecting healthy wood. But the arborist and homeowner's concern is just one piece of the honey mushroom pie. The other is that it is a choice edible mushroom, and one that has people driving around local parks to fill up the trunks of their cars with clusters of young honeys to take home to make into sauces for pasta, or into ketchup, or to be canned for the winter. Ironically, the most dangerous thing about eating honey mushrooms is the risk of botulism from improper canning.

There are also honey mushroom look-alikes, including the deadly galerina, which is generally much smaller, grows on fallen logs rather than standing trees, grows singly to scattered rather than in clusters, and has a brown spore print rather than a white one.

Another common look-alike that grows at the base of hardwood trees is the big laughing gym (*Gymnopilus spectabilis*). It is intensely bitter and is not likely to be mistaken for honey mushrooms, and even cooking doesn't change its bitterness. But it does grow in clusters, can be large, is yellow to orange, has an orange to orange-brown ring on the stalk, and has orange gills that produce an orange-brown spore print (unlike the honey mushroom's white spore print). Eating the big laughing gym, either by mistaking it for the honey mushroom or by consuming it intentionally for its psychedelic properties, gives you, after an initial symptom-free half hour or so, a two- to three-hour period of intermittent laughter, often brought about by nothing more than an unexpected sound or by trying to focus on something, anything at all. The top three most cosmopolitan of these "backyard" mushrooms occur worldwide, in all nine regions highlighted on page 19. These are the shaggy mane (*Coprinus comatus*), meadow mushroom (or pink bottom, *Agaricus campestris*), and the white dunce cap (*Conocybe lactea*).

Jack-o'-lantern (*Omphalotus illudens*)

Honey (*Armillaria mellea* complex)

Big laughing gym (*Gymnopilus spectabilis*)

BEFORE YOU START

Gear

For local parks, you need no special footwear, no insect repellent, no whistle or compass, no emergency rations in case you get lost, nothing but a sharp eye, a folding pocket knife, a roll of waxed paper or paper bags, and any nonplastic collecting container, and you're good to go.

Know Local Laws

Oh, and one more thing. Assume that there may be laws regarding the picking of mushrooms in public parks, with heavy fines if you're caught. In some areas there are regulations prohibiting the picking of mushrooms on public lands. There is a no-pick policy in most national parks. National forests are a different matter, sometimes requiring a permit and limiting the amount collected, and picking on private land requires the permission of the landowner. When in doubt, ask before you collect and avoid an unpleasant and possibly costly encounter.

A Local Park Mushroom Hunt

Before venturing off into the deep dark woods, and after walking about grocery stores looking for mushrooms, and observing lawn and backyard mushrooms, it's best next to go to a local park. The surroundings are familiar; the walkways are usually paved; the mushrooms, though not as numerous or diverse as you find in the woods, are easier to learn; and there are usually no hordes of mosquitoes, dangerous snakes, lurking bears, or wild cats to contend with. And you can concentrate on looking for mushrooms without fear of getting lost, slipping into a swamp, or falling off a cliff.

Once in a park, you'll discover that urban and suburban parks have the same lawn, wood chip mulch, and tree mushrooms that front and backyards do. Even the trees are often the same, and the mushrooms that come up under the trees—that is, on the ground but associated with tree roots—are also often the same. These mushrooms, called mycorrhizal mushrooms because they form a symbiotic association with the root ends of certain trees, are distinctly different from basic decomposers in grass or wood chip mulch.

There is a community of these mycorrhizal mushrooms that occurs with hardwood trees and a different one that occurs with conifers. There are only a few kinds of trees that these particular mushrooms grow under, and once you learn what oaks, beech, and birch look like, and what pine, spruce, fir, Douglas fir, and larch look like, you know most of the trees that host mycorrhizal mushrooms. The mushrooms that are symbiotic with these trees, and that come up under them in people's yards and in parks as well as woods, are a distinctive group that includes species in the gilled mushroom genera *Amanita*, *Lactarius*, *Russula*, *Cortinarius*, *Inocybe*, and *Tricholoma*.

Some of these are good edibles, such as some species of *Lactarius* or *Russula* or the matsutakes. Some of these contain poisonous, even deadly poisonous mushrooms, including species in the genera *Amanita* and *Inocybe*. The best nongilled genera include the chanterelles (genus *Cantharellus*) and the boletes (genera *Boletus* and related groups). It doesn't take a beginner long to realize that among wild mushrooms, the nongilled kinds present fewer problems in identification and edibility. The gilled mushrooms—even though these are well known mushrooms and any outing to collect mushrooms is likely to procure more gilled mushrooms than anything else—are not the first mushrooms you should try to learn. This is especially so given how many nongilled mushrooms are about, how good the best ones can be, and how relatively little risk is run by making a mistake with the nongilled mushrooms.

Where to look

Morels, for example, can be found in many parks, but people who want morels want lots of them, not just a token amount. Come spring these folks drive up into the mountains, to burn sites, flat-land elm woods, apple orchards, and sycamore bottomlands. The more enterprising get a pH meter and check the soil for a high pH reading. Acid soils are not conducive to morel growth, but limestone areas are, and maps showing geological formations can be helpful in choosing a site to hunt morels. (For extensive information on morels, refer to pages 56–65.)

Contact a local mushroom club in your area. Hunting with others is more fun than hunting alone, it's safer, and you can benefit from the collective experience of the group.

Fish milk cap (*Lactarius volemus*)

Corrugated milk cap (*Lacterius corrugis*)

Hygrophorus milk cap (*Lactarius hygrophoroides*)

The northern flying squirrel, a nocturnal animal, glides down from trees to alight on underground truffles that it can detect from afar. Its diet can be largely composed of truffles and trufflelike mushrooms, and just its presence in an area can tell us that there are several, perhaps as many as twenty, different truffles growing underground that cannot otherwise be detected. One solution here is to go out at night wearing headlamps, spot the flying squirrels in the trees, and wait and watch where they glide onto the ground to unearth a truffle.

Chanterelles can be found in summer under oaks, which is also the best time to find delicious fish milk caps (*Lactarius volemus*), which are called "bradleys" in some regions, or one of its close equally choice look-alikes. The boletes, but not the king bolete, come up all summer and autumn under oaks and conifers, and even the large cauliflower mushroom, just like the giant puffball, is no stranger to public parks. Although there are any number of mushrooms that do not seem to occur in urban and suburban parks, or that are rarely abundant, there is more than enough for most people.

For example, in New York City's iconic Central Park, there are more than 300 different kinds of mushrooms, and at least twenty of these are choice to very good edibles that come up in quantities to satisfy the lucky few who hunt for them. With its lawns, wood chip mulch, and wooded areas, it has what most other parks have, including largely the same mushrooms.

A Walk on the Wild Side: The Big Bad Woods

Part of the pleasure of a mushroom hunt is the walk in the woods, the search in what feels like a trackless forest for something thought to be rare and precious. Here, trails replace paved pathways, and trees that fall across the trails have to be climbed over or got around. Wearing good walking or hiking shoes is essential. Wearing long pants and long-sleeved shirts is a good idea to avoid scrapes and insect bites. Some people even tuck their pant legs into their socks to prevent insects or ticks from climbing up their legs.

Trails, when they are blazed by markers on trees every so many yards, can be lost sight of, especially where trails are just worn paths often obscured in the autumn by a covering of fallen leaves. Dry footing can be scarce where wet areas abound, and these trails can be messy or slippery. Daylight can be deceptive in a forest and night can come on all too quickly. Finding your way out of a dark wood, especially if you're alone, can test the best of us. The Hansel and Gretel story is just a story, but it is based on real fears—the fear of getting lost in the forest, and the fear of something there that can harm you.

Mushroom hunters do get lost from time to time, and occasionally there are accidents, tripping, slipping, getting hurt. It's a good idea to have a cell phone (if it works in the woods). It's a good idea to carry a day pack with a few first-aid items, with some emergency rations just in case (I always like knowing that I have food in my pack even though I rarely need it). Whatever you do, don't eat the good edible mushrooms you are collecting raw.

Mushrooms can be highly indigestible unless well cooked. Getting an upset stomach in the woods will only compound an already difficult situation. It's also a good idea to carry rain gear, a flashlight (that works), and an emergency all-weather blanket (a tiny package that expands when opened). You may never need any of these things, but you never know: better to be safe than sorry.

In addition, there are thorny plants that can tear your clothes, and animals, such as snakes and bears, and insects too small to see. Mosquitoes in some areas, and ticks in others, can cause diseases that, though treatable, are best avoided by using permethrin-based sprays. Although rattlesnakes (United States) and vipers (Europe) can be deadly, people are sometimes the worst threat you face in the woods. During hunting season there are so many game hunters in the woods that wearing something bright orange is only common sense, as is making human sounds, such as talking, singing, and whistling. There are, in some places, other people who are also picking mushrooms or engaging in some kind of illegal activity that it would be better not to confront, and there are, in some places, government officials who will insist you pay a fee to collect, or who will issue you a summons for collecting either too much or in a prohibited place. Mostly, however, in the woods there is just you and the mushrooms, and your job is to find them and bring them back "alive."

Collecting Equipment

In the storybook forest no amount of care can prevent disaster, but in a real world forest good footwear is essential, not just to keep your footing, but to do so while carrying a basket full of mushrooms. What you take so much care collecting you don't want spilled on the ground because you tripped or stumbled. Choose a basket that has a broad bottom and, if it doesn't close, at least one that is deep enough to contain what you plan on collecting. Carrying a roll of waxed paper to wrap your collections in, or paper lunch bags to put them in to keep them separate from one another, helps prevent damage or loss on the trail: if you trip and the mushrooms spill out, if they are wrapped in separate waxed paper containers they will not break apart on hitting the ground, and they can be gathered up and put back in the basket intact. It will also allow the mushrooms, once you are home, to be examined again, to be certain that everything collected is edible. If any prove on home inspection to be poisonous, having kept the collections separate in the basket reduces the risk that a poisoning could occur. Broken pieces of a poisonous mushroom can mix in with an edible one.

Clothing

- A hat. Wear something that can double as a container to hold mushrooms or one giant or fragile mushroom.

- A vest with lots of pockets. This is essential for your field guide, knife, hand lens, notebook, note cards, pens and pencils, etc.

- Long-sleeved shirt. This will prevent you from being easy prey for mosquitoes, etc., a major distraction from hunting mushrooms!

- Long pants that do not get easily wet or that dry quickly. Do not wear blue jeans in the woods. Where biting or stinging insects or infected ticks are prevalent, use a spray and tuck your pants into your socks.

- Shoes that are broken in and comfortable, preferably with a nonslip sole. Do not wear flip-flops, rubber clogs, or open-toed shoes.

- During hunting season remember to wear bright clothing and to talk, sing, or whistle. Mushroom hunters wearing dark clothing and moving quietly can be mistaken for game prey.

- A soft brush to clean debris from collected mushrooms.

- A bottle of water (as there is very little safe potable water in the woods).

Necessary Gear

- Repellent for clothes and skin. Pants can be sprayed or dusted with anti-tick compounds. Skin can be protected with a variety of products.

- Sunscreen. Being in the woods is not being entirely out of the sun. Besides, getting into and out of the woods can involve walking in the open.

- Foul-weather gear. Bring a rain slicker or, if it's late autumn, something warm to wear just in case you're in the woods longer than you intend.

- A compass and a whistle. Make sure you know how to use a compass. Test your whistle before going into the woods to make sure it is effective.

Mushroom Hunting Equipment

- **A FIELD GUIDE.** If you find something you want to collect, a field guide can be consulted on the spot. A good one can tell you what features to look for and what poisonous look-alikes to be aware of, and photos and descriptions can help you compare what you found with what a field guide shows.

- **A BASKET.** Any flat-bottomed container will do, but it should be one that can be carried comfortably, and not too large or too small: experience will determine the right size for the woods you're in. In public parks, or places where mushroom hunting is frowned upon, such as cemeteries, it's best not to carry a basket. Carry something like a paper (flat-bottomed) shopping bag that won't advertise your mushroom hunting.

- **A KNIFE** (Swiss army or folding style). Do not bring a kitchen knife. The knife is necessary to dig up the complete mushroom. If you are collecting a gilled mushroom you need to know whether there is anything underground that could help you identify the mushroom. Digging up the mushroom does not prevent more mushrooms from growing. There is no good reason not to dig up the mushroom you want to identify. Once identified, use the knife to cut off the base of the stem so that the soil doesn't get into the container with the otherwise clean mushrooms.

Note: When collecting gilled mushrooms, always bring home a couple that are intact, that is, with the stem base still on; that way, you can retain all the features you'll need to see to identify your mushroom correctly.

- **A HAND LENS OR MAGNIFYING GLASS.** It's useful to have something that is 5x or 10x. Nothing fancy. Just something that lets you see features on a mushroom that you otherwise might miss, features mentioned in field guides.

- **A LIGHTWEIGHT CAMERA.** A point-and-shoot digital allows you to record what the mushroom looks like when you find it. Later, it can be used to show you just where the mushroom was growing or what color it was when found. (Many mushroom caps fade before you return home. Accurate identification depends on knowing what color the cap was when first found.)

- **NOTE CARDS AND PEN AND PENCIL.** When you find a mushroom that interests you, write a few notes about it right there, not later. Jot down what it's growing on or under what tree it's growing, whether it's single or clustered, what color the cap is, and what other features you notice, such as a ring on the stem or a distinctive smell. Put this note card with the mushroom in a piece of waxed paper that you enclose the mushroom in (or in a paper bag). A card can also be used to set up spore prints in the field. The cap can be placed gill-side down on a white card, and then wrapped in a waxed bag or waxed paper to hold it in place. Soon after returning from the field the spore print can be examined for a detectable color to assist in the ID process.

- **WAXED PAPER OR PAPER BAGS.** Do not use plastic: mushrooms sweat in plastic and deteriorate quickly. Place mushrooms on a sheet of waxed paper, fold over, and twist both ends, creating a little package that protects the mushrooms in your basket. Paper lunch bags work well also; just fold over the top of the bag to keep it closed.

- **A BRUSH.** This is useful in cleaning dirt and bits of leaves and debris off the collected mushrooms. A small paintbrush or an old-fashioned shaving brush is perfect. Too stiff a brush can break off or obscure essential identifying characteristics.

- **A STICK** to carry along in the woods is helpful for some people. Sticks (5 feet [1.5 m] long or so) can assist you in walking and climbing and help you find mushrooms by pushing aside fallen leaves.

A basket full of choice edible many-colored mushrooms can be filled in no time.

Porcini (*Boletus edulis*)

Collecting chanterelles

Rules of the Road

There are some simple rules of the "road" when mushroom hunting in the woods: always go into the woods with a group, never wander off alone, and always maintain voice contact with others. Many mushroom clubs go out on scheduled hunts every weekend during the mushroom season, and it is easy to find the location and schedule of a club near you on the Internet. Otherwise, it is much better to go with a friend or two than to go into the woods alone. It is very easy to become disoriented and lost when you are in pursuit of wild mushrooms. You forget where you are when you are focused on the ground, or you are following the trail of choice edible mushrooms. You look up and don't remember where you came from, just that you are somewhere in the middle of the woods. If you are alone, a whistle might help more than yelling, but someone has to be there to hear it. If you go with a friend, and even if you get absorbed in conversation and get lost looking for mushrooms, two heads are often better than one in getting out of the woods, and to help keep you from losing yours.

Stepping Out: Where the Wild Things Are

Walking through a wooded area, a place not groomed or managed by park rangers, can provide delights that no backyard or city park can possibly offer.

MIXED HARDWOOD FOREST. Walking through a summer hemlock and mixed hardwood forest, for example, provides not only shade and relief from the summer heat but also views of a green world, a world of mossy banks and dark green trees. A basket full of choice edible many-colored mushrooms can be filled in no time. And, sitting like jewels, yellow chanterelles, orange hedgehogs, and bright red waxy caps glow in the beds of green moss. Boletes of all kinds are underfoot, and a few are even the king bolete, the porcini (*Boletus edulis*). The rest are a mixed assortment of boletes, some of which are good edibles. Then there all the various gilled mushrooms, white, pink, yellow, orange, brown, and purple ones, including poisonous *Amanitas*, beautiful but not edible *Cortinarius*, and endless numbers of brittle caps, russulas, and many types of milk caps. The best edible milk cap—the fish milk cap, and its equally choice edible look-alikes—are here, and in no time a basket is full of dinner fare.

AUTUMN DECIDUOUS. A walk through an autumn deciduous woods offers too many mushrooms to collect and identify. It's much simpler to focus on a few good edibles and just look at the others. For example, the hen-of-the-woods comes up at the base of large oak trees. This choice edible is a clustered polypore that can fill a mushroom basket in no time. Find more than two or three and the problem becomes how to get it all out of the woods. Looking up instead of down, the conspicuous white bear's head tooth fungus can be found growing on several trees during a day's walk in the woods. The problem here is not identifying the mushroom, but in how to get it down intact. This is usually done by prodding and loosening the large mushroom with a stick and having someone catch it when it falls. Or, if birches are present, an area that resembles a charcoal-blackened burned site on the trunk could be the famous chaga mushroom, something now in high demand among those using mushrooms as medicinals.

SPRUCE AND ASPEN. A walk, hike, or climb through a mountain spruce and aspen woods in summer can give you all the choice edibles in a single day that are only available other places over a much longer season. A mountain summer season is very short and quite dramatic. There are often too many good edibles to pick. A basket of giant corals and hawk's wings can be filled in minutes. King boletes can weigh a pound each, and it only takes a few minutes to fill a basket. Chanterelles are smaller than those found elsewhere, but the forest floor can be carpeted with them, and a crawl up a hillside can produce basketsful of perfect chanterelles. Summer is also the season in some mountain regions for matsutakes, both the white and the brown. While looking for these, you are likely to come across a run of shrimp russulas, which is the mushroom of choice for making a seafood pasta without seafood. The mushroom basket is overflowing but the good edibles keep appearing. You've got to make room for the sweet coral club growing in the moss in the spruce woods; this is the perfect dessert mushroom to finish off a wild mushroom feast.

Rocky Mountain mushroom basket

Chanterelles
(*Cantharellus cibarius*)

Brown Matsutake
(*Tricholoma caligatum*)

Sweet coral club
(*Clavariadelphus truncatus*)

Pacific Northwest white chanterelles (*Cantharellus subalbidus*)

California chanterelle (*Cantharellus californicus*)

California Candy caps (*Lactarius rubidus*)

AUTUMN CONIFERS. In autumn conifer forests, you'll find baskets full of different choice edibles such as chanterelles, hedgehogs, bear's heads, and matsutakes. There are different kinds of chanterelles, called rainbows and whites, as well as king boletes and bear's heads, and more than likely you'll run into commercial collectors hunting for matsutake, a mushroom that fetches an astronomically high price in Japan.

WARM WINTER CLIMES. Overwinter, in warm climates, the mushroom season is in high gear, and people are out gathering chanterelles (such as *Cantharellus californicus*) in the oak woods and looking for candy caps (*Lactarius rubidus*) under oak and pine. Candy caps can smell like maple syrup, and large quantities can be brought out of the woods and turned into savory dishes, a sweet quiche, and candy cap cookies and pies.

EXTREME MUSHROOMS: GOING FOR THE GOLD

Mushroom hunting is not a contact sport—at least it's not supposed to be. Whether done alone or with a few friends or family or with a mushroom club, mushroom hunting is a day in the woods, a romantic throwback to a hunter-gatherer life-style, and a walk about looking for something good for dinner, preferably something not otherwise available.

There are those among us, primarily in parts of Europe, who are collecting mushrooms in large quantities for winter use. There are also those who are hunting mushrooms for survival, not to eat themselves but to sell, either for additional income or for their only income, and these people can be found in almost every country that has mushrooms that can be sold locally or exported. Some of these people hunt mushrooms the way some people hunt animals. They track their quarry into the most inhospitable terrain, set up camp to wait for their prey if the mushrooms haven't appeared yet, and are prepared to haul out of the wilderness whatever they are able to bag.

Reports of wildfires get people studying maps to see how to enter burned areas the following spring for the expected mother lode of morels. The morels that pop up the following spring are more than people can harvest. A few people will travel deep into a wilderness, flying in if there's no other way and, like gold prospectors from another time, will set up camp and pan for mushrooms. What they collect they dry on the spot, and thousands of pounds of dried morels come out of wilderness sites every year.

By the time the morel season is over in the late spring, the spring king boletes (*porcini*) are starting to appear. People race off to collect truckloads of these boletes. Come summer in the high mountains, caravans are driving up to areas above 10,000 feet (3,000 m) to find porcinis, the dense,

hard-fleshed mushroom with not an insect hole to be seen. These are as good as it gets, if, at this elevation, you can breathe and pick mushrooms at the same time. Some of these are no sooner picked than shipped out to restaurants and suppliers across the country.

Avid hunters drive up and down the mountain roads in vans they hope to fill with chanterelles and matsutakes. People using GPS and cell phones co-ordinate their strategies to bring as many of these choice edibles as possible out of the vast mountain forests, before others get them first.

Wherever one forays these days, if it's mushroom season, you are more and more likely to run into mushroom buyers. This is an international miscellany of people scouring the earth to buy wild mushrooms on the cheap to export to countries that will pay dearly for them. In British Columbia it could be people collecting matsutake to ship to Japan. Others show up in the Atlas Mountains of Morocco to buy truckloads of matsutakes growing under cedars. In Madagascar it's chanterelles, in southern Africa it's king boletes, and in northern India it's morels, all being shipped to Europe. There's even a growing market demanding desert truffles from Israel and Namibia, and a hot market for summer truffles from China and Tibet.

But these are stories about people turning mushrooms into money, not what we're about here—turning mushrooms into memorable meals.

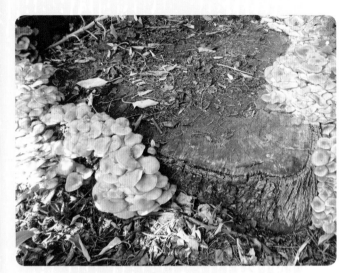

Honey mushroom
(*Armillaria mellea* complex)

Eating Like There's No Tomorrow

Imagine baskets full of mushrooms, large baskets full of big mushrooms, baskets full of morels, chanterelles, and king boletes, and not just a few mushrooms, but more than any one person could eat at one time. If a tree is covered with chicken mushrooms, there is a desire to collect every one, even if it means 50 pounds (23 kg). The satisfaction in finding the mother lode of any choice edible mushroom is too hard to resist. For whatever deep-seated reason, we crave abundance, something more than we can ever use. And the most common cause of mushroom poisoning is eating too many good edible mushrooms at one time! It's not a life-threatening event, to be sure, just a sense of unease, a queasiness, a heaviness, nausea, and then a release of sorts, and you're as good as new, if a little worn out.

Going out to find some mushrooms for dinner and finding too many and eating them like there's no tomorrow is not the best way to get to tomorrow. Sometimes it's just too many mushrooms. Sometimes it's the butter—too much of it. Sometimes it's the alcohol consumed with the meal, or the combination of too many mushrooms and too much alcohol. Sometimes, and probably more frequently than anyone knows, it's an upset brought about because a choice edible mushroom has been eaten when it, or some part of it, is no longer fit to consume, any more than are wilted greens in a grocery store. After blaming the mushrooms and blaming yourself, consider the possibility that what brought you down was a virus, something having nothing to do with either the mushroom or the way you ate them. More often than you'd imagine, people have been on the verge of getting flulike symptoms, then eat wild mushrooms, get sick, and blame the mushroom!

Cleaning Mushrooms for Cooking

Brush leaves and debris off the mushroom and cut the stem base (preferably before you get home) to keep soil from falling into the mushroom cap. It's a good idea to cut mushrooms in half lengthwise to make sure the mushrooms are free of bugs and undamaged inside and out. Mushrooms are not usually washed unless forest debris adheres to them. If you do wash them, pat them dry with paper towels to absorb as much water as possible.

Consider wearing kitchen gloves when cleaning mushrooms; sometimes certain mushrooms can stain hands.

Contending with Excess

What do you do with 5 pounds (2.5 kg) of chanterelles? There's almost no waste on them, nothing to trim off, like there often is with king boletes. What you collect is what you get to eat, but how much can you eat, and what do you do with the leftovers? Some people brag that they've eaten more than a pound of cooked chanterelles, or that they've eaten so much porcini that they can't get up from the table. Some people feel the need to eat every bit of chicken mushroom they collect—at one sitting— even though it means stuffing themselves.

The same thing happens in the spring with morels, when people can't stop eating them. Even thoroughly cleaned and cooked wild mushrooms can bring on indigestion, sometimes acute, to put a mild word on a sometimes extended stay in the bathroom. Sometimes eating chicken mushrooms that have been cooked with a quarter pound of butter can give you "mushroom poisoning" that is anything but that, just time spent in the bathroom to contemplate the sin of gluttony. Although there are traditions of gorging on particular foods—think hot dog– and pie-eating contests—the only award that should be given if there ever are any mushroom-eating contests is a bottle of Pepto-Bismol.

Freezing the Surplus

The problem with finding too many choice edible mushrooms is not something about which those who never find so many can sympathize. After all, you've been out all day in the woods, in the fresh air, walking about, collecting a basketful of good edibles. You should have nothing to complain about. But there is no rest for those who have great success in the field. Now you've got kitchen counters piled high with mushrooms. There's cleaning, trimming, cutting, and cooking to do, and, for all you are not going to eat immediately, there's preserving. This can mean four skillets going simultaneously on four burners, and once cooked, the mushrooms left to cool before freezing while the

A kitchen counter lined with chanterelles

skillets are refilled with the next batch. This takes hours. (See Chapter 5 for details.)

Drying the Surplus

If you choose to dry some of your mushrooms, the mushrooms have to be cleaned and trimmed and sliced into sizes to be dried. Sometimes there are so many mushrooms to dry that there's no room to dry them all. The odor of drying mushrooms, as pleasant as it can be for a moment or two, is not necessarily an odor you want to sleep with. Like cooking mushrooms, drying them also takes hours of work. The end result—the pleasure of eating mushrooms throughout the year—may well justify the labor involved, but it is labor. It is laborious, and there's no point complaining to your friends who can't find as much as you do because you won't get any sympathy from them; you might even feel the sting of their resentment. Who knew there could ever be too much of a good thing?

CHAPTER 3:

Mushroom Identification

Above: A cauliflower mushroom; **Opposite page:** A young mycophile with chanterelles

In a newly greening spring woods peppered with morels, on a summer mountain slope carpeted with golden chanterelles, or driving past an autumn meadow and seeing a fairy ring of soccer ball–size giant puffballs—how can you know for sure that you've identified these mushrooms correctly? How can you be sure that they're edible? People who know the names of hundreds of different kinds of plants, even professional botanists, will tell you that they can't tell one mushroom from another, that they all look alike, and that just one mistake can kill you. What chance do you stand?

It is generally believed that plants, somehow, are easy to identify, but mushrooms are hard. This belief might come from the observation that plants have lots of parts to help you identify them, such as stems, leaves, flowers, and fruits, while mushrooms just have, well, the mushroom.

For those of us who know both the flowering plants and the mushrooms where we live, it's always an eye-opener to travel and find that the plants we see, whether we're in Thailand, New Zealand, California, or France, are new and strange, while the mushrooms we encounter in those places are familiar.

What we discover the more we travel and learn is that mushrooms have a finite number of field forms. These dozen or so forms, whether resembling soccer balls or underwater coral, show up in nearly every country. Although there are thousands of different kinds of mushrooms, by just choosing a dozen or so choice edibles that have few if any poisonous look-alikes, learning these, and ignoring all the rest for the time being, you'll discover that, with luck and good timing, you can find and correctly identify choice edible mushrooms just about anywhere on the planet.

To accomplish this feat, this chapter gives you the information you need to recognize the different groups of mushrooms by sight, and to learn about particularly good examples of each group that are common, conspicuous, and found everywhere you are likely to go in the world. We explore in-depth information on poisonous look-alikes and mushroom poisoning, and a look at magic mushrooms rounds out this chapter.

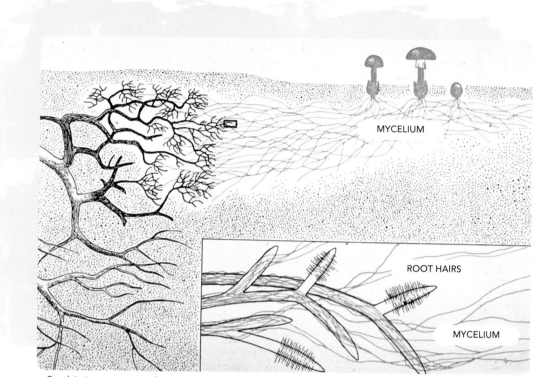

MYCELIUM

ROOT HAIRS

MYCELIUM

Symbiotic connection between mushrooms and trees (Bunji Tagawa)

What Are Fungi?

Fungi are spore-bearing microorganisms that cannot make their own food and must live as parasites on living organisms, as saprophytes or decomposers of dead organic matter, or in symbiotic relationships with plants and other organisms. In a traditional two-kingdom classification system, like the kind Charles Darwin followed, fungi were considered plants and called cryptogams, like ferns, that is, plants that had a hidden means of reproduction, as opposed to phanerogams, the seed plants, such as conifers and flowering plants, that can be readily seen to bear seeds. A five-kingdom classification of organisms recognized in the late 1960s elevated the fungi to a kingdom of their own, equal to the macroscopic kingdoms of the plants and animals, as well as the microscopic kingdom of the bacteria and the mostly microscopic kingdom of the protists (a miscellaneous group of organisms that include algae and amoebas).

What Is a Mushroom?

A mushroom is a macroscopic fruiting body of some microscopic fungi that produces and disperses the spores of these fungi. Many fungi do not produce mushrooms. Yeast, for example, are single-celled fungi. Mushrooms are just a part of the life cycle of many fungi, most of whose lives are lived as a network of microscopic filaments underground or in wood or manure. This book is about those fungi that produce mushrooms, and in particular those that produce mushrooms big enough to pick and put in a basket, and appealing enough to want to eat—if they are identified correctly as being edible. The term *toadstool* is sometimes used to refer to poisonous mushrooms, or to all mushrooms by some people. There is no scientific distinction between mushrooms and toadstools. There are edible and poisonous mushrooms as well as a great many that are not "eatable" because they are too tough, too bitter, or too small.

What Is a Mushroom Species?

A species in biology can be defined differently depending on which techniques are available for studying an organism. A biological species concept states that two organisms are members of the same species if they can be bred and the offspring are both viable and fertile. Most mushrooms have never been bred in a laboratory. Some mushrooms, those known as mycorrhizal fungi because they have a symbiotic root relationship with plants, cannot be bred independent of their plant associates. Some of these include our favorite edible mushrooms, the king boletes, chanterelles, and black trumpets.

The traditional way in which plants, animals, and mushrooms have been identified and recognized as distinct from other similar kinds is known as the morphological species concept. This bases a species on what an organism (or a population of organisms) looks like and assumes that if an organism looks different from other similar organisms it is because there is no effective interbreeding between them. Almost all our plants, animals, and mushrooms are known to us this way. Some people use an ecological species concept, which recognizes distinct species based on the particular habitats in which they occur. A mushroom thought to be a single species but found growing under conifers or oaks or in moss can be recognized in some cases as three distinct species. The most recent approach to identifying species is to use DNA sequencing techniques. This allows us to see that what seems to be a single species is often a complex of many distinctive populations that are assumed not to be interbreeding even though there doesn't appear to be any reliable and conspicuous field characteristics by which we could separate these populations into different species.

Spores being dispersed from the mushroom fruiting body of a *Calostoma*, a stalked puffball

For field purposes, for learning to recognize edible mushrooms, for example, and reliably distinguish them from any and all poisonous look-alikes, the method used is not very different from a preschool approach that teaches a child to look at a picture of six almost identical white puppies and recognize that the one with a spot is different. In other words, microscopes and DNA sequencing techniques are not necessary for you to be able to recognize the commonly collected edible mushrooms and tell them apart from their poisonous look-alikes.

WHAT IS THIS MUSHROOM CALLED?

Mushrooms have names just like animals and plants do. We use two kinds of names to refer to particular mushrooms. One kind of name is called the *common name*. There can be many common names for any given mushroom because the names used are ones that would differ by region, culture, language, and history. *Merkels*, *dry land fish*, and *sponge mushrooms* are just a few of the common names used to refer to morels. The other kind of name used for mushrooms is the *scientific name*. Like the scientific names we use for animals and plants, the names for mushrooms follow a set of rules that requires all species to be binomials, that is, composed of two words, a genus and a species epithet.

King trumpets oyster (*Pleurotus eryngii*)

The gray wolf is known as *Canis lupis*, which is thought to be a distinct species from the red wolf, *Canis rufus*. The beautiful coral-pink seaside rose is *Rosa rugosa*, a distinct species from the weedy multiflora rose, *Rosa multiflora*.

Similarly, the cultivated oyster mushroom is known as *Pleurotus ostreatus*. It is the same species as that found most commonly on wood in backyards, city parks, woods, and forests. There are different species in the genus *Pleurotus*, and some of these are hard to distinguish in the field from *P. ostreatus*.

TIP

A Rose (or Chanterelle) by Any Other Name Would Smell Just as Sweet

*Until fairly recently, mushroom names were reliably stable ways to refer to the mushrooms we find. Because so many new techniques are now being employed in studying mushrooms, the names we use for many of our most familiar mushrooms change regularly. The chanterelle (*Cantharellus cibarius*) is still a chanterelle, but it's no longer reliably known as the scientific binomial* Cantharellus cibarius. *This is understandably confusing and frustrating to many people, especially those who learned their mushroom names decades ago. It doesn't change the edibility of the mushroom.*

Can I Eat This Mushroom?

This is a risk-benefit analysis. When you decide to eat a wild mushroom that you have never eaten before, you are taking a risk. Even if the mushroom is correctly identified and is known to be edible, that doesn't mean that you, in particular, can digest it. Just as some people are allergic to peanuts or strawberries, some people can eat certain mushrooms with impunity, but other people cannot. This is sometimes referred to as an idiosyncratic reaction. You get an upset stomach, and it's over.

When you look at the diversity of wild mushrooms out there, from lawns to woods, you might think it's quite impossible to gauge your risk, but that's not true. The nongilled mushrooms, for example, except for the false morels, do not include any mushrooms, or extremely few, that have caused human fatalities. The gilled mushrooms, on the other hand, include a number of common species that can cause digestive upset, many others that can cause muscarine poisoning, and a few that cause human fatalities. Given this information, the cautious mushroom hunters will focus their attention on the less risky groups of mushrooms. Some genera of gilled mushrooms contain both edible and poisonous species. The cautious mushroom hunters will avoid these genera until experience has shown them just how to recognize the edible ones and avoid those that are poisonous. In this sense, mushrooms are not just another vegetable, like lettuce. Outside of the grocery store, where it is presumed only edible mushrooms are being sold, the mushroom hunter must be willing to learn the important differences in identification before deciding to eat unfamiliar wild mushrooms.

Anyone interested in eating wild mushrooms, and sufficiently motivated to get all the available facts beforehand, can discover that there are mushrooms thought to be edible but that are not. That is, they are not safe to eat raw (e.g., morels, chanterelles),

Mushroom Russian Roulette: Are You Game or Sane?

When it comes to eating wild mushrooms, there seems to be two kinds of people: those who choose only to eat mushrooms known to be edible and those who choose to eat mushrooms not known to be poisonous. Which kind are you?

You may assure yourself that you belong in the first group, that you would never eat a mushroom you didn't know for certain is edible. Still, when you've been out hunting mushrooms all day, and you haven't found what you've been looking for, but you do find a lot of something else, something you have reason to believe is not known to be poisonous . . . what do you do? Answer: stay out of the kitchen until you have finished reading this book!

or undercooked (e.g., honey mushrooms, blewits), or with alcohol (some inky caps). Some, including maitake and chicken mushroom, are safe for most people, but not for people taking MAO-inhibitor medications (some antidepressants, for example). A few other mushrooms are unsafe but they have been reported mistakenly as edible in some field guides (e.g., some boletes and coral fungi).

On the other hand, some mushrooms that are believed to be poisonous can be processed in a way that renders them safe to eat (e.g., some acrid species of *Lactarius* or milk caps).

Mica cap (*Coprinus micaceus*)

Mushroom Morphology

The terms we use to describe mushrooms are the terminology of morphology. The mushroom cap is referred to as the *pileus* and the stem as the *stipe*. If the mushroom has gills, they are often referred to as *lamellae*. The "ring" on the stem of some mushrooms is called an *annulus*, and it comes from the *partial veil* that covered the immature gills. The *universal veil* is the name of the egglike membrane covering the developing *Amanita* mushroom. When the mushroom rises up out of this membrane, there is often material left stuck to the mushroom cap and a cup of some kind (referred to as a *volva*), or remnants thereof, left about the base of the stem. The mushroom is the fruiting body, sometimes called a *sporocarp*, because it is the structure that bears the spores. In the soil, wood, or manure, you will find the *mycelium*, the vegetative structure of the fungus. Individual elements of this mycelial network are called *hyphae*, microscopic filaments that compose the fungus.

Mushroom Taxonomy

Mushroom taxonomy is the way in which we use mushroom morphology to recognize mushroom species. Recognizing the shaggy mane mushroom, *Coprinus comatus*, is done by assembling the various distinguishing characteristics that make it both recognizable and distinctly different from all other mushrooms, especially other species in the genus *Coprinus*, such as the mica cap (at left).

The fungi are in a kingdom of their own. The kingdom fungi, as it is generally recognized, is composed of two major groups that mushroom hunters come across. There are the ascomycetes, which include the cup fungi, the morels and their look-alikes, the true truffles, a group of fungi that cause molds, and a large number of tiny to very small fungi that most conspicuously act as plant pathogens or as part of a symbiotic relationship with algae called lichens. The great majority of fungi are ascomycetes. The term *ascomycetes* refers to the microscopic spore-bearing structures that are variously designed enclosures in which spores are developed and from which they are liberated.

The mushrooms that we collect on mushroom hunts, except for the morels and a few others, almost all belong to a different group, the basidiomycetes. These mushrooms include all the bracket fungi (the polypores), the boletes, the puffballs, the coral and tooth fungi, the jelly fungi, and all the gilled mushrooms. This group clearly represents nearly all of the mushrooms we would put in a mushroom-collecting basket. The term *basidiomycetes* refers to the microscopic spore-bearing structures that are clublike with minute external appendages in which the spores are developed and from which they are liberated.

Identifying Mushrooms Using All Our Senses

Mushroom identification is not just an activity that depends on the brain or a good memory. Mushrooms have color, odor, taste, and feel to them, as well as structure. Some people can recognize particular mushrooms by their distinctive shape or color, or by an unmistakable aroma, or by a certain sweetness or sourness or acridity in the taste, or by the feel, a dry velvety quality rather than a slippery smooth cap. Some people can identify mushrooms in place—in a given woods with all the cues that that woods offers—but not back at home once the mushrooms have been collected and separated from their natural environments.

That mushrooms have remarkably different colors and shapes is readily apparent, but noticing their distinctly different odors requires a good nose for smells and a good memory. Assuming that the mushroom is fresh and not in some stage of decay, where odors can be deceiving, let's look at a few examples of conspicuous mushroom odors.

◎ The common chanterelle smells like apricots.

◎ The shrimp russula smells like shrimp or crab.

◎ The candy cap lactarius smells like maple syrup.

◎ Matsutake has a distinctly complex odor that includes cinnamon, and is a smell remembered from childhood by many Japanese adults.

◎ Other detectable odors include anise, almond extract, coconut, cumin, garlic, butterscotch, chocolate, bleach, radish, corn silk, Mercurochrome, and rotting meat, and all these odors are important characteristics that help us identify particular mushrooms.

Daring to Taste

Tasting edible mushrooms raw is not dangerous because you are not swallowing anything, just tasting to see whether the mushroom flesh is sweet, mild, peppery, bitter, or acrid. Knowing its taste can help identify some mushrooms. Bring hard candy, mints, gum, or water on a mushroom hunt to clear the palate after a tasting. Only taste those you think are edible and that the book describes as tasting sweet or mild.

However good we are at using our various senses, we still need to confirm our hunches, especially if we hope to eat the mushroom, by trying to place the mushroom in some kind of field-based group, then to genus, and finally to species, if possible. The closer we can get to identifying the mushroom to species, the more certain we can be of our identification, the more we know about any poisonous look-alikes that could confuse us, and the more we know about the edibility of the particular group, the less reason there should be for anxiety and fear, and the less chance that we will make a disastrous mistake.

WORLDWIDE MUSHROOM FIELD GROUPS

Mushrooms are not endlessly different in appearance. There are only a dozen or so field-based shapes that mushrooms can take, whether you find them in a city park, in the Amazon, on a mountainside, or in a desert. These dozen or so field-based categories of mushrooms have recognizable species throughout North America, South America, Europe, Africa, Asia, and the Pacific—that is, worldwide. However different the languages, culinary traditions, or customs may be between populations or regions, these groups of mushrooms are consistent. Once you are familiar with the categories, you can find them wherever you live or wherever you travel. You may find they are a good way, whether or not you ever eat them, to center you in an unfamiliar country, to give you something you can recognize when everything else, whether it's the local language or the flora, seems strange and alien to you.

What follows is a synopsis of the most familiar field groups of the mushrooms. The two main groups are the nongilled mushrooms and the gilled mushrooms. The nongilled mushrooms are the safest group for beginners because nearly all the seriously poisonous mushrooms are gilled mushrooms.

Nongilled Mushrooms

MORELS AND CUP FUNGI

These mushrooms are usually small and shaped like cups, or sometimes saucers. The cup fungi are a recognizable group of mushrooms that occurs worldwide. There are some cup fungi look-alikes, such as the bird's nest fungi, that are tiny cuplike containers in which spore-filled bunches of "eggs" sit, waiting to be splashed out and dispersed by a water drop. The most important edible group of cup fungi are the morels, which consist of a hollow head of fused cups attached to a hollow stem.

TRUFFLES (AND OTHER UNDERGROUND BALL-LIKE FUNGI)

True truffles are only one kind of roundish underground mushroom, usually recognizable by their marbled interior. Truffles are easy to identify as a group but difficult to narrow to a species, and there are many more nontruffles growing underground near trees than there are truffles. Very little is known about the edibility of most underground fungi except that they seem to be edible for the various animals that are known to eat them.

CHANTERELLES AND BLACK TRUMPETS

Chanterelles and black trumpets are at first not obviously similar to each other. However, when the whole range of chanterelle and black trumpet species are examined, there is a strong sense that one shape and color merges into the other, so that looking at the extremes gives no clue to their relationship. The chanterelles, at least the common chanterelle (*Cantharellus cibarius*), appears to have "gills" under its cap. That is, there are thick-edged ridges that are forked between the cap margin and the stem, and in addition are cross-veined. This is readily apparent on the large chanterelles. The black trumpets have wrinkled undersides, but rarely except in a few species do they show any gill-like appearance.

TOOTH FUNGI: BEAR'S HEAD AND HEDGEHOGS

Mushrooms with spines or "teeth" under their caps are a distinct field group that can be recognized on sight. Although most of the genera are recognizable in the field, telling the species apart requires technical literature and microscopes. Only a few of the tooth fungi are commonly eaten, and these include the hedgehog (*Hydnum repandum*) and the various species of *Hericium*. Other tooth fungi are leathery tough or bitter. Some of these are important dye fungi, but nothing fit for the table.

CORAL FUNGI: SWEET CORAL CLUBS AND CAULIFLOWERS

What is true of the tooth fungi is doubly true for the coral fungi, all the mushrooms that look like underwater coral in the woods. The species are often so difficult to determine that only specialists will put in the time and effort. Coral fungi range in shape from a cluster of unbranched, wormlike stalks to huge multibranched underwater coral-like growths, and they range in color from white to purple to bright red to many shades of yellow and orange. Only two examples are given here because the others are too unknowable to recommend for food, even though some are eaten by people in some parts of the United States, Europe, and Asia.

BOLETES

The boletes are mushrooms that grow on the ground and have fleshy caps, with a spongelike underside attached to a fleshy stem. Boletes grow with forest trees such as conifers and particular hardwoods, including oak, beech, and birch. Field identification to the genera of boletes is not difficult, although learning individual species can be time-consuming. Very few boletes are known to cause stomach upset, and these can be learned and avoided. The boletes are the safest of the groups of large, fleshy mushrooms that can be gathered for food, except as noted, without knowing the identity of every species.

POLYPORES: CHICKEN MUSHROOM AND HEN-OF-THE-WOODS

Polypores are like boletes, with a spongelike surface under their caps, but many or most are stemless and occur as brackets or shelves on wood rather than on the ground. All but a few are either woody or leathery tough. A few are choice edibles because they can be abundant, and they are large, meaty, and flavorful.

GIANT PUFFBALLS (AND OTHER ABOVE-GROUND BALL-LIKE FUNGI)

There are puffball-like mushrooms, including false puffballs, stinkhorn "eggs," and destroying angel buttons. Giant puffballs come in two sizes: a softball—11 to 12 inches (28 to 30 cm)—and a soccer ball—26 to 27 inches (68 to 70 cm). No mushroom the size and shape of a soccer ball or larger can be anything but a giant puffball. If solid fleshed and pure white inside, it is the only puffball that can be recommended for beginning mushroom hunters.

MOLD FUNGI: LOBSTER MUSHROOM

There are many mold fungi covering everything from houses to plants to other fungi. The best of the lot, a choice edible mushroom, is a single species of a mold that parasitizes a white gilled mushroom, a *Lactarius* or a *Russula*. Only the orange to orange-red mold fungus, *Hypomyces lactifluorum*, is thought to be unquestionably safe to collect and eat. Even upscale food stores stock it on their shelves, and it is known commercially as the lobster mushroom.

JELLY FUNGI: WOOD-EAR

There is a small group of gelatinous fungi, called jelly fungi, that occurs everywhere. A few of these in Asia are considered to be crucial to one's well-being, and two of these, the wood-ear and the white jelly fungus, are cultivated and sold in markets wherever there is a Chinese community. Jelly fungi are mostly small, either jellylike and bubbly or leafy and rubbery, and do not break or crack when handled.

Corrugated milk cap
(*Lactarius corrugis*)

Oyster mushroom
(*Pleurotus ostreatus*)

Salmon-pink spore print of
Pluteus cervinus

Gilled Mushrooms

Gilled mushrooms can be found everywhere in the world where it is not too dry for their caps to open and disperse their spores. That is, you wouldn't look for gilled mushrooms in deserts any more than you'd expect to find gilled mushrooms in city parks or nearby woods if there's been a prolonged drought. Gilled mushrooms can be found from the Alaskan tundra to the southern tip of South America, more in north and south temperate zones, but also throughout the tropics around the world.

The gilled mushrooms are various and diverse, extremely abundant at times, and exasperatingly difficult to identify to species most of the time. Still, there are a number of popular edibles among the thousands of gilled mushrooms in our woods, but I am restricting our choices here to a half dozen or so of the best edibles and the most commonly collected and readily recognizable of them all.

Despite the fact that our most familiar mushroom is the gilled button mushroom (*Agaricus bisporus*) and that people around the world collect and eat some of the gilled mushrooms, this is not a group easily differentiated by beginners. Mistakes can be easily made and some of them can lead to poisonings, even fatalities. To avoid any unpleasant consequences, be especially cautious in identifying gilled mushrooms. What you overlook or don't know can kill you.

The nongilled edible mushrooms can be described briefly by field group, that is, by what they look like in the field, and misidentifications made within a given group, with appropriate caution taken where indicated, are not life-threatening mistakes. Edible gilled mushrooms have no such margin of error. The edible gilled mushrooms and their poisonous look-alikes can be so similar that a mistake can be deadly. For this reason, rather than describing the field groups of the gilled mushrooms, that is, their genera, these mushrooms will be described only as particular species. Because edible and poisonous species are often in the same genus of gilled mushrooms, knowing the genus is no guide to safe eating. You must know the species you intend to eat, and you must know its poisonous look-alikes, or you are taking an unreasonable risk with your health and well-being.

MAKING SPORE PRINTS FOR IDENTIFICATION

The gilled mushrooms can be divided up in a number of convenient ways. The most reliable way is to make a spore print first. Removing the cap from the stem and placing it gillside down on a white note card, and leaving it overnight (preferably with a glass or bowl over it to maintain the humidity), will give you a ready means to begin the identification of a gilled mushroom. The spore print can be (1) white (to somewhat yellow or ochre), (2) pink (meaning salmon-pinkish brown), (3) a brown ranging from yellow-brown to gray-brown to rusty brown to chocolate brown, (4) a purple-brown to almost purple-black, and (5) black. There is also one gilled mushroom with a green spore print, at least one with a lilac-gray spore print, and one (or a group) with a pinkish tan spore print, but these are exceptions. Most mushrooms in the woods will produce either a white or a brown spore print. With the spore print and the various structures observed on the mushroom, you can begin to identify the mushroom using any of several guides available in books or on websites. This book is not a general guide to identifying all kinds of mushrooms, but a guide to identifying the best of the edible mushrooms.

Why make spore prints of gilled mushrooms? The gill color is often not a good indication of the spore print color. Immature gills on many mushrooms are white to off-white. Even the mature gills of many mushrooms are a color other than the spore print. Usually, when the mushroom cap is expanded and thought to be mature, the color of the gills will become the color of the mature spores. Unfortunately, this is not always the case.

EXAMPLES:
- The gill color of the young green-spored lepiota (*Chlorophyllum molybdites*), a very poisonous mushroom, is white to off-white, while the mature gills and spore print are gray-green to green.
- The gills of the young meadow mushroom (*Agaricus campestris*), a good edible mushroom, is bright pink, while the mature gills and spore print are chocolate brown.
- The gills of an immature deadly galerina (*Galerina autumnalis*) can be a pale yellow, while the spore print is rusty brown.
- The gills of young and poisonous *Entoloma* species can be white, while the spore print is salmon-pink.

CULTIVATED AND WILD
Cultivated mushrooms can sometimes look very different from the wild form of the same mushroom. Oyster mushrooms, for example, can be grown to look more like white trumpets (similar in gross appearance to black trumpets) than to flat-capped, stemless oyster mushrooms. Similarly, the enoki is a smooth white, small-capped, long, thin-stemmed mushroom that in the wild is an orange-capped mushroom with a relatively short, densely hairy stem. The difference in their appearances lies in the conditions under which they are grown. Using a "field" guide to identify cultivated store mushrooms can be frustrating.

There are many other edible wild mushrooms in lawns, backyards, parks, woods, and forests, but these are the best and the safest ones. Becoming familiar with all of the variations in all of these can take years of hunting, gathering, comparing mushrooms with descriptions and illustrations, and testing them for their edible and digestible qualities.

See the chart on pages 54–55 for comparisons of selected edible, gilled mushrooms and their poisonous look-alikes. The chart references these mushrooms by four major criteria: habitat, spore print color, gill attachment, and veils.

The habitat can be on wood or on the ground. If the latter, then the habitat might be grass or buried wood, or associated with forest trees (trees typically within 20 feet [6 m]). Spore print color can be white, pink-salmon, some shade of brown, purple-brown, or black. (One mushroom, the blewit, has a pinkish tan spore print, distinct from either white or pink.) Gill attachment can be free (from the stem), attached (to the stem), or decurrent (running somewhat down the stem).

FIELD CHARACTERISTICS
Veils refer to two structures. The partial veil covers the immature gills and, on the expansion of the cap, breaks and typically hangs as a ring or skirt on the upper stem; sometimes this veil is cobweblike and just leaves faint hairlike marks on the upper stem. The universal veil is a membrane that encloses the entire undeveloped mushroom in some genera, such as *Amanita*. It ruptures as the mushroom grows up, and leaves either remnant patches on the cap or a sacklike cup or remnants about the base of the stem, or both.

With the exception of the spore print, all of these characteristics are readily observable in the field. A spore print can be made on a note card in the field, and then carried home, by which time the spores may have dropped, revealing the spore print color of the mushroom.

Seasonal Guide to Edible Nongilled Mushrooms

Mushroom seasons and growing location for the edible nongilled mushroom groups are presented here. For definitions of the nine major regions of the world listed here, see page 19. Consult local or regional mushroom guides to pinpoint precise growing seasons.

Mushroom	1. NA	2. RM	3. CAPNW	4. SA
MORELS (*Morchella* spp.)	in old apple orchards, near dead elms, Apr–May	under poplars and conifers, Apr–May, but into July at higher elevations	under hardwoods and conifers, esp. after fires, Apr but into late spring in higher elevations	under Austrocedrus and southern beech, Oct–Dec
TRUFFLES (*Tuber* spp.) **AND RELATIVES**	under oaks, pecans or conifers, July–Dec	under conifers, summer	under conifers, Jan–June, Oct–Feb	N/A
CHANTERELLES (*Cantharellus cibarius complex*)	under oaks and pines, summer	under spruce, summer	under live oaks, Oct–Apr; conifers, autumn	N/A
BLACK TRUMPETS (*Craterellus cornucopioides*)	under hardwoods, summer–autumn	N/A	under hardwoods, Jan–Apr	N/A
SWEET CORAL CLUBS (*Clavariadelphus truncates*)	under conifers, late summer–autumn	under conifers, summer	under conifers, Oct–Feb	N/A
CAULIFLOWER MUSHROOMS (*Sparassis* spp.)	on the ground in woods, summer and autumn	N/A	at base of conifers, Nov–Feb	N/A
BEAR'S HEAD (*Hericium* spp.)	on hardwood trees, autumn	on hardwood trees (aspen), summer	hardwoods and conifers, Oct–Feb	N/A
HEDGEHOG (*Hydnum repandum*)	under conifers, summer and autumn	under conifers, summer	under conifers, autumn; Jan–Apr	N/A
CHICKEN MUSHROOM (*Laetiporus* spp.)	on hardwood trees, summer and autumn	N/A	on hardwoods, Aug–Oct; on conifers, autumn	on hardwood trees, Feb–Apr
HEN OF THE WOODS (*Grifola frondosa*)	at base of oaks, autumn	N/A	not reported	N/A
KING BOLETE (*Boletus edulis complex*)	under hardwoods and conifers, June and Aug–Oct	under conifers (spruce), summer	under pines and hardwoods, Oct–Jan, June	N/A
GIANT PUFFBALL (*Calvatia gigantea complex*)	in grassy areas, late summer–autumn	in grassy areas, summer	in grassy areas, Jan–June	in grassy areas, April
WOOD-EAR (*Auricularia* spp.)	on hardwoods and conifers, summer and autumn	on hardwoods and conifers, summer	on hardwoods and conifers, Oct–Jan	on hardwoods, Feb–June
LOBSTER MUSHROOM (*Hypomyces lactifluorum*)	on *Russula brevipes*, under oaks and conifers, late summer–autumn	on *Russula brevipes*, under conifers, summer	on *Russula brevipes*, under oaks and conifers, autumn	N/A

N/A= not reported or not yet found
1. (NA) Eastern and Central North America from Canada to Mexico and through Central America
2. (RM) Rocky Mountains of North America
3. (CAPNW) California and the Pacific Northwest of North America
4. (SA) South America

5. (EUR) Europe (including western, central, and eastern Europe)
6. (MED) Mediterranean (including southern Europe, North Africa, and parts of the Middle East)
7. (AFR) Southern Africa
8. (ASIA) Asia (from India to Japan)
9. (ANZ) Australia and New Zealand

5. EUR	6. MED	7. AFR	8. ASIA	9. ANZ
sandy soils, orchards, burn sites, March–May	in sandy soils, spring	in gardens, mulch sites, Oct–Nov	under hardwoods, spring	in relatively high pH pumice soils, Sept–Oct
under oaks and hazels, Nov–Jan	under hardwoods and pines, Apr–Nov	in sandy soil near Acacias, Apr–June	under oaks and conifers, early winter	native: Jan–May; introduced: June–Sept
under hardwoods and conifers, autumn	under oaks and pines, late autumn	under indigenous trees, Apr–June	under hardwoods, autumn	on the ground in woods, Apr–Jun
under beech and oak, summer and autumn	under hardwoods, autumn	N/A	under hardwoods, autumn	N/A
under conifers, autumn	under conifers, autumn	N/A	N/A	N/A
at base of pines, autumn	at or near base of pines, autumn	N/A	at base of trees, late summer–autumn	N/A
on hardwood trees, autumn	on hardwood trees, autumn	N/A	on hardwood trees, autumn	on hardwood trees, Apr–May
under hardwoods and conifers, autumn	under hardwoods and conifers, autumn	N/A	under conifers, autumn	under hardwood trees, Apr–June
on hardwood trees, summer–autumn	on hardwood trees, autumn	on hardwood trees, Mar–May	on hardwoods, autumn	N/A
at base of hardwood trees, autumn	not reported	not reported	at base of oaks, autumn	at base of tree, Apr
under hardwoods and conifers, autumn	under hardwoods and conifers, autumn	under introduced oaks and pines, Dec–June	under hardwoods and conifers, autumn	N/A
in grassy area, summer–autumn	in grassy areas, autumn	in grassy areas, Mar–May	in grassy areas, summer–autumn	in grassy areas, pastures, Mar–May, Aug–Nov
on hardwoods, summer and autumn	on hardwoods, autumn	N/A	on hardwoods, summer and autumn	on hardwoods, Mar–May
N/A	N/A	N/A	N/A	N/A

Four yellow morels that were picked near the same apple tree. Note the differences in shape and color.

Morels

Many natural occurrences are harbingers of spring: the first shoot of color that appears when the trees are still bare, new growth that promises spring is just around the corner. For mushroom enthusiasts, the first sign of spring is the morel. The morel reassures us that life, color, and leafiness are returning. Edible, delicious morels reappear like clockwork every spring—along with the crocus in the garden, the first robin in the yard, and fresh asparagus in the market—and are one of the best eating mushrooms on the planet.

By early spring, emails are flying across the Internet among mushroom hunters: "Have you seen any morels yet?" Photos of morel collections—on the ground, in baskets, on car hoods, in skillets, and on dinner plates—are posted online on social networking websites (such as Facebook) and mushroom club websites as the season progresses. The "blacks" are up. There is a quickening after a long winter, a drive to get out and about in the still bare woods, a rising excitement, an anticipation of a great harvest, a need that can only be satisfied by finding that poster child of spring: the morel mushroom.

Elusive Locations, Varied Names

The morel is the one mushroom for which people actually count how many they find and make every effort not to disclose to anyone else where they find them. A few actually auction off their sites if they move out of town, or leave them as gifts in their wills; others would rather carry the secret of their morel sites to their graves. Morel hunting is not for the kindhearted, the absentminded, or the slow of foot, and the prize brings with it an incomparable satisfaction.

Morels are called many different things in different places. *Morel* is the market name, and that known and used most commonly. Morels are also called merkels, Molly moochers, or dry land fish, because the halved morel can resemble a cooked fish. Usually, though, hunters in the field just talk about the "blacks" and the "yellows."

The scientific names are as various as the common names. The yellow morel is a complex, as is the black. Scientific names for the yellows, which might be several species, include *Morchella esculenta* (yellow in color), *Morchella deliciosa* (more white in color), and *Morchella crassipes* (often 12 inches [30 cm] high).

A gray-colored morel occurs under eastern tulip poplar trees and is sometimes considered a distinct species. Scientific names for the blacks include *Morchella angusticeps*, *Morchella conica*, and *Morchella elata*. The differences among them are not as clear as their unique names might suggest.

Yellow morel in the woods

Black Morels and Yellow Morels

COMMON NAMES:
Morels, merkels, Molly moochers, dry land fish

SCIENTIFIC NAMES:
Black Morels: *Morchella angusticeps*, *Morchella conica*, *Morchella elata*, and others (species differences not yet resolved)

Yellow Morels: *Morchella crassipes*, *Morchella deliciosa*, *Morchella esculenta* (species differences not yet resolved)

FIELD DESCRIPTION:
- Grows on the ground, singly or scattered; (yellows) under hardwood trees, in old apple orchards; (blacks) under ash and sycamore, and under conifers and in recently burned areas.

- Reaches 3 to 6 inches (7.5 to 15 cm) or more when mature.

- Cap is cream-colored to yellowish, light brownish, brownish black, or gray, never reddish; conical, honeycombed (a cone of ridges and pits), hollow, and attached to stalk at base of cap.

- Stalk is whitish, hollow.

- Field differences between blacks and yellows: the ribs on the black morels are darker than the pits.

LOOK-ALIKES:
The poisonous look-alike group is called the false morels, species of the genus *Gyromitra*. When cut in half lengthwise, morels are hollow. *Gyromitras* that are typically brownish red or reddish brown are chambered or stuffed.

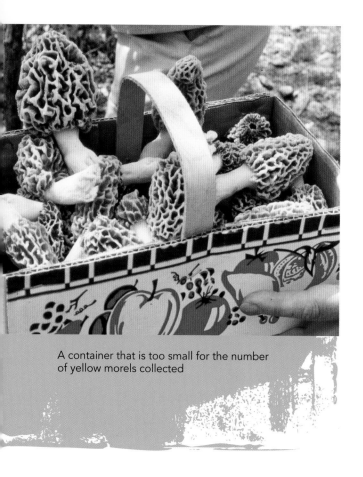

A container that is too small for the number of yellow morels collected

Seasonality

Black morels come up as early as March in the United States and Europe, and sometimes into June in northern areas and higher elevations (such as the Canadian Rockies). Yellow morels come up two to three weeks after the black morels appear. There can be overlap in some places at some times. Yellow morels fruit through May, and into early June in northern regions.

WHERE THE TREES ARE

In certain regions, morels are found by locating particular trees. It might be old apple orchards, a wood of tulip poplar trees, ash trees, or dead or dying elms. In lowland, wetland, areas with cotton-woods or sycamore trees can be very productive, especially for the early black morels.

The common denominator appears to be the soil pH. The higher the pH, and thus the more alkaline the soil, the more likely it is that morels will be found in the area. Knowing an area has heavy limestone (North America) or calcareous (Europe) deposits is all you need to know to determine where to start hunting for morels. Alkalinity in soil varies by region.

Morel Season

Morels occur throughout the Northern and Southern Hemisphere temperate zones. There are two criteria that are usually present when and where morels show up: the spring season and alkaline soil. In March through May in the Northern Hemisphere (September and October in the Southern Hemisphere), morels are among the first signs of spring. The local plants or birds that are conspicuous at the same time will differ from region to region, but if it's spring, the morels are as regular as taxes.

TIP

What are referred to as limestone soils in the United States are similar to the alkaline soils in Europe called calcareous. The Jura Mountains, for example, which comprise parts of France, Germany, and Switzerland, are calcareous and are famous for their morels.

APPLE ORCHARDS

Apple orchards are traditionally limed to produce good crops, and a limed soil has a high pH—a good reason to look for morels in old apple orchards. A downside of apple orchards, however, is the possibility that they may been sprayed with lead arsenate, a compound that does not degrade in the soil and that can, possibly, be present in apple orchard morels. Nevertheless, there have been no confirmed poisonings of people who pick and eat morels collected in apple orchards.

Some people have used Geologic Survey maps that were developed in the 1950s. The maps show the locations of apple orchards, a favorite place for morel hunters. Even though the areas searched in are often now housing and business tracts, the morels still come around old and forgotten apple trees. A systematic search for morels using these maps has netted some morel hunters thousands of morels a season. Envy is the expected response when you hear about harvests of this magnitude, but secrecy is part of the process, and friends who would risk their lives to save yours are still not good enough friends to share their morel sites with you.

WHERE THE TREES *WERE*

It is well known that burned forests are a good habitat for morels. Morels will come up in droves the spring following the fires. Across central and eastern Europe, from Munich to Moscow, fires are set by people hoping for a good morel harvest the following spring. A forest fire in Austria not long ago netted 45,000 pounds (40,211 kg) of morels! Late summer forest fires in the western United States provide some of the best morel collecting on the planet.

MORELS ARE WHERE YOU FIND THEM

One mushroom hunter recently found 100 morels in an olive orchard in California. She walked the paths between the plants, and she found morels coming up between the pruned branches that had been cut at the end of the previous season and left on the ground. The explanation for why morels could come up in olive orchards is likely to be the same as that for morels fruiting in apple orchards: the orchards are limed to increase the pH of the soil, and morels love to grow in alkaline soil. Similarly, forest fires produce ash, a transient alkaline layer that favors morel growth. Morels have even been found growing alongside cement paths in parks, feasting on the lime leaching out of the cement!

Cross-section of yellow morel showing hollow interior

MUSHROOM FESTIVALS IN THE UNITED STATES

In the midwestern United States, morels are so much a part of popular culture that there are festivals held every year to hunt, cook, and celebrate them. In Boyne City, Michigan, the annual morel hunt and hoopla is around mid-May. People come from all over to participate in a timed hunt: a gun goes off signaling the start, and contestants run into the woods to see who can collect the most morels in 90 minutes. Each person submits his or her bag of morels for the official count, and every morel is counted as carefully as votes in an election. One year the winner collected more than 900 morels in 90 minutes.

In Magnolia, Illinois, there is an annual morel-hunting championship. The hunt and count are just the beginning, though, because the cooking and eating are an essential part of the fun, and regional preferences in how morels should be prepared can be an eye-opener as well as a crowd-pleaser.

Morel Season: Europe and Beyond

Morels are a popular spring food in parts of Europe, but although they occur throughout Europe and northern Asia, most people see them only in the marketplace. In France, for example, morels are brought to market, and fresh French morels are expensive, but not because they are the best quality. Morels sold in the markets in France also come from Turkey, northern Africa, and northern India.

Some people consider the Turkish morels the best. Indian and Pakistani morels are usually sold dried, and because drying methods include slow drying over dung fires, there is a *je ne sais quoi* about them that some people mistakenly think is the flavor of the morel (which, incidentally, they then say has a taste that reminds them of aged ham!).

In France, as elsewhere in Europe, the main problem morel hunters face has to do with local regulations that prohibit or limit mushroom collecting. In the American Midwest, by contrast, where morels are most abundant, there are few if any restrictions on collecting them; in fact, morel festivals are promoted by local chambers of commerce.

Morel Highs and Lows

One of the best morel areas in Europe is in the Pyrenees, the limestone-rich mountain chain in southwestern France and northeastern Spain. The demand for morels in Europe, especially quality morels, far exceeds the local supply available in France, Germany, and Switzerland. Morels are imported in ever growing quantities.

In northern India, where there is a significant morel export business, as in Pakistan, the black morels come up above 8,000 feet (2,426 m)—in Himachal Pradesh, for example—while the yellow morels come up at lower elevations. As elsewhere, both favor alkaline soils, and their order of appearance follows that of morels elsewhere.

In the western Himalayas, Kashmiri forests in India, and adjacent northeastern Pakistan, limestone deposits are rich sites for morel harvesting, so much so that both countries export more than 50 tons (455,000 kg) each of dried morels for the European market.

High-quality morels, not the sometimes sandy, watery morels often available in Europe, or the sometimes smoky-flavored morels from the Himalayas, are imported from Turkey.

Interestingly, with one notable exception, morels are not eaten in India, Pakistan, or Turkey, just collected for the export trade. Madhur Jaffrey, a noted authority on Indian cuisine, reproduces in one of her books a recipe for a rice dish with morels that her mother used to make, but that seems to be the exception to the rule.

Two baskets of black morels

HUNTING AT CAMP DAVID

The last weekend in April can be a good time for a weekend camping trip just outside the gates of Camp David, the U.S. presidential retreat outside Washington, DC, in the Catoctin Mountains of Maryland. One year, a group of us walked side by side with our baskets in hand, making our way slowly toward Camp David. We must have been observed by the sentries, who could not have understood what we were doing. Had we found morels any closer to the perimeter of Camp David, we might still be trying to explain ourselves.

Half-free morel showing its cap, which is not attached at its base to the stalk

Related Species and Morel Look-Alikes:

The half-free morel (*Morchella semilibera*) appears at the same time as other morels in some regions. Its cap is not attached at its base to the stalk. Rather, it is attached halfway up the cap, giving it a skirtlike appearance. These are collected with the other morels, but are usually too thin-fleshed and flavorless to bother with if enough yellows can be found.

There are also species of *Verpa* that occur at the same time, and these have caps that are attached only at the apex of the hollow stalk. One *Verpa* (*V. conica*) has a thimblelike cap, the other (*V. bohemica*) a somewhat pitted one, but neither can be confused with the yellows or blacks because their caps are not attached at their bases to the stalks.

False morels (*Gyromitra* spp.) occur at the same time as the yellows and blacks, but they look brainlike or convoluted or saddle shaped, and not honeycombed. In addition, the false morels are not hollow when cut in half longitudinally, but visibly chambered or stuffed. False morels are usually reddish brown or brownish red, colors not found on morels. The reason for pointing this out is that some of the false morels have caused poisonings, even a few fatalities. Although some false morels are collected and highly esteemed as choice edibles, they are not mushrooms beginners should ever consider picking to eat.

The highly esteemed false morel (*Gyromitra esculenta*) of Europe is collected and eaten there by many people, and it is a popular offering in many restaurants. However, it must be very carefully prepared. Boiling the mushroom and discarding the cooking water is an essential part of the preparation. Even inhaling the vapors coming up out of the cooking pot has produced serious life-threatening poisonings. Dried false morels are thought to be safe to eat, but when it comes to eating false morels, it's better to err on the side of caution and avoid them all!

False morels, showing their brainlike fruit bodies rather than the honeycombed ones of the morels

Yellow morel above two false morels (*Gyromitra korfii* and *G. infula*)

Cross-sections of a yellow morel above two false morels: the morel is hollow while the two false morels are chambered or stuffed.

Characteristics of Morel Look-Alikes:

Mushroom	Appearance
MORELS	◉ Has a honeycombed cap (with longitudinal ribs and pits); blonde or light brown to black, sometimes gray, even off-white, attached to stem at base of cap. ◉ Mushroom is hollow in cross-section.
LOOK-ALIKE	
HALF-FREE MOREL	◉ Has a honeycombed cap (with longitudinal ribs and pits); light-brown, skirtlike, attached to stem halfway up cap. It is typically short compared to length of stem. ◉ Mushroom is hollow in cross-section.
VERPA BOHEMICA	◉ Has a honeycombed cap (with longitudinal ribs and pits); brownish, skirtlike, attached to stem at apex of stem. ◉ Mushroom is hollow in cross-section.
VERPA CONICA	◉ Has a thimble-shaped cap, brownish, smooth, skirtlike, attached to stem at apex of stem; typically short compared to length of stem. ◉ Mushroom is hollow in cross-section.
FALSE MORELS (*GYROMITRA* SPP.)	◉ Has a brainlike, convoluted, or folded drapelike cap; reddish brown, brown, sometimes yellow-brown, or darker. Caps are typically broader than length of stem, sometimes as broad as high. ◉ Stem is typically (not all species) thick and branched or ribbed. ◉ Mushroom is chambered or stuffed in cross-section.

Sautéed morels on toast

Eating Morels

Morels have been brought under cultivation, so it is now possible to find them in fine food stores everywhere. The cultivated ones are readily distinguished by their uniformity of size and appearance. Fresh cultivated morels are also expensive, and they have yet to prove to morel hunters that they have any flavor worth discussing.

With fresh morels, the rule is simple: do not eat morels raw. Moreover, if eating black morels, restrain your alcoholic intake because even cooked black morels can cause stomach upset.

Not everyone likes morels. They taste best when cooked in butter or cream sauces; in culinary traditions in which dairy is not dominant, such as Japan's, morels are not usually eaten.

Even those who love morels don't agree on the best way to prepare them. With deference to regional culinary differences, people have batter-fried morels until they resemble a light tempura; made cream of morel soup with a hint of nutmeg; and even stuffed morels with a forcemeat of seasoned veal, flaming it over with an apple brandy.

Some people love to eat fresh morels; others prefer drying them, then rehydrating them in something other than water, such as heavy cream, and then cooking them. The simplest and quickest way to prepare morels, though, is just to pan-fry them in butter and/or oil, season, and serve.

Drying Surplus Morels

Whether you have five morels or 5,000, if you have too many to eat at one time, the best solution for enjoying them all is to dry them. Dried morels develop an intense flavor; a little goes a long way. The safest drying method for long storage should include some heat, though air-drying is fine.

The simplest method for air-drying morels: Cut them in half lengthwise and lay them on paper towels. (Morels are hollow, and any insects discovered inside them can be easily removed.) Turn them a few times over the next two days so they dry evenly. Finish the drying in an open oven with the heat turned down to the lowest temperature setting. Leave in the oven for one hour (and make sure the morels are not cooking).

A more efficient means of drying mushrooms: Use an electric food dehydrator. Decent quality dehydrators are available for a reasonable price, and some come with stackable screens that accommodate mushrooms well. The halved morels can be placed on the screens and left to dry for a day or so inside the food dehydrator. They can be stored in jars (preferably clear) with tight lids. Dried morels retain their flavor for more than a decade.

A miscellany of morels: a single day's harvest

Truffles

Truffles are the food of voles and moles and flying squirrels. They are eagerly rooted up by pigs, smelled out by dogs, and found out by truffle flies that hover over them. Truffles are underground mushrooms that resemble round balls or clods of soil, and emit a complex odor that is part earth and part garlic, cheese, chocolate, spice, and something too pungent to be with in a closed room for any length of time. Truffles are also the mushroom par excellence of haute cuisine. The demand far exceeds the supply, its price is exorbitant, and, as legend has it, it's the aphrodisiac of choice for humans of a certain age and financial security.

Where the Truffles Are

Spoleto is a hill town about an hour and a half from Rome. It's famous for its summer Festival of Two Worlds, but if you are there in the late autumn, the local pizzaria offers something you won't find elsewhere: pizza topped with truffles! In Florence, restaurants add polenta with a truffle sauce to their autumn menus. In Alba and Asti, in northern Italy, there are truffle festivals where during October and November, when the Italian white truffle is being harvested, these and other truffles, including black truffles, come to market, and people travel great distances to see, smell, taste, and buy the season's best truffles. These festivals have all the exuberance of a state fair and the frenzied air of a stock exchange.

BLACK TRUFFLES

A little later, in December and January, in the Perigord region of France, the French black truffles are ripe and are being harvested and brought to market. In French towns early in the morning, often before people are even going to work, groups assemble at various locations wherever the truffle market is set up. There are sacks of black truffles and dealers. There is no hoopla, no festival, just people who come together in twos or threes, there is conversation, and notes are taken. No truffles change hands and no money changes hands. Later, the truffles are delivered and the money is paid. It is explained, perhaps accurately, as a way to prevent French tax inspectors from seeing any taxable transaction taking place.

In late autumn, European truffles start appearing in markets and high-end restaurants. The press coverage can be so pervasive that it's no wonder people think the only truffles are the French black and the Italian white, and that truffles are beyond the budget of any working American. Yet there are other European truffles, as there are truffles in Asia, Africa, and North America.

North American truffles occur in greatest diversity and abundance in the Pacific Northwest, where there are twenty species of true truffles (genus *Tuber*). Truffles can occur almost anywhere their plant hosts grow. There are at least a dozen truffles in the eastern United States, and a few are even relatively common, though difficult to find.

The summer truffle (*Tuber aestivum*) is collected in Spain, France, and Italy and can be found in some places at a tenth to a quarter of the price of French black truffle.

There are two or three species of Asian truffles that are exported to various markets. *Tuber indicum*, *Tuber himalayense*, and *Tuber sinense* all come from China. Although each has its unique characteristics, the sense of them all is that they have the color and size of the French black truffle, and at least one has the fragrance, but the flavor is either insipid or somewhat bitterish and disappointing. To conceal this, these truffles are sometimes mixed in with European truffles.

A desert truffle is collected by the San people in the Kalahari Desert of southern Africa. Some European entrepreneurs have been exporting these desert truffles from Namibia and selling them in markets in Switzerland and Germany. While not the equal of the Italian white truffle or the French black truffle, desert truffles have a texture and flavor all their own, and there is a growing demand for them.

Black Truffles and White Truffles

Oregon black truffle
(*Leucangium carthusianum*)

COMMON NAMES:
Black truffle and white truffle

SCIENTIFIC NAMES:
Black Truffles: *Tuber melanosporum* (French black truffle), *Leucangium carthusianum* (Oregon black truffle), *Tuber aestivum* (summer truffle, also marketed as the burgundy truffle), *Tuber sinensis* (Chinese truffle), *Tuber himalayensis* (Himalayan truffle). A brown truffle (*Leucangium brunneum*) occurs in the Pacific Northwest.

White Truffles: *Tuber magnatum* (Italian white truffle), *Tuber canaliculatum* (Eastern white truffle), *Tuber lyonii* (pecan truffle). The Oregon white truffle is currently recognized as two distinct truffles: the spring white truffle (*Tuber gibbosum*), which occurs from January to June, and the autumn white truffle (*Tuber oregonense*), which fruits from October to January.

Oregon white truffle
(*Tuber gibbosum*)

FIELD DESCRIPTION:
- Grows underground under hardwood trees such as oak, and under conifers, such as Douglas fir.

- Unearthed at times by animals.

- Roundish, 2 inches (5 cm) or less, up to 5 inches (12.5 cm).

- Outer surface is black, brown, reddish brown, or yellowish.

- Cross-section is distinctly marbled, showing veins.

- Odor is often intense and complex, with different truffles having a mixture of odors, including the perfume of flowers, cocoa, garlic, cheese, spices, pineapple, and fresh earth.

LOOK-ALIKES:
There are many look-alikes, but a mature cross-section will reveal the marbled context of the truffle. Lacking that character, assume what has been found is not a true truffle! (There are several field guides available and many websites to be used as resources for identifying the different kinds of truffles.)

CAUTION:
Even if the mushroom is a true truffle, it does not mean that it is a good edible. There are many described species of true truffles and there are undoubtedly truffles in the ground under our feet that have yet to be discovered or described. The edible qualities of the true truffles refer here only to those species that are well known and relatively readily available, and only when they are mature or ripe. Blacks should be black, and the veins should be white. Truffles are not for the novice to identify; check with a mushroom club in your area.

Oregon white truffle
(*Tuber gibbosum*)

Trained truffle dog

Propagating truffle-inoculated oak
seedlings

TRUFFLE ALLERGY

It was a dream trip: traveling to Italy and France during the late-autumn truffle season, getting a chance to eat truffles until they come out of our ears. And we did. Every day, sometimes twice a day, we ate truffles. We ate white truffles grated over a bowl of steaming pasta near Spoleto, Italy. We ate black truffle–coated trout in southern France. We ate truffles in salad dressing, truffles with chicken, truffled pâté. Many of us thought if this wasn't heaven, it was close enough.

Except for the one person in our group who got sick. Her symptoms included trouble breathing. The concierge in our hotel called the local hospital. Eventually, a doctor came, but she spoke only Italian and none of us could understand her or explain the problem. After an examination, she prescribed Benadryl, presumably for the relief of allergies. When we tried to tell the doctor, through a translator, that the trouble was with the truffles, that there wasn't any other possible cause that we could imagine, the doctor rose to the defense of Italy's beloved truffles. Impossible, she said, nobody gets sick eating our truffles. She was indignant that we even considered such an absurd idea.

Our traveling companion recovered but avoided truffles for the rest of the trip. All the more for the rest of us.

Truffles: Not Just for the Wealthy

For many people, truffles are just food for thought, or fantasy. They are not even thought to be mushrooms, even by people who should know better. But they are mushrooms, just mushrooms that grow underground. The French black truffle (*Tuber melanosporum*) and the Italian white truffle (*Tuber magnatum*) appear in the late autumn in some high-priced food markets and on the menus of some very expensive restaurants. A simple baked potato with black truffles or a simple pasta with white truffle shaved over the steaming bowl can have an exorbitant price. The classic truffled dish is pâté de fois gras, a black truffle–studded goose liver pâté, something more heard about than eaten. The implication is clear: truffles are for the very rich. Or so it would seem. There are more falsehoods about truffles than truths, and a little attention to detail can yield rich dividends.

Sniffing Out Truffles

There are plenty of truffles lurking in woodlands. The problem has always been the same with truffles: how to find them.

If there is one characteristic in common with choice edible truffles, it is that they are fragrant. Although there is no agreement on exactly what each smells like, there is no doubt that they have an in-your-face aroma. The reason is simple: growing underground, they cannot disperse their spores in the wind the way other mushrooms can, so they are dependent on animals, such as rodents, to find, eat, and excrete them, thereby spreading their spores.

Because truffles rarely break the surface of the ground, people in Europe used pigs to smell them out. There is a pheromone in truffles, androstenol, resembling one a boar emits to attract sows, and sows detecting this will eagerly dig into the ground to find it. The question is not whether sows think boars are hiding underground, but rather how you keep the sows from eating the truffles, which they do unless they're muzzled. Being large animals, they are also hard to handle, so dogs have been trained to find truffles. Any dog can be trained, and there are schools set up to do just this, and dogs don't eat truffles. A simple pat on the head, a little treat, and the dog will smell out the desired truffles.

Cultivating Truffles

In Europe it's not a matter of walking aimlessly through the woods waiting for the dog to detect the truffle odor. Truffles are being cultivated. However, truffles cannot be grown like the white button mushroom (*Agaricus bisporus*) because they are in a group of fungi that are known as mycorrhizal: they form a symbiotic relationship with certain trees. The trees produce sugars, which feed the truffles, and the vegetative stage of the truffles, attached to the tree roots, bring in essential nutrients, such as nitrogen and phosphorus, that the trees need to grow.

Nurseries inoculate oak and hazel seedlings with a truffle extract. These young trees are then planted in orchards where the soil is alkaline or maintained at a high pH. After seven or eight years of maturation, the ground under the trees shows what looks like burned areas. This is the sign that the truffles are being produced and are ready for harvest. A truffle tree can then produce pounds of truffles every year for decades. For a long time the French had a monopoly on their black truffles. Now, these truffles are being grown successfully elsewhere.

Eating Truffles

As exotic as truffles are, the cooking instructions for them are quite simple. Do not cook white truffles; they are best slivered or shaved over steaming hot pasta or rice. As for the blacks, the less heat the better; just heat enough to let their flavors seep into

Evolution of a New World Trend

Truffles and Europe have always gone hand in hand. In literature, in movies, in French or Italian cuisine, in the marketplace, European truffles always seem to have been the whole story. But no longer. Everyone wants in on the act. Truffles collected in Tibet and China are finding world markets, as are desert truffles from southern Africa. But it is in North America where a new truffle industry has been developing just since the 1990s. A truffle hunting club has been formed in the Pacific Northwest (The North American Truffling Society, www.natruffling.org) that has, so far, found more than 100 different kinds of truffles growing under conifers. None of these is known to be poisonous, and several are reported to be delectable edibles. There is an annual three-day winter truffle festival in Oregon (www.oregontrufflefestival.com) that offers everything you need to find them, eat them, and grow your own. Not to be outdone, Ashville, North Carolina, hosts an annual national truffle festival, and North Carolina is the home of Garland Truffles. Franklin Garland has been successfully growing the perigord truffle and others in quantity now for several years. What has been for more than a century a European monopoly has the makings for a growth industry, international in scope.

and spread through a fat-based or buttery sauce. Black truffles are perhaps best heated very lightly in a pâté or encrusted on trout or buttered toast.

Preserving Truffles

Freeze truffles or turn them into butter or paste. Truffles can be stored in the refrigerator with rice, flavoring it over time, or, if put into a bowl with eggs, their flavor will penetrate the shells.

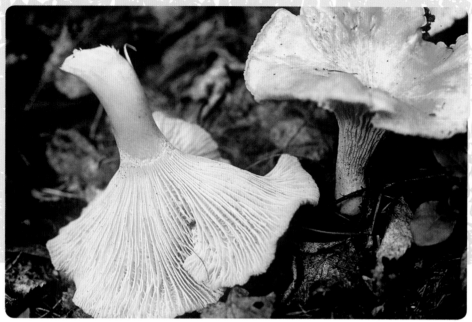

European chanterelle (*Chantharellus cibarius*)

Chanterelles

The chanterelle is one of the very few mushrooms you can identify blindfolded. Its fragrance is so distinctive that it need not be seen to be recognized. Even in spicy food its flavor comes through intact. The golden chanterelle and its charcoal gray relative, the black trumpet, are popular wherever they occur, which includes most of the Northern Hemisphere. The chanterelles and black trumpets form a distinct group of mushrooms that with just a little attention to detail can be reliably recognized in the field and separated from any potential look-alikes. Nearly everywhere where edible mushrooms are ranked, chanterelles place among the top five choice edible mushrooms. That they are easy to see, that they can be abundant, and that they are free for the picking should place them at the top of everyone's list of best edible wild mushrooms to find. Of course, the primary reason is because they taste so good.

Chanterelles in Europe

Come summer, chanterelles appear like wildflowers, their yellow to orange colors contrasting nicely with the greens and browns of the woodlands of the northern hemisphere. Their fragrance compares favorably with the sweetest flowers, and they are a choice edible, free for the picking if you can find them.

Many Europeans flock to their forests to find these summer jewels, and there are as many common names for chanterelles in Europe as there are languages: girolle, eierschwamm, pfifferlinge, leseechki. There is even a late fall chanterelle that appears in the mountains and markets of Europe, and restaurant menus across Europe offer dishes made using a mushroom that can't be grown, only found in the wild. The demand for chanterelles across Europe far outstrips the supply, and buyers ply the cities and towns of African countries, like Morocco, Madagascar and Zambia, wherever chanterelles occur, to satisfy a seemingly insatiable demand.

Their taste is so distinctive, so fruity-aromatic, that no amount of seasoning can conceal them, and they are especially loved in risotto and pasta dishes. There are even restaurants that offer a to-die-for chanterelle sorbet. Because their aroma and flavor are so unmistakable, a few chanterelles, in just a day, can flavor a bottle of Lillet, a French aperitif wine.

Chanterelles

COMMON NAMES:
Chanterelle, golden chanterelle, true chanterelle, smooth chanterelle

SCIENTIFIC NAMES:
Cantharellus cibarius, *Cantharellus lateritius* (smooth chanterelle), *Cantharellus subalbidus* (white chanterelle)

FIELD DESCRIPTION:

◉ Grows on the ground, singly or scattered, in oak woods and in various conifer woods.

◉ Reaches 2 to 3 inches (5 to 7.5 cm) high or larger.

◉ Cap is 2 to 4 inches (5 to 10 cm) across, lobed or wavy edged, yellowish.

◉ Underside of cap has gill-like folds—thick-edged, distinctly forked, and cross-veined—running down and into stalk, yellowish.

◉ Stalk is 2 to 3 inches (5 to 7.5 cm) high, up to 1 inch (2.5 cm) thick, off-white to pale yellowish.

◉ Aroma is distinctly fragrant, smelling somewhat of apricots.

LOOK-ALIKES:

The jack-o'-lantern (*Omphalotus* spp.), causes severe stomach upsets, and it occurs throughout much of southern Europe, the Mediterranean region, and North America. The jack-o'-lantern grows in big clusters at the base of trees or on stumps, or in lawns on buried wood; it has circular caps, not wavy-edged ones, and sharp-edged gills that are not forked. The color difference is between yellowish chanterelles and orange jack-o'-lanterns. There is no distinctive odor.

The false chanterelle (*Hygrophoropsis aurantiaca*) is a look-alike but it is not poisonous. It grows in clusters on wood and is usually bright orange, with forked gills and slender stalks.

An orange group of *Cortinarius* species has been mistaken for chanterelles in Europe, and most recently in the United States, with life-threatening consequences. Such mistakes can happen if only the color of the mushroom is considered, as if nothing else mattered. *Cortinarius* is a gilled mushroom, without forking gills; it has a veil covering the young gills, and the mature gills turn a rusty brown, the color of the spore print.

The clustered habit and unforked gills of the jack-o'-lantern (*Omphalotus illudens*), a poisonous look-alike

Close-up of the gill-like forked ridges of a chanterelle

California chanterelle (*Cantharellus californicus*), a humongous chanterelle

SECRET CHANTERELLES

We were driving through a forested and mountainous area about two hours away from home. I was in the back as we wound our way up and down roads looking for mushrooms. When the man sitting on the window side to the left started to shout "chanterelles," his wife elbowed him so hard that I felt it. It shut him up at once. The gesture alerted all of us that we were passing chanterelles, that she knew we were passing chanterelles, and that she didn't want us to know it. It's little things like that that show you who your friends really are.

Chanterelle Seasons

Chanterelles are the mushrooms of summer. These mushrooms grace the menus of upscale restaurants everywhere. People just hunting chanterelles for fun often cannot stop picking. One person gathered 100 pounds (45 kg) in one day and then had the unenviable task of trying to find a way to preserve them. Being a tourist, she had no kitchen of her own and chose to dry the lot of them. Not only did they not dry well, in part because it was too wet and humid the entire time, but even if she had dried them, they would have proved very disappointing upon rehydration. Sometimes there is no good solution for what to do with too many good things.

By September the chanterelle hunt is over in some regions, but it'll just be beginning in others. Large patches, even fields of chanterelles, come up under conifers. Competition can be fierce because commercial collectors are not just collecting for dinner, but often to make a living.

Regional Variations

Chanterelles in California can be two or three times the size of chanterelles in the Rocky Mountains. During winter in Northern California, live oak hillsides are regularly checked for patches of chanterelles. A hazard that comes with the territory here is poison oak, a woody shrub that grows under live oaks, and a harvest of chanterelles can sometimes cost you more than you might think. Fortunately, local people are well prepared for this, and they have a number of products that they apply to their hands before going into the woods.

Eastern smooth chanterelle
(*Cantharellus lateritius*)

The smooth chanterelle is found in the eastern United States. It looks just like a chanterelle except that where there are gill-like folds on the true chanterelle (*Cantharellus cibarius*), there is a mostly smooth surface on the smooth chanterelle (*Cantharellus lateritius*). In fact, it looks somewhat like the black trumpet except that it is orange, and was not long ago placed in *Craterellus*, the same genus with the black trumpet. It's a summer mushroom and is often found along with the true chanterelle, especially under oaks in urban and suburban parks and open oak woodlands in eastern states.

California and Eastern Species

There are two species unique to California that are of worldwide interest, and both can be humongous. One is the California chanterelle, formerly just referred to as *Cantharellus cibarius* but now known as *Cantharellus californicus*, and the white chanterelle, *Cantharellus subalbidus*. Both are easily seen and collected, and both are superb edibles.

Eating Chanterelles

The best way to prepare chanterelles is to sauté them slowly. To preserve chanterelles, first sauté and then freeze them; rehydrating dried chanterelles often results in mushrooms whose texture is too tough to enjoy.

Black Trumpets

COMMON NAMES:
Black trumpet, trompette de la mort, horn of plenty

SCIENTIFIC NAMES:
Craterellus cornucopioides, Craterellus fallax

FIELD DESCRIPTION:
- Grows on the ground, singly, but often scattered in great numbers; under beech, oaks, and other hardwoods.

- Reaches 3 inches (7.5 cm) high.

- Cap and stalk are a trumpet-, vase-, or funnel-shaped fruiting body, 1½ inches (3.8 cm) across at the top, narrowing to the base.

- Outer side of trumpet is gray to blackish.

- Black trumpets, except for color, resemble the smooth chanterelle (*Cantharellus lateritius*) and are distinctly fragrant.

LOOK-ALIKES:
There are no poisonous look-alikes. Other species of *Craterellus* are not often seen but are equally edible.

CAUTION:
Be careful to eat only fresh mushrooms. Older, somewhat decayed, usually shiny black mushrooms are often strongly perfumed but not digestible.

Black trumpets (*Craterellus cornucopioides*)

Black Trumpets

Black trumpets are among the most fragrant of all mushrooms. However, if any choice edible wild mushroom is harder to see than the morel, it's the black trumpet. It can look like withered leaves and can grow in among last year's fallen leaves, and many people miss them until they're pointed out. Then, once you see one, with patience and luck, you can find hundreds of these fragrant "horns of plenty" in the summer woods in the eastern United States, often fruiting well into September, and in the autumn and winter woods in California and Pacific Northwest.

Hunting mushrooms in Europe is much more an affair of the heart than the stomach. When hunting black trumpets in the woods of France in the late summer and autumn, you will hear them called "trompette de la mort," the trumpet of death. If your high-school French isn't as good as your mushroom-hunting skills (and if you are romantically inclined), you may hear "trompette d'amour" instead, the trumpet of love. Everyone wants to eat the good edibles, but there is a passion, nostalgia, and a *je ne sais quoi* that makes mushroom hunting much more than a simple pastime.

Black trumpets (*Craterellus cornucopioides*)

Their fragrance is perhaps best brought out in omelets or in plain grain dishes where the black trumpet can be the principal seasoning. Any meal can be enhanced using this mushroom.

Eating Black Trumpets

They are easily picked and cleaned. If growing in sandy soil they can be washed and dried with paper towels without losing flavor or texture in the process. They incorporate well into omelets and can be made in a fragrant sauce for a fish dinner.

Black trumpets are easily dried and stored in tight-fitting jars for later use, which is the best way to preserve them. Jars of dried black trumpets, when opened, are typically quite fragrant for years. They rehydrate easily and can be used in any number of dishes with good results.

VACATION HARVEST

Bicycling about in late summer, it's possible to go slowly enough past the trees to stare at the ground beneath them. With luck, a single odd thing might stick out and make you stop to get a closer look. It might be a black trumpet mushroom, a small gray to black mushroom in the shape of a ram's horn. Where there's one, as they say about a mouse in the house, there's got to be more. A crawl about the woods on hands and knees can yield quantities of black trumpets that cannot be seen from a standing position.

During one summer bicycling trip, we filled our saddlebags with black trumpets and bicycled to a nearby bed and breakfast. We bought a roll of paper towels and put them along every flat surface we could find in the room, spreading our black trumpets out to dry overnight.

Black trumpets are a very aromatic mushroom. On drying they give off a very sweet smell. We had no choice but to sleep with them as best we could. They were still damp the next morning when we packed up to leave, so we rolled them up in paper towels, placed them back in our saddlebags, and took off. We continued to find black trumpets and other mushrooms, and stayed at another B&B overnight, spreading out our mushrooms to dry as best they could. After several days of bicycling we had four bags full of drying black trumpets, which we took home to dry and store.

Bear's Head (*Hericium erinaceus*)

Tooth Fungi

"Tooth Fungi" is the name given to mushrooms that produce toothlike projections or spines instead of gills or pores. The mushrooms can have caps and stems, with downward-pointing spines beneath the caps, or the mushrooms can be stalkless, growing on wood, and bear a mass of downward-pointing spines, sometimes branched, sometimes not. The tooth fungi, as a group, is readily identifiable in the field, but only a few are worthy of culinary attention, notably the bear's head complex (species of *Hericium*) and the hedgehog or sweet tooth (*Hydnum repandum*). The bear's head is now in cultivation and is a well-known medicinal mushroom in China. Both of these are sold in fancy food markets and served in high-priced restaurants (where the bear's head is called "pom-pom").

Bear's Head (*Hericium americanum*)

Bear's Head

Wandering about urban or suburban parks in the autumn, or hiking through an autumn hardwood forest in northern Japan, Europe, or North America, if your eyes aren't glued to the ground searching for mushrooms, you might just see the bear's head adorning a variety of trees just above your head or growing along a fallen log. Sometimes it's hard to get them down intact, but once secured, you've got the "crabmeat of the woods," a mushroom whose appearance, texture, and flavor can be favorably compared with the best crabmeat available. And you just need one bear's head to provide enough for a dinner party.

The bear's head is a white mushroom composed of a base attached to the tree and a proliferation of fleshy spines that hang downward. On aging, these spines turn a yellowish color, and the quality quickly degrades.

Bear's Head

COMMON NAMES:
Bear's head, monkey head, lion's mane, pom-pom, icicle or waterfall fungus

SCIENTIFIC NAMES:
Hericium abietis, H. erinaceus, H. coralloides (H. ramosum, H. caput-ursi), H. americanum

FIELD DESCRIPTION:
- Grows attached to trees or logs; singly on a given tree or log, but there may be several in the area; hardwood trees and logs; one on conifer in the West.
- Reaches 3 to 12 inches (7.5 to 30.5 cm) or more.
- Are either roundish or elongated vertically, but not shelving or bracketlike.
- Surface is a mass of white (when fresh) downward-pointing, soft fleshy spines either unbranched or variously branched.

LOOK-ALIKES:
There are no poisonous look-alikes. The inedible northern tooth (*Climacodon septentrionale*) is tough-fleshed and appears as shelving on trees, with spines hanging down from broad, imbricated bracketlike caps.

TARGET PRACTICE, OR MUSHROOM HUNTER BEWARE

It was too good to be true. There, growing on a tree in a big city park, was a bear's head hydnum, a choice edible mushroom. Bear's head mushrooms are common on some trees in autumn woods, but always a pleasant surprise when they show up in your backyard, as it were. It was even within reach instead of way above my head, as it usually is. Still, it was small, no bigger than a baseball, so I photographed it and planned to return later in the week to gather it, hopefully after it had doubled in size. When I returned, I wondered whether anyone had seen it in the interim, whether it was even still there.

It was. And there was an arrow through the center of it. As I stood in front of the bear's head, I thought, if that arrow was just shot, the person using the bear's head for target practice might find me better sport. I didn't bother to turn around. I just moved away from it at a normal walking pace, and kept walking until it was out of sight. I never did go back to that tree, or anywhere near that tree, the rest of the autumn.

I never learned who shot my bear's head hydnum. I do often wonder what that person thought he was shooting at.

Bear's head (*Hericium americanum*)

Bear's head (*Hericium erinaceus*)

Bear's head (*Hericium erinaceus*)

NAMES AND LOCATIONS

Although there are a great many edible mushrooms and very few kinds that are seriously poisonous or life threatening, most mushrooms are just not eaten. The reason usually is that there is no particularly attractive attribute of flavor or texture that makes people want to eat these mushrooms. They can serve as bulk but little else. The mushrooms we dream about and walk through parks and woods searching for are those that have a special quality, a fragrance, a flavor, a texture that makes them stand out from the crowd. The bear's head is one of these. This is a large, fleshy, tooth or spine mushroom that grows on trees and, when cooked, has the appearance, flavor, and texture of crabmeat!

The bear's head is a complex of several species, all of which are choice edibles, that occur throughout the temperate forests of the Northern Hemisphere. It is easily cultivated and is known as pom-pom in the restaurant business. The bear's head name comes from the scientific name of a mushroom first described in Europe, *Hericium coralloides* var. *caput-ursi*. We now use that name to refer to any of several look-alike species. The lion's mane is the common name used for the medicinal preparation that is made from the cultivated *Hericium erinaceus*. Monkey head is a translation of the Chinese name of this species. Sometimes *Hericium erinaceus* is referred to as the bearded tooth (because it is unbranched), and two other branching spine look-alikes are called the bear's head (*Hericium americanum*) and the comb tooth or the icicle fungus (*Hericium coralloides* or *H. ramosum*). Out west, the waterfall tooth (*Hericium abietis*) occurs on conifers; the other *Hericium* species occur on hardwoods.

Despite its size and color it is easily overlooked, or rather underlooked. People looking for mushrooms in the autumn walk about the woods with their heads down, intently scanning the ground for something that looks different than the multicolored leaves now piling up. They walk right by and under trees bearing bear's head mushrooms. These mushrooms are often 8 feet (24 m) or more above the ground. They can be 6 to 12 inches (15 to 30.5 cm) high or more and up to 12 inches (30.5 cm) across. Finding them is the necessary first step. Getting one down intact is the next but equally important step. It sometimes takes two people to bring one down successfully. One person gets a long branch and pushes up on the bottom of the mushroom; the other person stands ready to catch it when it comes loose and falls. Failing to catch it and letting it hit the ground will cause it to break into too many pieces to try collecting. Once caught, however, and assuming it is in prime condition, a great dinner is assured.

EATING BEAR'S HEAD

The bear's head is a fleshy mushroom that can and should be pulled apart and washed carefully. It doesn't become waterlogged. You will notice the pieces bear a striking resemblance to crabmeat.

One popular way to cook this mushroom is to cut it into bite-size pieces, sauté it in butter and shallots (or garlic), season it, and just before serving, squeeze a little lemon juice on it. It will have both the appearance and the texture of crabmeat. Sometimes this mushroom will be a little bitter at first; if this is the case, parboil it first, throw away the water, and then cook as desired. The bear's head can be cooked until almost dry and then frozen for future use.

Hedgehogs

COMMON NAMES:
Hedgehog, sweet tooth, pied de mouton

SCIENTIFIC NAMES:
Hydnum repandum (formerly *Dentinum repandum*)

RELATED SPECIES:
Hydnum umbilicatum (almost as good to eat)

FIELD DESCRIPTION:
- Grows on the ground, singly or scattered; under trees, primarily conifers.
- Reaches to 4 inches (5 to 10 cm) high, 2 inches (5 cm) or more across, becoming much larger at times.
- Caps are orange or creamy but bruising yellowish orange on handling.
- Underside of cap is a covering of soft, fragile orange spines that are easily broken.
- Stalk is off-white to lightly pigmented.

LOOK-ALIKES:
There are no poisonous look-alikes. Other tooth fungi are either not orange or not fleshy-soft and fragile. Although hedgehogs and chanterelles are sometimes confused in the restaurant trade because they can be similar in color, the underside of the caps are entirely differently constructed.

CAUTION:
Be 100 percent certain of your identification and that the mushroom is firm and clean, not spongy or decaying.

Hedgehog (*Hydnum repandum*)

Hedgehog (*Hydnum repandum*), white variety

Hedgehog (or Sweet Tooth)

A casual summer walk through a mixed hemlock/hardwood forest to escape the heat and humidity can be surprisingly productive. Even the unobservant can hardly fail to notice the occasional bits of bright yellow and orange dotting the tree canopy–darkened hillsides or poking out of the moss. The yellow ones might be chanterelles and the orange the small hedgehog (or sweet tooth) mushrooms. Although they can be much larger in the autumn, and can then be found in large patches, the summer hedgehogs are often plentiful enough to transform a pedestrian dinner into a midsummer night's dream.

Hedgehog (*Hydnum repandum*)

NAMES AND LOCATIONS

The hedgehog or sweet tooth mushroom is a name given to one of several look-alike species of a tooth fungus that is often mistaken for a chanterelle. The orange colors of both can be similar, as can the size.

Because hedgehogs are European animals and do not occur in the United States, the name *sweet tooth* has been coined there for this well-known edible that is found throughout the temperate regions of the world. Both names are used in U.S. markets.

The hedgehog (*Hydnum repandum*) has a look-alike species, *H. umbilicatum*, which differs primarily by its cap being visibly indented (*umbilicate*) in the center. There are other differences, but perhaps the main one visible in the field is that the hedgehog is typically larger and more robust. Both grow under conifers or in mixed conifer/hardwood combinations.

EATING HEDGEHOGS

The hedgehog (or sweet tooth) is best sautéed in a butter or an oil-based sauce, some kind of liquid that can both moisten it and absorb its flavor. Adding ground hazelnuts or almonds will heighten its hint of nuttiness. If the hedgehogs are detectably bitter (before cooking, take a piece of cap in your mouth, chew it up, and see whether it's a tad bitter), boil them in water for a minute, throw off the water, and proceed as described above. The hedgehog can be cooked and preserved like chanterelles.

IMPASSE

One French restaurant owner wanted to show me the "chanterelles" he had just received. He dumped the contents onto the bar and it was immediately obvious to me that he had both chanterelles and hedgehogs. He insisted they were the same thing. I told him that one had gill-like folds under the cap while the other had short spines, but he said that wasn't important. I showed him that the chanterelle smelled fruity, like apricots, but that the hedgehog didn't. I told him to cook the two mushrooms separately and taste them: the chanterelle has a fruity, faintly peppery taste; the hedgehog is somewhat tangy or even nutty. He listened but had no patience for hearing that he had been buying and serving a mushroom mixture rather than just chanterelles. No harm would be done by serving this mixture because both mushrooms are good edibles, but the diners will be paying chanterelle prices for eating the less expensive hedgehog. This is not unheard of in the restaurant business, but among us mushroom hunters, who train ourselves to look for differences and to recognize the significance of such differences, this mistake, as harmless as it is, should never happen.

Hedgehog (*Hydnum repandum* complex)

Sweet coral club (*Clavariadelphus truncatus*)

Coral Fungi

Coral fungi look like underwater coral and can be very abundant and colorful mushrooms in our conifer forests, especially in the autumn and sometimes in the spring. Corals also fruit in hardwood forests but are rarely as large or attractive. There are more than 100 different kinds, but very few are identifiable to species. Their colors range from bright red to yellow, orange, orange-brown, and various shades of purple. A few are white. They range in size from 1 inch (2.5 cm) high to 12 inches (30.5 cm) or more across. Some are small but grow gregariously and abundantly on the forest floor. Some are collected for food. Some, without being identified to species, are sold to restaurants. Only a few have been reported to cause diarrhea or cramping, and none is known to be seriously poisonous. Still, because there are so many kinds of coral fungi and because so little is known about their edibility, none can be recommended here. Instead, I am presenting two easily recognized "corals" that are popular among mushroom hunters and that come into the marketplace, especially farmers' markets, in the autumn.

MUSHROOMS FOR DESSERT

Some mushrooms are not mushroomy; that is, they have a distinctive taste. Chanterelles and black trumpets are fruity, the prince agaricus tastes like marzipan, and candy caps taste like maple syrup. Sweet coral clubs taste so sweet that no one who tastes them imagines them as anything other than a dessert mushroom.

One of the pleasures of mushroom hunting is finding all the ingredients for a full-course dinner using just mushrooms, from soup to dessert. Sweet coral clubs make a perfect ending to so special a dinner.

Sweet Coral Clubs

While almost all the choice edible wild mushrooms can be found in most of the mushroom regions of the world, there are a few, such as the termite mushrooms of Asia, that are geographically limited and rarely even available outside their home territory. Sweet Coral Clubs is an example of a uniquely sweet tasting mushroom, but it has come into commercial supply as demand for it increases. Although the sweet coral club (*Clavariadelphus truncatus*) can be found widely, it's the Rocky Mountain region where it is found in quantities and where it is enjoyed as a dessert mushroom. The 3-inch (7.5 cm) -high orange clubs come up in bunches and stand out in bright contrast to the green mossy ground and the dark conifer forests. They can be spotted from a distance and are easily collected, and, best of all, there are no look-alikes in these mountains to confuse with the sweet coral club. In other areas where they occur, it's usually best to chew a bit of one of the clubs to make sure it's the sweet club: it actually tastes sweet, and there are no good-tasting look-alikes.

If the mushroom is used in soups or sautéed dishes its main contribution to mushroom gastronomy will be missed. It should be used in making a mushroom dessert. A simple one is to dip the clubs in a thin batter and fry in a light oil until golden brown. The clubs can then be drained on paper towels, dusted with confectioner's sugar, and served alone or with an accompanying dish of seasonal fruits.

Eating Sweet Coral Clubs

Cook in water, then serve with fruit; or dip in tempura batter, deep-fry, and sprinkle with orange juice and confectioners' sugar.

To preserve, cook to taste and freeze.

Sweet Coral Clubs

COMMON NAMES:
Sweet coral clubs, flat-topped coral

SCIENTIFIC NAME:
Clavariadelphus truncatus

FIELD DESCRIPTION:
- Yellow to orange fleshy clubs reach about 3 inches (7.5 cm) high and 1 inch (2.5 cm) or so thick at the top, appearing flat-topped, narrowing to the base, often in moss in conifer forests, summer and early autumn

- Has a distinctly sweet taste

LOOK-ALIKES:
Clavariadelphus pistillaris is not flat-topped but is otherwise quite similar. It is bitter to the taste and easily distinguished this way from the sweet coral club.

Cauliflower Mushrooms

COMMON NAME:
Cauliflower mushroom

SCIENTIFIC NAMES:
Sparassis spathulata (in the eastern United States),
Sparassis crispa (in the western United States)

FIELD DESCRIPTION:
- The cauliflower mushroom is large (up to 12 inches [30.5 cm] across, 12 inches [30.5 cm] or more high), rounded, with off-white to yellowish fleshy, flattened leaflike branches.

- The eastern cauliflower is stalkless and grows near the base of hardwood trees; the western cauliflower has a long rooting stalk attached to conifers.

LOOK-ALIKES:
Nothing really resembles cauliflower mushrooms except, perhaps, aging coral fungi (genus *Ramaria*). The cauliflower mushroom has flattened, almost elasticlike leafy fronds while the coral fungi are more pencil-like in shape and more fragile. A much smaller jelly fungus, *Tremella foliacea*, might be confused with the cauliflower mushroom, but the jelly fungus is truly jelly-like and rubbery, not dry and stiff.

CAUTION:
Clean carefully and thoroughly. Cook well before eating.

Eastern cauliflower (*Sparassis spathulata*)

Eastern cauliflower (*Sparassis spathulata*)

Western cauliflower (*Sparassis crispa*)

Cauliflower Mushrooms

Although common across Europe and Japan, the cauliflower mushroom's culinary home is North America, where summer and autumn people are out looking for it because it is large, it has a great texture, and it can be cooked in any number of pleasing ways. This mushroom grows on the ground and looks somewhat like an Elizabethan ruff. The cauliflower mushroom is a species of a small genus known as *Sparassis*. There are no look-alikes. The eastern *Sparassis*, now known as *S. spathulata*, can occur as early as July, though it's more common later into September in urban and suburban areas and local woods, and is unique to eastern North America. Another species, *S. crispa*, grows at the base of trees and fruits in the autumn and winter, and is unique to western North America. Both kinds of cauliflower mushroom can be quite large, with the western one sometimes being a couple of feet across. Coming up as they do, they need to be cleaned carefully of any soil, plant parts, and debris that get caught in its folds as it rises up out of the ground.

Although some mushrooms should not be washed because they'll become too waterlogged to maintain a pleasing texture, the cauliflower mushroom can and should be washed to make sure that what you cook and eat is just the mushroom. Both kinds also are best precooked or heated in water that is then discarded before preparing the mushroom for a meal. Although cauliflower mushrooms can be sautéed with success, their texture is such that they could stand in for a noodle and be used in making a cauliflower mushroom pasta. The mushrooms can be preserved by cooking and freezing.

Eating Cauliflower Mushrooms

This mushroom is best sautéed and added to mixed cooked vegetables. To preserve, sauté and freeze.

THE QUEEN OF THE FOREST

The woods can be a magical place; you are taken out of your normal environment and placed in a fairyland world of soft green moss and towering trees. So it was one day when we were hunting mushrooms and someone found a large eastern cauliflower mushroom, shaped like an Elizabethan ruff. A fellow mushroom hunter held it beneath her neck and announced to us all that she was the Queen of the Wood. Without missing a beat, someone who had found a large scaly vase chanterelle raised it to his mouth and pretended to blow it like a trumpet, calling us together for the coronation. Someone placed a large funnel-shaped mushroom on her head. Someone else, kneeling, presented the queen with a large chicken mushroom bouquet. And another person handed her a stick covered with turkey tail mushrooms as her scepter. Someone came over with a giant artist's conk, a shelf mushroom that you can write on, and offered to be her scribe. The Queen of the Wood then demanded gold from us, and we complied with all the golden chanterelles we had found. She was pleased as only a queen can be, and next ordered a feast to be held to celebrate this grand occasion—a good thing, too, because with all the destroying angels we found that day she could easily have sentenced any one or all of us to death.

King bolete, porcini (*Boletus edulis*)

California queen bolete (*Boletus regineus*)

Boletes

The mushroom known in Italy as *porcini*, in Germany as *steinpilz*, in France as the *Cèpe*, and in Russian as *belyi grib*, is the premiere edible wild mushroom of Europe, preferred even over morels and chanterelles, and much more available and affordable than truffles. While gathered in quantities in China and southern Africa, it is not adored in either place, and finds itself exported for sale elsewhere. In summer in the Rockies, in the autumn in the Northeast, and in winter in California, the king bolete is sought after, gathered, and cooked as one of the best of the wild mushrooms. This is the secret ingredient in mushroom barley soup that makes it such a memorable dish among a generation of European immigrants. The king bolete is one of the five most highly esteemed mushrooms in the world, along with morels, truffles, matsutake, and chanterelles.

Bolete Groups

There are hundreds of boletes, stalked mushrooms growing on the ground under trees, with caps that have a soft spongelike layer underneath. Some of these are good edibles, but most are of an indifferent quality. Still, many are cooked and eaten by mushroom hunters because the boletes, as a group, are one of the safest kinds of mushrooms to eat without knowing the exact species eaten, given the boletes to be avoided, which are listed in this book.

The boletes can be recognized in the field as belonging to distinctive groups. One group, now placed in the genus *Suillus*, grows under conifers and has caps that are usually slimy, a quality that allows them to withstand frost in the autumn. If the caps are not peeled or wiped clean, a meal of *Suillus* can have a laxative effect. Another group of boletes, the *Tylopilus* genus, has species, such as the bitter bolete, *T. felleus*, that looks surprisingly like the king bolete when young. If tasted, however, it is strikingly bitter, and the bitterness doesn't dissipate with cooking. Many a chef has inadvertently included one or more bitter boletes in a dish of the king bolete and ruined the meal!

California spring king bolete (*Boletus rex-veris*)

The boletes that are regarded as poisonous are in the group where the spongy layer beneath the cap is orange or red, turning blue or blackish on bruising. Some of these are edible; however, there are some species in this group that are known to be poisonous, though not life threatening. A number of boletes stain blue on bruising, an oxidizing condition that doesn't indicate anything in terms of edibility. However, there are a few of these that stain blue instantly on bruising. This is best seen by cutting the bolete in half and noting that the yellow flesh is indigo blue almost before the knife cuts through the mushroom. One of these, *Boletus sensibilis*, is known to cause stomach upset, something that can put a damper on an otherwise successful dinner party. Occasionally, you can find a bolete, such as *Boletus huronensis*, that gives no outward sign of its indigestible nature, but cooking and eating it will give you a bad night nonetheless.

This said, there are more than 100 boletes, many found in large quantities, that are edible and can be good eating if collected when young and firm. These are:

◎ **LECCINUMS:**
Often found under birch or aspen trees, and recognized by a stalk covered with blackish scabers, or hairlike scales

◎ **TWO-COLORED BOLETE:**
(*Boletus bicolor*)
East Coast of the United States

◎ **BUTTER BOLETE:**
(*Boletus appendiculatus*)
Primarily California; fruiting with autumn (November) rains

◎ **CHESTNUT BOLETE:**
(*Gyroporus castaneus*)
Primarily eastern North America

SERENDIPITOUS BOLETES

No matter how devoted a mushroom hunter you are, sometimes mushrooms just aren't on your mind. One day, we took a day trip to an art park to see giant sculptures by Isamu Naguchi and Mark DiSuvero in an outdoor setting. We no sooner walked from the car to the sculpture park than we noticed giant mushrooms coming up under the conifers that had been planted as a screen around the parking lot. Under the Norway spruce trees were many large, perfect porcini, king boletes. No one in attendance seemed to have noticed them. We tried to wait until we had viewed the sculptures before we picked them. It was hard to concentrate on any of the sculptures, though, and we were constantly looking back to see whether the mushrooms were still there.

Finally, we gave up. We hurried back to the parking lot to harvest the porcini. Driving home we passed a restaurant with an adjacent parking lot that also had a border of Norway spruce trees. We drove around the parking lot and found even more porcini. Now, come autumn, when we want porcini, we drive around looking for Norway spruce trees, which are most commonly used in landscaping.

King Boletes: Regional Variations

In California, there is now a recognized spring king that fruits in late June, as well as a king and a queen bolete that fruit in late autumn and winter. In the eastern United States, there is a king bolete that fruits under Norway spruce and a different one that fruits under Eastern hemlock, which is sometimes referred to as *Boletus clavipes*. The king bolete in Colorado, which fruits under Engelmann spruce, is different from any of these others, and may need a new scientific name, although it will continue to be called a king bolete, or even *Boletus edulis*, and be as highly esteemed whatever its scientific name becomes.

In Russia not so long ago, a map was published showing dots representing all the locations where *Boletus edulis* has been found throughout the country. Now we know that this map represents between a half dozen and a dozen distinct species, often distinguished from one another by cap color or mushroom shape or tree association, and that the map has to be redone to represent our new understanding of this species complex.

Eating Boletes

You may need to discard the stem if it is tough or fibrous and cut away the spongy layer under the cap if it is too soft. Cooking soft caps and tough stems together is not a good idea because when the caps are cooked, the stems are still mostly raw and indigestible. Cooking the caps with the spongy layer still attached, if it is thick and soft, produces a dish more like okra than meat. The cap flesh cleaned of the spongy layer can be sautéed or grilled and can resemble steak. This is especially true of the king bolete. (Alternatively, if the king bolete is too old or soft to eat, it can be used in stock.)

Calfornia queen bolete (*Boletus regineus*)

Boletes

COMMON NAMES:
King bolete, cèpe, porcini, steinpilz

SCIENTIFIC NAMES:
Boletus edulis complex (which includes a number of closely related species, such as *B. clavipes*, *B. pinicola*, and *B. pinophilus*)

Note: The king bolete is now generally recognized as a group name. *Boletus edulis* is the mushroom most people think they're picking when they find the king bolete, but it is often something closely related, not the same species.

FIELD DESCRIPTION:
- The bolete is a large mushroom, up to 12 inches (30.5 cm) high, with a reddish brown bunlike cap and a white (when young) spongy layer underneath the cap.

- A brownish stalk often flares out near the base and becomes bulbous.

- The upper part of stem bears a conspicuous white fishnetlike pattern.

LOOK-ALIKES:
Boletus huronensis (see page 87). The bitter bolete (*Tylopilus felleus*) has a white spongy layer under the cap when young, but it turns pinkish as the spores mature, and the upper part of the stalk has a black, not white, fishnetlike pattern; besides, it's distinctly bitter.

CAUTION:
Everyone wants every bolete they find to be the king, but few are, and even these are a complex of different species. Therefore, caution is strongly advised before committing a collection to the dinner table.

A sauce made with the king bolete can be spread between layers of polenta or cornmeal cakes and poured over the top. Another way to prepare boletes is sautéed in oil and seasoned lightly. Some people prefer rehydrated dried king boletes to fresh ones; the flavor is more intense. Whatever the preparation, boletes are best paired with a grain, such as wheat (pasta), rice (risotto), corn (polenta), or barley (soup).

The best way to preserve boletes is to dry them and store in tight-fitting jars. The cap flesh alone is dried, unless the boletes are very young and the spongy layer is too thin to bother removing. Dried bolete caps can be stored in jars for years and maintain their quality when rehydrated. This is how they are usually seen in markets, as packages of dried porcini or cèpe caps.

Polypores

Polypores are the bracket or shelf fungi that are so familiar on trees, fallen logs, and stumps. There are hundreds of different kinds, almost all of which are woody or too tough to consider eating. Many polypores are known in Asia as important medicinal mushrooms, and some of these are common around the world but go unused.

Polypores are named for their pore surface, the layer underneath the cap or shelf, which is composed of a great number of tiny pores, or openings, through which the spores fall to be dispersed by the wind.

White chicken (*Laetiporus cincinnatus*)

Chicken Mushrooms

There are only a few polypores that are considered edible, and among these, the chicken mushroom is one of the best. It has a texture somewhat reminiscent of chicken and a pleasant flavor. Perhaps best of all, it is easily spotted by its colors, is often in quantities too great to even consider collecting it all, and is hard to misidentify.

As early as February in Argentina and as late as November in Malaysian Borneo, the chicken mushroom has one of the longest fruiting seasons of all edible wild mushrooms. Not only does it occur nearly throughout the planet, but it fruits almost year-round, and in some places it can fruit again and again for nearly a six-month period. It can also fruit in quantities that cover the trunk of a standing tree, or spreading out across fallen logs, providing 50 pounds (22.7 kg) or more of often choice edible wild mushroom.

The chicken mushroom grows on standing hardwood trees, often in shelves ascending 10 feet (3 m) or more, or on logs or stumps, looking much like a bouquet. A very similar species, *Laetiporus cincinnatis*, white chicken mushroom, grows at the base of hardwood trees and, like *L. sulphureus*, causes root rot. Aside from the position of the mushroom on the tree, the only other easily discerned difference is that the white chicken mushroom has a white pore surface rather than a bright yellow one. When collecting either of these mushrooms, make sure the mushrooms appear fresh and firm. As they age they dry considerably and whiten, and lose their culinary appeal.

Other species occur on conifers and one favors introduced eucalyptus. These are sometimes reported to cause digestive upset. Even where this mushroom is a favorite edible, there are people who complain that the mushroom causes symptoms that make them feel uncomfortable. One person said it made her lips swell. Still, it's on most people's Ten Best list.

Left: Chicken mushroom (*Laetiporus sulphureus*)

THE SEVEN DEADLY SINS OF MUSHROOM HUNTING

Unlike other choice edible mushrooms that are very hard to see because they blend so well into their environment, chicken mushrooms stick out like a sore thumb. Hiking through a summer or autumn woods, chicken mushrooms can be seen from more than 100 feet (30 m) away. They sometimes produce a giant 3-foot (1 m) -high bright orange bouquet on a spot where a tree limb once was, or 20 feet (6 m) of bright orange-yellow shelves running up the tree trunk.

The problem, if there is one, is that the proverbial Seven Deadly Sins are never far away.

The Lust for the mushrooms can be so great that every last one of them has to be collected. You fill with Pride at carrying 20 pounds (9 kg) or more of chicken mushroom through the woods or to the car, and this is Greed personified. Gluttony comes next because it's almost impossible not to pig out by eating more than you ever thought possible. If you're home with 20 or more pounds (9 or more kg) of chicken mushroom in prime condition and you simply cannot eat it all, what do you do? The processing time for cleaning and cooking, and then cooling and freezing packages of chicken mushroom will take you well into the night. It might seem better to do nothing, as Sloth would recommend. The last two of the Deadly Sins, Envy and Wrath, are what you feel when someone else has found the mother lode of choice edible mushrooms. You're not happy for her good fortune; you envy her success and are angry at her for finding it and at yourself for not finding it. Mushroom hunting is often thought of as a bucolic, romantic, pleasant way to spend a few hours in the woods. For some people, though, it falls just short of a contact sport.

Eating Chicken Mushrooms

It's best (and most easily digestible) to eat chicken mushrooms when they are very young and juicy. The best way to prepare it is to cut it into small pieces and cook it covered in some butter and water or broth. Let it stew for about half an hour, then season it and serve. Or add to soup. Some people like to cook it uncovered until it is almost dry, but this sometimes requires using too much butter, which disappears quickly, and ¼ pound (115 g) can be used up in no time. The temptation is to eat the chicken mushroom as an entrée rather than as one dish in a meal. If there is any problem with this, it might be that it's very easy to overeat this mushroom, especially when there is so much of it, and it tastes so good. Large amounts can be somewhat difficult to digest, leaving you feeling "heavy" or slightly queasy. It's best to enjoy this mushroom in moderation. If a large number of shelves are found, it might be best to call some friends and share the harvest, knowing that you might benefit later from a harvest of some other mushrooms they find. Besides, it takes a lot of work and time and space in the freezer to preserve quantities of chicken mushroom.

The chicken mushroom is best preserved by cooking and freezing. It doesn't rehydrate well after drying.

Chicken Mushrooms

COMMON NAMES:
Chicken mushroom, chicken-of-the-woods,
sulfur shelf

SCIENTIFIC NAMES:
Laetiporus sulphureus, L. cincinnatis

FIELD DESCRIPTION:

⊙ Grows in clusters, often very abundantly, on both
standing and downed hardwood trees.

⊙ The chicken mushroom is a large (often 12
inches [30.5 cm] across), shelving fleshy polypore
with an orange cap and yellow pore surface.

⊙ The white chicken mushroom (*Laetiporus cincinnatis*) is similar but is pinkish to orange above and
with a white pore surface; it typically grows at the
base of hardwood trees.

LOOK-ALIKES:
Other polypores that might resemble the chicken
mushroom in size do not resemble it in color; any
that resemble the chicken mushroom in color will
be found to be tough in texture.

CAUTION:
People taking MAO-inhibitor medications should
avoid polypores because they contain tyramine.
Also, some people cannot digest this mushroom and
complain of cramps. A few people complain that it
makes their lips tingle.

Chicken mushroom (*Laetiporus sulphureus*)

Hen-of-the-Woods (and Maitake)

The hen-of-the-woods is known as *maitake* in Japan, where it has been cultivated for decades. The Japanese have long treasured this mushroom and have used it as a medicinal food for treating almost everything that ails them, from allergies to graying hair.

This mushroom, which can grow to be 1 yard (1 m) across, occurs at the base of oak trees across much of the northern hemisphere, except for the Rockies and West Coast of North America. Sometimes several mushrooms occur at the base of a given tree, and an oak tree area can yield a dozen or more mushrooms with very little effort.

One of the first signs of autumn in northeastern and north central North America is the hen-of-the-woods. Recognized by different names in different places, it is the mushroom we look for at the base of big oak trees from early September to mid-October. It is one mushroom that people can pick more of than they know what to do with. A single clump growing at the base of one oak tree can weigh 5 pounds (2.5 kg) or more. Some people, when they find young ones, will cover them with leaves so others won't see them, and then gather them a few days later when they are larger. An eager collector can find dozens, even hundreds, of these fruitings. They can be so abundant some years that country restaurants will use them as decoration. Among some groups, such as Italians, it can be the only mushroom sought after, and elderly men with walking sticks and large bags wander through urban and suburban woods looking for it every autumn.

The mushroom is a polypore, a fleshy bracket fungus composed of numerous small caps attached to a central base. It can appear like a woman's skirt swirled out in a dance, and the Japanese call it maitake, the "dancing" mushroom. Health food stores stock maitake tablets, which are used as an immune enhancer.

Hunting the mushroom in backyards and city parks and outlying woods, however, is part of the pleasure of the mushroom experience.

Quite unexpectedly, the mushroom turned up in New Zealand one April at a foray. It had not been seen there before, and it was going to be photographed and preserved for later study when it mysteriously disappeared from the premises. It turned up that evening as an entrée at dinner. The advance of science must always be balanced against the needs of a chef preparing dinner.

DRUG INTERACTIONS

Every mushroom seems to come with a caveat, as do any number of choice fruits and vegetables. The hen-of-the-woods, like many polypores, contains tyramine. People taking certain antidepressant medications, especially MAO inhibitors, are told to steer clear of any food or beverage containing tyramine, including cheddar cheese and red wine. Not knowing this about polypores, susceptible people will experience gastric distress, and learn to avoid these mushrooms in the future.

EATING HEN-OF-THE-WOODS

The mushroom is best prepared by sautéing it for 5 minutes or so in a little butter and oil. Its flesh is thinner than that of the chicken mushroom, so it needs less cooking. A little seasoning is all it needs. It can be served alone or with mixed vegetable or fish or meat. It enhances every food it's eaten with. Some people take the young and small caps and make a light pickle as a tasty hors d'oeuvre.

The mushroom can be cooked and frozen for later use, but a great harvest will quickly fill up a freezer, and hen-of-the-woods can be dried. It keeps well, rehydrates well, and can be used in soups or mixed dishes.

GUARDIAN OF THE HEN

It was autumn, and we were in the park looking for hens. Hen-of-the-woods is one of the best eating mushrooms around, and it comes up like clockwork every September at the base of old oak trees. A "good" tree can be visited every autumn for several years. We were thinking such thoughts as we wandered through the park woods. We weren't finding much of anything except for one person who was sleeping there. Naturally, right near him we found a large hen-of-the-woods. Getting it meant approaching him, disturbing him, and hoping he wouldn't mind. We tried making noise but nothing seemed to rouse him. We raised our voices, but he didn't move. We wondered whether he was on anyone's Most Wanted list. We wondered whether he was armed or crazed or sleeping off a drug overdose. We thought a sleeping bear would be easier to read than the mind of someone sleeping in the afternoon in the wooded part of a big city park.

Eventually, the man turned over, saw us, and sat up. We told him about the mushroom that was growing nearly within arm's length of his head. He said he didn't eat mushrooms. We said we did. He invited us to take it, for which we thanked him, and we stole away with our trophy. It was the best-tasting hen-of-the-woods we could remember eating.

Hen-of-the-woods (*Grifola frondosa*)

Hen-of-the-Woods

COMMON NAMES:
Hen-of-the-woods, maitake

SCIENTIFIC NAME:
Grifola frondosa

FIELD DESCRIPTION:

⊙ Grows at the base of old oak trees in the autumn.

⊙ The hen-of-the-woods is a large, often 1 to 2 feet (30.5 to 61 cm) across, clustered mass of small, grayish brown fleshy caps with white pores below.

⊙ Caps are attached by short lateral white stems to a base.

LOOK-ALIKES:
The black-staining polypore (*Meripilus sumstinei*) often grows on buried wood, appearing to grow in the grass. Its edges bruise black and the whole turns blackish on aging or with cooking. Very young fruiting bodies are edible, but older ones are just too tough to chew. The umbrella polypore (*Polyporus umbellatus*), an equally good edible, is much lighter in color and occurs on the ground in summer and early autumn in the eastern United States, rising up out of a tuberlike mass of compacted mycelium.

CAUTION:
People taking MAO-inhibitor medications should avoid polypores like this that contain tyramine.

Giant puffball (*Calvatia gigantea*)

Giant Puffball

HOOP DREAMS

I noticed some kids throwing a ball back an forth in a big city park. It was hard not to see its distinct wobble in flight. When the kids tired of their game and left it to go on to something else, I examined the "ball." What they had been tossing about was a mushroom, a large, round, soccer ball–size giant puffball. Although it had been handled a bit, when I cut it open it was pure white inside, indicating that it was fresh and edible. It didn't take much cleaning, with some water and a paring knife, plus a little cooking and seasoning, to turn the kids' game ball into a tasty meal. You could call it secondhand food, if you must, but it was a delicious find.

Some people go to New Zealand just to see tens of millions of sheep grazing in pastures. Mushrooms grow in these pastures, and the largest and most conspicuous of them is the giant puffball. It's smaller than a sheep, it's roundish and smooth, and it's much easier to "catch," prepare, and eat; and you're not poaching someone else's property. Wherever there's grass or open woods on planet Earth, there could be giant puffballs, and there are no poisonous giant puffballs, and no look-alikes, except for soccer balls and dinosaur eggs.

Caveat: While small puffballs species, those 1 inch (2.5 cm) or so in diameter, can be good eating when young (with an unadorned white context when cut in half), there are too many easily confused look-alikes for beginners to attempt to identify small puffballs with any confidence. Look-alikes include destroying angel and death cap buttons, as well as panther Amanita and fly-agaric buttons, stinkhorn eggs, and false puffballs (species of *Scleroderma*). All of these have been mistaken for puffballs, and some have caused poisonings.

Where the Giants Are

There are many kinds of small puffballs and their look-alikes, but nothing looks like a giant puffball.

They occur in lawns, in grassy areas, in parks in big cities, and in meadows in the mountains. They are easily spotted from a car window or walking into a clearing in the woods, or in the middle of the city.

Sometimes they are growing in fairy rings, and there can be twenty or more basketball-size or larger giant puffballs. If they're in prime condition for eating, you can still only eat a few slices from one of these. Even a giant puffball party would still only consume one or two. Huge fairy rings of fifty or more giant puffballs have been found in several locales.

Eating Giant Puffballs

There are a couple of different kinds of giant puffballs, and all are edible. When they are cut in half and are white throughout, they are in prime condition for the table. Unlike some other mushrooms that can be sliced and sautéed in butter or oil, giant puffballs cooked that way are usually rejected as oily or greasy. The best way to cook giant puffballs is to cut them into thin slices, dredge them in a light batter of egg, a little water, and panko bread crumbs, and then sauté to a golden brown on both sides. Because they can be so large, some as wide as 1 yard (1 m) across, it is tempting to want to preserve it in some way. Giant puffballs could be cooked and frozen, but the texture is best when they are used fresh and in prime condition.

Giant Puffballs

COMMON NAME:
Giant puffball

SCIENTIFIC NAME:
Calvatia gigantea (eastern United States), *Calvatia booniana* (western United States)

FIELD DESCRIPTION:
- The giant puffball is a huge (2 to 3 feet [61 to 91 cm]) white sphere.

- Smooth in *C. gigantea*, pure white and firm-fleshed within when young and fresh. Matures within to greenish yellow spore powder; the whole cracking and splitting on maturity to release the spores.

LOOK-ALIKES:
There are many smaller puffballs. One, *Calvatia cyathiformis*, is the size of a softball (12 inches [30.5 cm] in circumference). When mature, its white flesh becomes a dingy dark violet color from the maturing spore case. While this one is edible when immature and solid white within, many others are poisonous. When sliced in half, a conspicuously thickened skin is the hallmark of a toxic false puffball, a species of *Scleroderma*, even if the immature context is white.

CAUTION:
Use only soccer ball–size (27 inches [69 cm]) puffballs that are pure white inside. Avoid any that are discolored within.

Giant puffball (*Calvatia gigantea*)

One of the first things I learned about mushrooms was that there are some squat-looking white mushrooms that are very common in the woods but are of no value whatsoever as food. One is the peppery milk cap (*Lactarius piperatus*), and the other is the short-stemmed white russula (*Russula brevipes*). They don't taste good raw, and sautéing them doesn't improve their flavor. They are just mushrooms that you find and leave where they are.

Then, around midsummer, something orange seems to attack them. What results is a deformed-looking mushroom whose gills are largely obscured by tiny bumps. The whole becomes a bright orange to orange-red color. This is a mold (a parasitic fungus) attacking these two mushrooms, without which it could not live independently. It turns out that the mold transforms its host from something not palatable at all into something that has a memorable flavor and texture.

Lobster mushroom (*Hypomyces lactifluorum*)

Lobster Mushrooms

From Eastern and Western Canada down through Mexico a choice edible mushroom appears in the woods, and then in the markets, that occurs no where in the world. A decidedly unpalatable mushroom in North American woods is parasitized by another fungus that totally transforms the color, texture, and flavor of its host. The result is a parasitized mushroom that is better eating than the uninfected mushroom could ever be. The mushroom goes by the common name lobster mushroom. Its scientific name is that of the parasite, *Hypomyces lactifluorum*. Its host, most likely a white russula (*Russula brevipes*), is rarely visible when the lobster mushroom is found. Forty years of researching this phenomenon has turned up only one other likely host, a milk cap (*Lactarius* sp.).

This mushroom, once unknown outside North America, is now a major market wild mushroom, something which cannot be grown, only gathered, and which is available in such quantities that upscale markets can keep it in stock during its summer and fall seasons.

The lobster mushroom is a solid mass and somewhat meatlike in texture. A single fruiting body can weigh close to 1 pound (455 g), so that one large lobster mushroom can be enough for dinner for two.

Eating Lobster Mushrooms

It is imperative to clean lobster mushrooms thoroughly before cooking. They are best used in soups and are also good grilled. The best way to preserve them is to dry or cook them and then freeze them.

Lobster mushroom (*Hypomyces lactifluorum*)

 Lobster Mushrooms

COMMON NAME:
Lobster mushroom

SCIENTIFIC NAME:
Hypomyces lactifluorum

FIELD DESCRIPTION:

◉ Grows on the ground near conifers and hardwood trees.

◉ Reaches 3 to 6 inches (7.5 to 15 cm); appears deformed, orange to orange-red.

◉ Underside of cap is covered with tiny pimplelike bumps, a parasite covering a white mushroom (*Lactarius* or *Russula*).

Wood-Ears

COMMON NAMES:
Tree-ear, wood-ear, cloud-ear, mu-her

SCIENTIFIC NAMES:
Auricularia auricula; *A. polytricha* (the name given to the cultivated wood-ear found in Chinese markets)

FIELD DESCRIPTION:
- Grows single to several, on both conifers and hardwood trees.
- Reaches 2 inches (5 cm) or so; brownish to charcoal colored, ear-shaped, thin-fleshed, rubbery.

LOOK-ALIKES:
Brown cup fungi are very fragile, and bending one breaks it easily.

CAUTION:
Because this mushroom is known to lengthen the clotting time of blood, if you are on a blood-thinning medication you should check with your doctor before making this mushroom a regular part of your diet.

Jelly Fungi

Every bowl of Chinese hot-and-sour soup contains pieces of a jelly fungi, the wood-ear mushroom. It has no flavor to speak of, and its texture is crunchy, almost like some seaweeds. For the Chinese, this mushroom is not a condiment; instead, it is a medicinal food. It is so important to the Chinese diet that its production accounts for nearly 9 percent of all cultivated mushrooms. Wherever Chinese can be found working in other parts of the world, in Indonesia, in Africa, in North America, they cultivate and market this mushroom, and it is something that only the Chinese are likely to purchase and use. Given its reputed anticoagulant, cardiovascular-supporting, antiviral, tumor-suppressing, and immune-enhancing benefits, it's no wonder that the Chinese have brought this mushroom into their daily diet. Where foods are valued for their flavor, a tasteless mushroom, especially one whose texture might resemble for some people a thin sheet of rubber, people may not use this mushroom, or know what to do with it if they find it or buy it.

Dried wood-ear mushrooms can be found in Chinese markets, and fresh wood-ears are now turning up in many upscale grocery stores. That a significant part of the world's population is eating this mushroom suggests that many are missing out on something everyone should at least try.

Wood-ears occur on standing conifers and hardwood trees and fallen logs in parks and woods throughout North America and Europe. Similar species occur in the subtropics and tropics. The mushrooms appear shaped like human ears. They are brown and rubbery. Folding them over doesn't break them the way it would a cup fungus. They can be a common sight in summer and autumn woods, even in late autumn, because, being rubbery, they are resistant to frost. However, because of their dark color growing on dark wood, they are easily overlooked. They are easily collected and cleaned.

Wood-ear jelly fungus (*Auricularia auricula*)

Eating Wood-Ears

Cooking is simple: slice into thick strips and cook in a soup. Dried cultivated wood-ear mushrooms, at least some of what is sold in markets, expand to more than 6 inches (15.2 cm) across when rehydrated. These enormous dark rubbery mats have to be cut into small bite-size pieces to be able to cook and eat. The best way to preserve wood-ears is to dry them and store in tight-fitting jars.

WRETCHED EXCESS

It was an autumn mushroom hunt in the woods. We were a large group walking along woodland paths, bushwhacking, looking for whatever mushrooms we might find that day. We had our eyes tuned to our favorite autumn mushrooms—hen-of-the-woods, honey mushrooms, blewits, and oysters—when we heard a commotion and chatter in the woods to our left. A Chinese family that was part of our group, two parents and their two children, were dragging a large tree limb out of the woods, all the while speaking rapidly in Chinese. They spoke almost no English, but it was clear from their excitement that what they found was very important to them.

The tree limb was full of the jelly fungus known as the wood-ear mushroom (*Auricularia auricula*). This family tried to explain to us how happy they were to find this mushroom growing outside China.

There was so much of it on the tree limb that they insisted on cooking it for the entire group. We could not say no. Back at the camp, they took the wood-ears into the kitchen and made a stir-fry with vegetables. Then they served it to us and watched as we ate it. It was the kind of moment when two cultures are brought together by a common passion for something but then discover that they don't share the same degree of love for it. We laughed over the event to conceal our mutual embarrassment.

Edible Gilled Mushrooms

Because the one edible mushroom everyone knows is the white button mushroom (or common cultivated mushroom, *Agaricus bisporus* or *A. brunnescens*), and because it has gills under its cap, it might seem that gilled mushrooms as a group are safe to eat. Nothing could be further from the truth.

In fact, the gilled mushrooms include our most dangerous mushrooms, such as the destroying angel and the death cap. Even the genus of the white button mushroom, *Agaricus*, includes many species that will make people sick. In most groceries the only mushrooms for sale are gilled mushrooms; in addition to the white button mushroom there are its variants, creminis and portobellos. In parks and woods the most common and conspicuous mushrooms are gilled mushrooms, perhaps 5,000 different kinds, including many that are either poisonous or whose edibility is simply unknown. Their presence and abundance in the field and our familiarity with the commercial white button mushroom lead us to underestimate the difficulties involved in identifying them or determining just which ones are safe edibles.

Gilled mushrooms, except for the white button mushroom and its variants and the few kinds that are commonly sold in markets or served in Asian restaurants, are not mushrooms for beginners to experiment with. People who grow up in a mushroom-picking culture—such as France, Italy, Germany, Austria, Switzerland, the Czech Republic, Slovakia, Poland, Romania, Bulgaria, the Scandinavian countries, and the entire Russian landmass—where pink bottoms (*Agaricus campestris*) and honey mushrooms are well known to the

Popular Wild Gilled Edible Mushrooms

- Meadow mushroom group (*Agaricus campestris* complex)
- Oyster mushroom (*Pleurotus ostreatus* complex)
- Honey mushrooms (*Armillaria mellea* complex)
- Shaggy mane (*Coprinus comatus*)
- Matsutake (*Tricholoma magnivelare* complex)
- Shrimp russula (*Russula xerampelina* complex)
- Orange-milk milk cap (*Lactarius deliciosus* complex)
- Fish milk cap (*Lactarius volemus* complex)
- Candy cap (*Lactarius rubidus*)
- Blewit (*Lepista nuda*)

general population and enthusiastically gathered, have no fear of gilled mushrooms. Many of them, however, gather only very few kinds of gilled mushrooms, ignoring the rest.

Most mushroom poisoning is caused by gilled mushrooms, and nearly all mushroom-related fatalities are a result of eating gilled mushrooms, specifically species in the genus *Amanita*. Travelers returning from Italy, for example, may tell stories about the delicious ovuli they sampled in Rome. They tell of eating the egg-stage or immature Caesar's mushroom, *Amanita caesarea*, sliced raw in salads. A closely related "ovuli" of the American

Blewits (*Lepista nuda*)

Amanita species is beginning to show up in farmers' markets in the United States. Although these market mushrooms are edible, the problem lies with trying to pick your own and successfully distinguish edible from poisonous species of *Amanita*—it is a hazardous activity, to say the least.

With that in mind, I present only a handful of choice edible wild gilled mushrooms here. There are others that are good to eat but require a level of care in recognizing them that is beyond the skills slowly acquired by beginners. Oyster mushrooms, matsutakes, and blewits are now frequently seen in American markets. *Agaricus* is included

because so many people collect one or another species and think they know them well enough. Honey mushrooms are a conspicuous and abundant mushroom in the autumn and are sometimes seen for sale in farmers' markets. Shaggy manes are included because, although they lack the shelf life necessary for selling in markets, they are distinctive and choice edibles. The shrimp russula and the candy caps are two choice edibles that, though they are gilled mushrooms, can be recognized by any beginner who has a nose for detecting seafood or maple syrup.

Seasonal Guide to Edible Gilled Mushrooms

Mushroom seasons and growing location for the edible gilled mushroom groups are presented here. For definitions of the nine major regions of the world listed here, see page 19. Consult local or regional mushroom guides to pinpoint precise growing seasons.

Mushroom	1. NA	2. RM	3. CAPNW	4. SA
MEADOW MUSHROOM GROUP (*Agaricus campestris* complex)	in lawns and grassy areas, summer–autumn	in lawns and grassy areas, summer	in lawns and grassy areas, Sept–Oct	in grassy areas, Jan–Apr
OYSTER MUSHROOMS (*Pleurotus ostreatus* complex)	on hardwoods, year-round, given rain and mild weather	on poplars (aspens and cottonwoods), summer	on hardwoods, Oct–Jan	on hardwoods, May–July
HONEY MUSHROOMS (*Armillaria mellea* complex)	at base of hardwoods, autumn	at base of conifers and aspens, summer	at base of hardwoods and conifers, Oct–Feb	at base of hardwoods, Jan–Apr
SHAGGY MANE (*Coprinus comatus*)	in grassy areas, May and Sept	in grassy areas, along roadsides, late spring–autumn	in grassy areas, along roadsides, Nov–Jan	in grassy areas, Feb–Mar
MATSUTAKE (*Tricholoma magnivelare* complex)	under conifers, autumn	under conifers, summer	under conifers, autumn	N/A
SHRIMP RUSSULA (*Russula xerampelina* complex)	under hardwoods and conifers, summer–autumn	under conifers, summer	under conifers, Nov–Feb	N/A
ORANGE MILK MILK-CAP (*Lactarius deliciosus* complex)	under conifers, summer and early autumn	under conifers, summer	under conifers, Oct–Jan	N/A
FISH MILK-CAP (*Lactarius voleumus*)	under oaks, summer and autumn	N/A	N/A	N/A
CANDY-CAPS (*Lactarius rubidus*)	N/A	N/A	in humus under hardwoods and conifers, Jan–Feb	N/A
BLEWITS (*Lepista nuda*)	in leaf mulch under oaks, autumn	in leaf mulch under trees, summer–autumn	in parks, in wood, in mulch under trees, Oct–Feb	N/A

N/A= not reported or not yet found
1. (NA) Eastern and Central North America from Canada to Mexico and through Central America
2. (RM) Rocky Mountains of North America
3. (CAPNW) California and the Pacific Northwest of North America
4. (SA) South America

5. (EUR) Europe (including western, central, and eastern Europe)
6. (MED) Mediterranean (including southern Europe, North Africa, and parts of the Middle East)
7. (AFR) Southern Africa
8. (ASIA) Asia (from India to Japan)
9. (ANZ) Australia and New Zealand

5. EUR	6. MED	7. AFR	8. ASIA	9. ANZ
in lawns and grassy areas, summer	in lawns and grassy areas, autumn	in lawns and grassy areas, Oct–Nov, May–June	in lawns and grassy areas, autumn	in lawns and grassy areas, Apr–May
on hardwoods, summer and autumn	on hardwoods, Oct–Jan	on hardwood stumps and logs, June–Aug	on hardwood trees, stumps and log, summer–autumn	on hardwoods, Apr–May, August
on hardwoods (esp oaks), autumn	on hardwoods (esp oak), autumn	on hardwoods and pines, Mar–June	at base of hardwoods, autumn	at base of hardwoods, Apr–June, Aug
in grassy areas, composted areas, bare soil, autumn	in grassy areas, autumn	in grassy areas, Jan–Mar, June (after rains)	in grassy areas, autumn	in grassy areas, Mar–May
under conifers, autumn	under conifers, Nov–Dec	N/A	under conifers, autumn	N/A
under conifers, autumn	under conifers, autumn	N/A	under conifers, autumn	N/A
under conifers, autumn	under conifers, Nov–Dec	under introduced pines, May–June	under conifers, autumn	under introduced pines, Mar–May
under hardwoods (oak), autumn	under hardwoods (oak), autumn		under hardwoods, autumn	N/A
N/A	N/A	N/A	N/A	N/A
in open woods, in compost piles, Nov–Jan	in mulch in open woods, Oct–Jan	lawns, in compost, Jan–Mar	in grassy woods, autumn	on the ground, July–Aug

Horse mushroom (*Agaricus arvensis*)
with veil covering immature gills

Agaricus Mushrooms

COMMON AND SCIENTIFIC NAMES:

Agaricus arvensis (horse mushroom): large, white
mushroom, bruising yellowish; habitat: lawns, often
large-capped and in fairy rings; odor: anise/almond
extract.

Agaricus augustus (the prince): large, yellowish
brown, scaly and almost square-capped mushroom,
bruising yellowish; habitat: woods; odor: anise/al-
mond extract.

Agaricus bitorquis (spring agaricus): large, brown
capped mushroom with short stem; habitat: urban/
suburban parks; odor: mushroomy; veil on stem.
appears to be double.

Agaricus campestris (meadow mushroom or pink bottom): smallish, white to brownish smooth-capped
mushroom with short, slender stem; habitat: lawns,
often massed or in fairy rings; odor: mushroomy;
young gills are bright pink.

FIELD DESCRIPTION:

Agaricus, as a genus, can be recognized as gilled
mushrooms growing on the ground, with a central
stem, a veil or sheetlike membrane covering the immature gills that usually remains as a ring or skirt of
tissue about the upper stem once the cap expands,
and gills free from (not attached to) the stem and
turning a dark brown on maturity. Its spore print is
chocolate brown.

**POISONOUS LOOK-ALIKES IN THE
GENUS AGARICUS:**

Agaricus xanthodermus complex
(poisonous *Agaricus* group): habitat: lawns; odor:
medicinal or phenolic

POISONOUS LOOK-ALIKES IN OTHER GENERA:

Amanita virosa (destroying angel): habitat: open
woods or lawns with oak trees or conifers

Chlorophyllum molybdites (green-spored lepiota):
habitat: lawns

CAUTION:

Be certain of your genus and your species. Always
make sure you have found a good edible *Agaricus*,
and be sure to cook it well. Even though the white
button mushroom is a species of *Agaricus* that is often eaten raw in salads, no species of *Agaricus* should
be eaten raw.

Agaricus Mushrooms

Species

⊙ **PINK BOTTOM:** *Agaricus campestris*
⊙ **HORSE MUSHROOM:** *Agaricus arvensis*
⊙ **THE PRINCE:** *Agaricus augustus*
⊙ **SPRING AGARICUS:** *Agaricus bitorquis*

The white button mushroom (*Agaricus bisporus*) is sometimes called the common cultivated mushroom, and sometimes referred to as *Agaricus brunnescens*. For decades it was only known as a canned food or in cream of mushroom soup. The white button mushroom comes in two color forms, white and brown. It also has spawned a couple of marketable variants: the small cremini and the robust portobello. Although these mushrooms look somewhat different from each other, they are the same species, grown under somewhat different conditions. Cremini, white button, and portobello are the mushrooms that are cultivated in mushroom "caves" in some regions. They are also cultivated in buildings that are designed to imitate cavelike growing conditions (temperature, for example).

Meadow mushroom, or pink bottom
(*Agaricus campestris*)

Common Species

More than 100 different kinds of *Agaricus* grow wild, and they pop up in urban and suburban parks and playgrounds, in nearby woods, and in large forests. Some are spring mushrooms, such as the spring agaricus (*Agaricus bitorquis*), that appear soon after the morels have stopped fruiting. Some are summer mushrooms, such as the common lawn pink bottom (*Agaricus campestris*), which is probably known by more Europeans than any other wild mushroom. One popular late summer mushroom is the prince (*Agaricus augustus*), which has a strong fragrance and cooked flavor of almond extract. The common autumn grassland species is the horse mushroom (*Agaricus arvensis*), which, like the pink bottom, often appears in fairy rings in open grassy areas. If all species of *Agaricus* were edible, it might not matter which one you find as long as it is a species of *Agaricus*. Unfortunately, there are species of *Agaricus* that are poisonous to eat, causing stomach upset.

Poisonous Look-Alikes:

There are also poisonous look-alikes in other genera. One is the green-spored lepiota (*Chlorophyllum molybdites*), which has a white cap and white gills when young (becoming gray-green on maturity); it can cause severe vomiting. A larger threat, however, is the genus *Amanita*, mushrooms that include the destroying angel (*Amanita virosa* and its closely related species), and that, if eaten, can cause a fatality.

A fair question to ask might be, "Why would people risk their lives, or the lives of loved ones they dine with, for a mushroom?" The usual answer is: because they are there. Often they are abundant, and cooked they are both meaty and flavorful. The risk is usually never considered, and indeed, there are very few serious mushroom poisonings. The victims are often visitors from outside the region who think they are picking something they recognize as edible back home.

Eating *Agaricus* Mushrooms

Best Preparation: Grill stuffed, marinated caps or use in duxelles.

Best Preservation: Sauté and freeze to retain aromatic flavors.

THE PRINCE AGARICUS

Sometimes it takes a village to identify a mushroom.

We had found a basketful of a large, meaty mushroom we all agreed was a species of *Agaricus*. They were growing singly and scattered on the ground in the woods. The mushroom had a skirtlike ring of tissue on the stem. The gills were dark brown and free, or not attached to the stem. Identifying it as an *Agaricus* was a slam-dunk. The problem was just what species it was. We wanted to know whether it was an edible or a poisonous species of *Agaricus*.

The caps were a yellow-pinkish brown color, somewhat scaly, and yellowed somewhat on bruising. The young caps appeared somewhat squarish around the stem, almost boxy. We hoped it might be the prince, *Agaricus augustus*, but that mushroom is strongly fragrant, smelling of anise or almond extract, and our mushrooms were odorless. We were at a loss to identify it with the certainty we needed to cook and eat it.

Someone in our group took a cap in his hand and squeezed a bunch of the gills between his fingers. Then he smelled the gills and passed the cap around

for the rest of us to smell. It smelled strongly of almond extract, just what we had hoped it would, but none of us had thought to squeeze the gills. The odor would also have become noticeable in the cooking pan if we had thought to cook the mushroom, which we wouldn't have done not knowing for sure what it was.

Prince agaricus (*Agaricus augustus*)

Oyster Mushrooms

The nearest thing there is to a year-round mushroom is the oyster mushroom. Even in climates where there are three months of winter, the oyster mushroom can fruit every month of the year, even during thaws in winter. Where it occurs, it recurs, sometimes for several years. So a particular tree can be visited every month or so to see whether fresh mushrooms have popped up. The spring, summer, and autumn/winter mushrooms might look a little different, the summer ones being thinner fleshed and whiter, while the late-season mushrooms are thick fleshed and almost rubbery (somewhat resistant to frost) and gray to grayish brown. All occur in the same places on the same trees, year in, year out. All are fruitings of *Pleurotus ostreatus*, or one of its equally edible and nearly indistinguishable satellite species.

Pleurotus as a genus can be recognized as wood-inhabiting white-spored* gilled mushrooms either without a stem or with one that is lateral or eccentric (not centered under the cap).

The oyster mushroom that is so common a sight on trees, fallen logs, and stumps in urban and suburban areas, as well as woodlands, is the same oyster mushroom that is grown commercially and sold in many grocery stores these days. Whether from the store or gathered wild, oyster mushrooms are used the same ways. They can be sautéed, roasted in the oven, or broiled, each preparation offering a different texture. In terms of quality, the younger and smaller the oysters, the better. The larger, older ones are sometimes too flabby or, if picked outdoors, can have insects in them. If the latter is the case, they can be soaked in water first, then patted dry with paper towels before cooking.

Oyster mushrooms are sometimes preserved when huge amounts are gathered. The autumn oysters freeze well. Some of those that are found frozen on trees or stumps in the autumn can still be good to eat. If they look "fresh" they can be used like oysters collected any other time.

*One "form" of the oyster mushroom has a lilac-gray spore print.

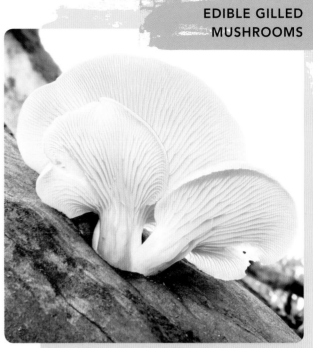

Oyster mushroom (*Pleurotus ostreatus*)

OYSTERS IN WINTER

A walk through a winter woods—say, in January—after a short warm spell and some rain can net you clusters of fresh oyster mushrooms that you may hope to see but are always surprised and pleased to find. Oysters come up year-round, given mild weather and rainfall, but are especially appreciated when nothing else is fruiting, when trees are bare and the ground is brown or still covered in snow. Winter oysters are particularly good eating because they are much firmer than summer oysters, and much less likely to be full of bugs. Somehow, they seem to taste better, too, when there are no other mushrooms to compete with them for attention.

Oyster mushroom (*Pleurotus ostreatus*)

Oyster Mushrooms

COMMON NAME:
Oyster mushroom

SCIENTIFIC NAME:
Pleurotus ostreatus

FIELD DESCRIPTION:

◉ Grows on stumps, logs, or trees.

◉ Reaches 2 to 5 inches (5 to 12.5 cm); appears as white, gray to brown fleshy-flabby smooth caps with whitish gills that descend down to the base of the mushroom, with white or pale lilac-gray spore print.

◉ Often has no stem or has a lateral stem or one that is noticeably off-center.

LOOK-ALIKES IN *PLEUROTUS* AND IN OTHER GENERA:
Lentinellus is a genus with toothed gill edges and a cap with a hairy surface; it is intensely bitter. *Crepidotus* is a genus with smaller caps and a brown spore print.

CAUTION:
Make sure the mushrooms are fresh and not buggy. To be sure they are clean, soak in a little saltwater, rinse thoroughly, and pat dry. They will have absorbed water that can be cooked out.

Oysters in the Marketplace

Marketplace oyster mushrooms include cultivated mushrooms that appear different because of the (CO_2/oxygen ratio) conditions in which they're grown. The white trumpet mushroom is an oyster mushroom. The king oyster, which looks like a giant white radish with a 1-inch (2.5 cm) gilled lined top, is a cultivated Mediterranean species of oyster mushroom, *Pleurotus eryngii*. A bright yellow oyster mushroom is known as *Pleurotus citrinopileatus*. The beech mushrooms, clusters of white or brown small-capped mushrooms, are most often sold fresh but marketed in plastic containers. They were formerly known as a species of oyster mushroom because they have somewhat decurrent gills and off-center stems; they are now called a species of *Hypsizygus*.

Remarkable Characteristics

The most curious discovery about oyster mushrooms, and subsequently about most other mushrooms that grow on wood, is that they are carnivores. That is, these deceptively innocent-looking, wood-inhabiting decomposers that appear to be as herbivorous as cows and deer have developed microscopic devices that go through the wood and capture tiny animals that they digest for their nitrogen. Much like carnivorous plants—Venus flytrap and pitcher plants, for example—many wood-decomposing fungi grow in nitrogen-poor environments. Tiny lassos wait for passing nematodes. Once a nematode is partway through, the lasso tightens around it and fungal hyphae invade the animal, kill it, and digest the needed nutrients. Similarly, a lethal lollipop, something with a sticky tip, waits for a luckless rotifer to touch it, get stuck on it, and become a meal for the fungus.

All the more remarkable is the new science of mycoremediation, and the oyster mushroom is the star in this field of oil spill cleanups. A mat, sometimes made of human hair, is inoculated with oyster mushroom. When the fungus has spread through the mat, the mat is placed on an oil spill. After several weeks, when the mat is lifted off the spill, the oil is gone. The oyster mushroom has metabolized the oil and cleansed the site. Over the next decade, we expect to see significant advances in oyster mushroom technology.

Eating Oyster Mushrooms

Best Preparation: Broil or grill the caps.
Best Preservation: Cook and freeze.

Honey Mushrooms

A popular trivia contest question is, "What is the largest organism in the world?". The answer that comes to mind first is the blue whale, which is the largest living animal in the world. When it was discovered that aspen trees grow in clones of thousands of so-called trees, and that each so-called tree is actually a stem of a single plant attached to a vast horizontally spreading underground root system, the aspen supplanted the blue whale as the world's largest organism. Now, it turns out, the honey mushroom also grows clonally, and each cluster of honey mushrooms in the clone is genetically identical to every other cluster in the clone. So, the honey mushroom is now known as the world's largest organism—the largest measures thousands of acres across.

Not only is it the largest, but it also seems to be one of the most widely distributed mushrooms on the planet. Because of the clonal way the honey mushroom lives, and its seemingly endless appetite to colonize every tree and plant it can, even potatoes, it has spread itself across the land masses of the world. Since the retreat of the glaciers at the end of the last Ice Age (some 15,000 years ago), great hidden clones have swept down from northern climes. Honey mushrooms also occur across the lands at the southern tip of the southern hemisphere. With some justification, Earth could now be called the Honey Mushroom Planet.

The honey mushroom is also known as one of the most aggressive, invasive, destructive mushrooms we have, attacking trees, shrubs, and even gardens, causing a deadly root rot, and moving from plant to plant.

Honey mushroom (*Armillaria melea* complex)

Honey Mushrooms

COMMON NAME:
Honey mushroom

SCIENTIFIC NAME:
Armillaria mellea complex

FIELD DESCRIPTION:

⊙ Appears as medium to large, clustered autumn mushrooms on wood, with yellow to buff-pinkish brown somewhat sticky caps with distinct erect black hairs or fibrils over the center.

⊙ Has off-white to pinkish buff attached gills, producing a white spore print.

⊙ Stems have skirtlike rings of tissue from a veil that conceals young gills.

COMMON NAME:
Ringless honey mushroom

SCIENTIFIC NAME:
Armillaria tabescens

FIELD DESCRIPTION:

⊙ Appear as medium to large, clustered late summer to autumn mushrooms on the ground (on buried wood or roots).

⊙ Have yellow-brown to salmon-brown dry caps with erect blackish scales over center.

⊙ White to pinkish buff gills, some descending stem.

⊙ Have fibrous, off-white stems, with no veil covering gills or ring on stem.

LOOK-ALIKES IN OTHER GENERA:
Galerina, Omphalotus, Gymnopilus

CAUTION:
Be especially careful not to confuse the deadly galerina (page 132), jack-o'-lantern (page 142), or big laughing gym (page 154) for honey mushrooms. Some honey mushroom populations, despite cooking, can still cause digestive upsets.

Honey mycelium (*rhizomorphs*)

One Name, Many Species

The honey mushroom is not a single species, as it turns out. In fact, there are a dozen or so biologically distinct look-alike species. These are not easily and reliably told apart, and most people who gather honey mushrooms for food pay no attention to these differences.

The ringless honey mushroom (*Armillaria tabescens*) looks just like the honey mushroom, but it lacks an annulus (a ring of tissue) about its upper stem, and it grows on the ground in large clusters in the autumn. It is also a root rot fungus, but it's most often found growing in grass and attached to underground tree roots or the roots of trees that died and have been removed from a yard or park. It's not as widely distributed as the honey mushroom complex, but it does occur throughout eastern and central North America and across most of Europe

Ringless honey mushroom (*Armillaria tabescens*)

and Asia. It is best eaten if picked as soon as it appears. Like many mushrooms, if it sits around a day or two it loses its "freshness" and starts to decay.

The genus *Armillaria,* as traditionally defined, is a group of white-spored, gilled mushrooms with attached gills covered by a veil of material that persists as a skirt or ring about the upper stem once the cap has expanded. Currently, *Armillaria* is restricted to two groups of species, the honey mushroom complex (a group of about a dozen nearly field-identical but biologically distinct species) and the ringless honey mushroom.

Eating Honey Mushrooms

Best Preparation: Sauté
Best Preservation: Sauté and freeze

A GANGLAND MUSHROOM HUNT?

We drove into a parking lot of a forested park outside a big city, and the first thing we saw were five parked cars with their trunks open, and nobody around. The same thought occurred to all of us: we had come upon a gangland rubout and they were dumping the bodies in the woods.

Under such circumstances, brimming with unwelcome possibilities, we decided to drive elsewhere. Right then, we saw one person, then another, emerge from the woods with buckets full of mushrooms. They dumped the contents of these buckets into the open trunk of their cars and promptly went back into the woods. We went over to see what they were getting, and it was all honey mushrooms—five car trunks full of honey mushrooms.

We asked one of the collectors what he intended to do with all those mushrooms. He said, in a strong Italian accent, that these were all going to be canned and made into sauce for pasta. The scale looked like a commercial operation, but it was just a couple of families that go out together every autumn to collect a year's supply of mushrooms. They preserve the harvest for the winter and the following year. We felt reassured that we had not stumbled upon a horrible crime being committed, unless, of course, someone were to be negligent in the canning process and everyone was "rubbed out" by botulism poisoning.

Shaggy Manes

COMMON NAME:
Shaggy mane

SCIENTIFIC NAME:
Coprinus comatus

FIELD DESCRIPTION:
Cylindrical 3- to 6-inch (7.5 to 15 cm) gilled
mushroom with shaggy-scaly white caps, opening
skirtlike at base of cap and expanding, flattening
out as it turns blackish and inky from the maturing spores

LOOK-ALIKES:
Other species of *Coprinus* do not have cylindrical
white shaggy-scaly caps.

CAUTION:
Eat only when young and white capped.

Shaggy Mane

From at least as far north as Fairbanks, Alaska,
to Tierra del Fuego at the southern tip of South
America (except for the tropics) and from sea
level to above 10,000 feet, the shaggy mane is the
preeminent mushroom of lawns and grasslands. It
occurs throughout Europe and Asia, in temperate
parts of Africa, such as Cape Town, South Africa,
and in New Zealand and Australia. Where the
mushroom season is foreshortened by drought or
frost, and everything more or less comes up in the
summer and at the same time, the shaggy manes
are no different. A day's collecting can provide
what in other zones would be a range of spring,
summer, autumn, and even winter mushrooms.

The shaggy mane has traditionally been placed in
the large group known as "inky cap" mushrooms.
This colorful name refers to the fact that soon after the caps of most of these mushrooms expand,
they dissolve into a black, inky, liquid mass. Other
mushrooms as they age dry naturally or decay, but
inky cap mushrooms are among the few that liter-
ally turn into a black inklike substance. This inklike
substance can be collected and used as paint or
even as actual ink.

Coprinus as a genus can be recognized as mostly
small, typically fragile, often abundant black-
spored gilled mushrooms that liquefy (deliquesce)
on maturity. Different species of *Coprinus* occur at
the base of trees, on stumps and wood mulch, in
grass, and on manure.

When it first appears in grassy areas, it has a long,
white, scaly cylindrical cap and a relatively short
stem. In deep grass the stem can be much longer.
In this young, unopened or unexpanded stage, it
can be a very good edible mushroom. Because it
is fragile, and easily crushed, care should be taken
when gathering it.

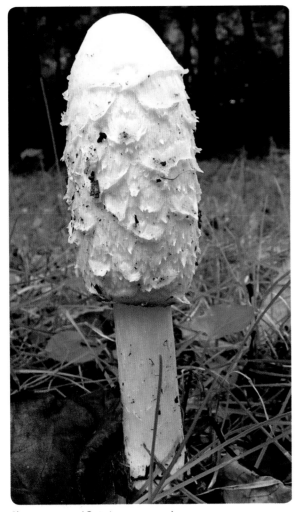

Shaggy mane (*Coprinus comatus*)

Eating Shaggy Manes

Rather than cooking them in butter or oil, you would do better to steam them and serve like asparagus, maybe with a butter or cream sauce. The fresh mushrooms can be stored in the refrigerator for a couple of days if placed in a jar of ice water.

Shaggy manes are best preserved by cooking them in a little water, seasoning them, letting them cool, and then puréeing them and storing the mixture in tightly sealed containers in the freezer. Then, when a soup stock is desired, the frozen parboiled shaggy manes can be put directly into a pot with water or broth and other soup ingredients and heated to a boil, and then served.

APARTMENT BUILDING SHAGGY MANES: A BONANZA FOR THE COLLECTING

One autumn day I happened to notice a huge quantity of shaggy manes coming up in the grass of a city apartment building's broad lawn. I couldn't believe my good fortune. I set to work collecting some of them. From an upper story window I heard a woman's voice call out loudly: "Get away from those mushrooms! They're mine! I pay the rent here!" A few minutes later she was running over to me across the grass, clearly out of breath, her arms waving. "Get away! These are my mushrooms!"

I tried to tell her that I was only taking a few for dinner. "They're all mine, every one of them. I live here. I paid for these mushrooms. Go away!" It was hard to discuss in a rational way just who owns mushrooms anyway, considering that they are "weeds" in lawns and mulched areas—they are not cultivated. She claimed property rights and that I was trespassing. There was no calming her. Nor could she have even used all the shaggy manes that had come up that day. They wouldn't even be usable after another couple of hours. It appeared she had no intention of collecting any of them herself. She just wanted to assert her rights over the mushrooms: they could rot for all she cared, just as long as I didn't get them.

A friend who always walked to work by a number of housing projects kept his eyes peeled for shaggy manes. Each autumn he said he bagged enough to can dozens of quarts of them. Perseverance can pay huge dividends.

DELICATE TOUCH

I led a group of mushroom hunters to Japan to meet our Japanese counterparts and collect mushrooms with them. In Japan, because people often live in small apartments, when they want to invite you to dinner, they take you to a restaurant. But our group wanted to be invited into a Japanese home for a home-cooked meal. We made a deal with our colleagues. We would supply matsutake mushrooms, the most prized mushroom in Japan, if the host and his wife prepared a dinner for us with matsutake. They agreed. We bought the expensive matsutake in a Kyoto market.

We were invited into our host's home with our gift and waited for at least an hour while the meal was being prepared. We were served a seven-course meal, each of which included matsutake mushrooms: soup, a rice dish, stew, a mixed vegetable dish, and so on. All ten of us feasted on the matsutake meal. As we departed, our hostess showed us the box we had given her: it still contained three untouched matsutake mushrooms.

She had extracted the flavor of the matsutake from only two mushrooms and incorporated it into all seven dishes she served to the ten of us. This was a remarkable feat, considering how inefficiently mushrooms are used in Western cuisine. Had an American host been preparing this meal, we would have expected at least one mushroom per person and we wouldn't have had a clue how to spread its flavor over seven courses. Learning that other cultures use mushrooms is nothing compared to learning how they use them.

Matsutakes

One of the most highly prized mushrooms in Japan is known as matsutake, the pine mushroom. It is very expensive, and single mushrooms cost as much as an upscale bottle of wine. A gift box of the mushrooms is often given as a present, and this present, or a part of it, is sometimes given to others because it is almost too valuable to eat and better used as a valued article of exchange. The Japanese matsutake mushroom is *Tricholoma matsutake*, a mushroom that grows associated with (mycorrhizal) the roots of Japanese red pine (*Pinus densiflora*). People lease a mountainside in red pine country for hundreds of thousands of dollars for the season. They are then allowed to harvest all the matsutake that they can find there. Although expensive and risky, it is thought of as a chance worth taking for the money you can make in a good year. The Japanese have a desire for this mushroom that can only be explained by a cultural association, a fond memory of the fragrance and flavor retained, perhaps, from childhood, and one that is treasured by succeeding generations.

Japanese matsutake mushrooms, like other mushrooms in Japanese cuisine, are medicinal foods. Like the shiitake, which is relatively easy to grow and, therefore, inexpensive, the matsutake, which can only be collected in the wild, is believed to be one of the best mushrooms to maintain good health and ensure a long life. Like the shiitake, it has also been shown to contain potent anticarcinogens, compounds that inhibit or reduce tumor growth. The demand is far greater than the supply, and a closely related species is imported from South Korea and sold for a slightly lower price in Japanese markets. Japanese matsutake buyers are always around in season in areas where any matsutake mushrooms occur. They're in the Pacific Northwest, up into British Columbia. They are also in the Atlas Mountains of Morocco, buying up carloads of matsutake occurring under atlas cedars.

Matsutake (*Trichloma magnivelare*)

Regional Variations

Everywhere there are mountains, there seem to be matsutakes. In North America there is a cluster of species similar to Japanese matsutake in odor and flavor, and sometimes closely resembling it in color as well. This matsutake includes at least three distinctly different kinds. The white matsutake of northeastern, Rocky Mountain, and northwestern conifer forests is a decidedly white mushroom, whereas the brown matsutake of the Rocky Mountains, while similar in odor and flavor, is more slender and of a different color. The eastern U.S. hardwood forest *Tricholoma caligatum*, while retaining the same name as the brown matsutake, is not a good edible. It lacks either the odor or the flavor or both, and is sometimes quite bitter. None are known to be poisonous.

Tricholoma as a genus can be recognized as white-spored gilled mushrooms that grow on the ground and are associated with forest trees, such as conifers and oaks. The mushrooms have fleshy caps and stems, and the gills are attached to the stem but don't descend it like a *Clitocybe*. One group of *Tricholomas*, which includes the matsutakes, has a veil covering the immature gills; it remains as a ring or skirt of tissue when the cap expands.

Eating Matsutakes

Best Preparation: Grill or cook in soup
Best Preservation: Best eaten fresh; flavor lost on drying

 ## Matsutakes

COMMON NAMES:
White matsutake, brown matsutake

SCIENTIFIC NAMES:
Tricholoma magnivelare (*Armillaria ponderosa*),
Tricholoma caligatum (*Armillaria caligata*)

FIELD DESCRIPTION:
- Matsutake is a fleshy, medium to robust mushroom.

- It has a white or brown cap adorned with scales, white attached gills, white spore print.

- Its stem has a white area above a sheathing skirtlike ring of tissue on upper stem and scales or patches below.

LOOK-ALIKES:
White matsutakes can be confused with white russulas and with the poisonous *Amanita smithiana* in the Pacific Northwest. The brown matsutake (*T. caligatum*) can be confused with *Tricholoma zelleri* in the western United States, but it lacks the odor and flavor of the brown matsutake.

A woman in Kyoto, Japan with a gift box of matsutake

Shrimp russula (*Russula xerampelina*)

Russulas

COMMON NAMES:
Shrimp russula, crabmeat russula

SCIENTIFIC NAME:
Russula xerampelina

FIELD DESCRIPTION:
- Russulas are fleshy-solid, 2 to 4 inches (5 to 10 cm) across, 2 to 3 inches (5 to 7.5 cm) high. Reddish to purple cap with attached off-white to yellowish gills, white spore print.

- Has a whitish stem with a pinkish blush near the base; rubbing the stem turns it olive-yellowish brown.

- Gills have an unmistakable shrimp or crab-meatlike odor. (If odor is lacking, put mushrooms in a paper bag and leave closed for 10 minutes or so, then open and smell. If the seafoodlike smell is still undetectable, discard the mushrooms and look for others.)

LOOK-ALIKES:
Other red-capped russulas include *R. emetica* and other acrid or bitter species. Do not confuse and eat these along with or instead of the shrimp russula.

Shrimp Russula

The genus *Russula* is one of the easiest genera of gilled mushrooms to recognize. They grow on the ground in woods, and many of the species have red or reddish, purple, or yellow caps, white gills, and brittle, chalky stems. Russulas typically look nibbled on by animals or look extremely weatherworn. They are sometimes called brittle caps because rather than breaking into a couple of pieces, the caps shatter into hundreds of fragments, something easily determined by throwing a suspected *Russula* against a tree or a rock. That said, the species of *Russula* are among the most difficult to differentiate from one another. There are more than 500 *Russula* species, and of all these species, only a few are recognized as choice edibles. The vast majority are either mild but unnoteworthy or acrid or bitter.

The best eating of all the *Russula* is the one known as the shrimp or crab russula (*Russula xerampelina*). The gills smell like shrimp or crabmeat, and when cooked the mushroom carries this flavor into the dish. Shrimp russula pasta is a seafood-like pasta without seafood. Although the shrimp russula or one of its closely related species can be found across most of northern North America, the best eating ones are found in the Rocky Mountains. They are free of any insects and are mostly in choice, firm condition when found. Sliced and cooked in a sauce to serve with pasta is the best and safest way to eat "seafood" in the mountains.

Eating Russulas

Best Preparation: Sauté and make into a sauce for seafood-flavored pasta
Best Preservation: Sauté and freeze

Milk Caps

Although milk caps are common in the temperate zone forests of the world, and there are hundreds of species known to science, only a few are good enough and safe enough to find a place on the dinner table. Three groups of these milk caps are readily recognized in the field and are choice and safe even for beginners to gather: orange milk caps (*Lactarius deliciosus* complex), fish milk caps (*L. volemus*, *L. hygrophoroides*, and *L. corrugis*), and candy caps (*L. rubidus*). *Lactarius* as a genus is recognized as a group of fleshy-gilled mushrooms that grow on the ground near conifers and hardwood trees and that exude a white or colored latexlike liquid when the gills are cut.

Orange Milk Caps

One group found in North America, Europe, Asia, and even the Southern Hemisphere wherever Northern Hemisphere conifers have been planted, has a bright orange latex (milky liquid) exuding from freshly cut gills. The mushrooms are also orange and, when bruised or aging, turn greenish or completely dark green. This is known as the *Lactarius deliciosus* complex, a group of several remarkably similar species, differing somewhat in edible qualities, but all edible, and often found in local markets.

Eating Orange Milk Caps

Best Preparation: Sauté or pickle
Best Preservation: Sauté and freeze or pickle

Orange-milk milk cap (*Lactarius deliciosus* complex)

Orange-milk milk cap (*Lactarius deliciosus* complex)

Orange Milk Caps

COMMON NAMES:
Orange milky, "delicious" milky

SCIENTIFIC NAMES:
Lactarius deliciosus, L. deterrimus

FIELD DESCRIPTION:

◉ Orange milk caps are a distinctive group of orange-colored mushrooms, often with concentric rings visible on the cap surface, and sometimes with large "age" marks on the stem.

◉ Exudes orange latex on cutting the gills or flesh, cream-colored spore print.

◉ Whole mushroom turns green with bruising or aging.

LOOK-ALIKES:
There are several species of orange milk caps, as well as a few that have a reddish milk. Many are eaten in different parts of the world, including Mexico, Spain, South Africa, Thailand, and China, and none is known to be poisonous.

CAUTION:
Look for the latex color to identify the mushroom correctly. Alternatively, lacking visible latex, look for a cap with concentric zones on its surface: any orange *Lactarius* that bruises or ages green is in an edible group of species.

Fish Milk Caps

COMMON NAMES:
Voluminous-latex milky (Bradley), hygrophorus milky, corrugated-cap milky

SCIENTIFIC NAMES:
Lactarius volemus, L. hygrophoroides, L. corrugis

FIELD DESCRIPTION:
- Grows on the ground under oaks.

- Appear as medium to large, meaty mushrooms with orange-brown caps and stems.

- White to buff gills exude abundant unchanging white latex on cutting, white spore print.

- The taste of all three species is mild (not a trace of bitterness); the odor of *L. volemus* is fishy.

LOOK-ALIKES:
Other similarly colored species of *Lactarius* with unchanging white latex are intensely bitter or acrid.

CAUTION:
Cleaning *Lactarius volemus* can stain your fingers; wear gloves when cleaning this mushroom.

Fish milk cap (*Lactarius volemus*)

Fish Milk Caps

In the fall, in the tropical hardwood forests outside of Bangkok, Thailand, a trio of beautiful mushrooms can be collected by the basketful. These fleshy orange to orange-brown mushrooms exuding a lush white latex when cut, are the choice edible fish milk caps, known to be three closely related species of *Lactarius*. This particular *Lactarius* complex also grows under oaks in summer woods in northern Japan and across Europe, and in the fall under cork oak in Morocco. While absent in western North America, these mushrooms fruit abundantly in the eastern United States, and are one of the favorite eating mushrooms of summer. Of all the milk caps, and there are a couple hundred species of *Lactarius*, the best eating ones are these three closely related species that all have orange caps and stems (sometimes as pale as yellow or as dark as cordovan leather), and a mild, abundant white latex when the gills are cut. These three are known as *Lactarius hygrophoroides*, *L. volemus*, and *L. corrugis*. The first has widely spaced gills and is one of the first of the genus to appear every year, fruiting as early as the summer solstice. All three can be found throughout the summer, sometimes well into September, but their peak is from mid-July to early September. These are eastern North American mushrooms, associated with eastern oaks and do not occur west of the 100th meridian. Even in hot, dry summers, you can fill a basket in an afternoon outing in just about any oak woods. Fish milk caps, to our current knowledge, are not found in the southern hemisphere.

Corrugated-cap milk cap (*Lactarius corrugis*)

Candy cap (*Lactarius rubidus*)

Candy Caps

COMMON NAME:
Candy caps

SCIENTIFIC NAMES:
Lactarius rubidus, L. rufulus

FIELD DESCRIPTION:

- Candy caps are small to medium-sized mushrooms on the ground in the woods.

- Orange to rusty brown cap with attached gills exudes a watery white latex on cutting, with as sweet odor (on drying, the odor intensifies to butterscotch), cream to buff spore print.

LOOK-ALIKES:
Other similarly colored *Lactarius* species have a white latex or a white latex that soon changes to yellow, or are acrid to bitter, and lack any distinctively sweet odor. To be 100 percent certain of your identification, dry the mushrooms and, before using any, smell each one to make sure the distinctive sweet odor is present. If not, discard.

CAUTION
Do not confuse with *Lactarius xanthogalactus*, which has white latex becoming yellow, and is acrid. Do not pick a mixed collection; examine each and every mushroom collected. Be alert for poison oak, which is often overlooked in winter when it's bare of leaves.

Eating Fish Milk Caps

Fish milk caps are best sliced and sautéed in a little butter and oil for 5 to 10 minutes, then seasoned and served. The fishy smell of *L. volemus* dissipates with cooking, and the texture of all three is meatier than just about any other mushroom. They are best preserved by cooking and freezing.

Candy Caps

Worldwide, the candy cap (*Lactarius rubidus*) has a very limited geographic range but it is such a unique, popular edible mushroom that it is worth exploring here. In western North America, in California in particular, where the mushroom season doesn't usually start until the eastern United States's season is over, that is, from November to February, this especially good edible milk cap mushroom tastes almost like maple syrup. A very similar second species (*L. rufulus*) can occur in the same areas, and it seems to be restricted to the northern California coast. It's found in mixed woods, often in large quantities (*L. rubidus* under pine and oak; *L. rufulus* under oak).

Eating Candy Caps

The candy cap is especially good in dishes where a butterscotch or maple syrup flavor is wanted, such as cookies or a quiche. It dries easily and retains its flavor for some time.

Best Preparation: As a dessert mushroom, in cookies and cakes.
Best Preservation: Dry and store in a tight-fitting jar.

Candy cap (*Lactarius rubidus*)

Blewits

COMMON NAMES:
Blewit (wild), bluefoot (cultivated)

SCIENTIFIC NAME:
Lepista nuda (wild), *Lepista personata* (cultivated)

FIELD DESCRIPTION:
- Reaches 2 to 4 inches (5 to 10 cm) across, 2 to 3 inches (5 to 7.5 cm) high.

- Appears as a fleshy mushroom with violet to tan cap, violet to pinkish buff attached (notched), and crowded gills, pinkish buff spore print.

- Has a violet to gray-brown stem.

LOOK-ALIKES:
Cortinarius alboviolaceus and related species have a cortina (or spiderweb-like veil) covering the young gills and leaving a rusty brownish hairlike band on the upper stem, and produces a rusty brown spore print. Entoloma species with blewit-like colors produce a salmon-pinkish brown spore print. *Laccaria ochropurpurea* has a grayish white cap and stem and broad, distant purple gills.

CAUTION:
Cook well.

Blewits and Bluefoot

The most beautiful mushroom in the market, perhaps, is the cultivated blewit (called bluefoot commercially), which has a distinctive, long purple stem; it is now available in some stores year-round. The wild blewit is something you have to wait for until autumn. It's as hard to see nestled in among the multicolored fallen leaves as the market bluefoot stands out. It's a hunt, to be sure, but well worth the effort, for most people consider it one of the best of the edible gilled mushrooms. In fact, it's one of the last of the year's good edibles available well into late autumn.

The name refers to its color. Blewit is short for "blue hats," and the mushroom, when young and fresh, has a blue cap and gills and a pale blue stem. As it ages or is exposed to light it fades considerably so that it can be hard to identify when it isn't blue. Even so, when it is blue it can still cause problems because there are other blue mushrooms out there and care has to be taken to identify the mushroom correctly.

The cultivated blewit is referred to as bluefoot. It's a different species but "field" distinguishable by its yellow-brown cap, pinkish tan gills, and long bright purple stem. Both the cultivated and the wild species share the same edible qualities. They can have a pleasant odor and, when well cooked, a pleasing, meaty texture and a pronounced flavor that is hard to describe but enjoyed and remembered.

Lepista as a genus can be recognized as a group of fleshy, often stout, pinkish tan spored mushrooms with attached gills, some species with blue to purplish cap, gill, and/or stem colors, that grow on the ground.

Eating Blewits
Best Preparation: Sauté or pickle
Best Preservation: Sauté and freeze or pickle

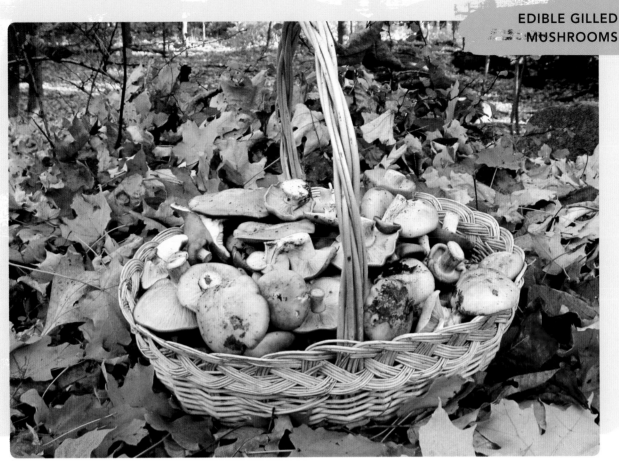

Blewits (*Lepista nuda*)

NO ONE LEAVES EMPTY-HANDED

Mushroom hunting is not about what you are looking for; it's about what you find.

It was autumn and we were in an oak-rich wooded part of a city park looking for hen-of-the-woods. We found nothing but a couple of elderly retired gentlemen walking about carrying sticks and large sacks. The hen-of-the-woods we were looking for were already in their sacks. It was when we thought we were just plum out of luck that we noticed the 3-inch (7.5 cm) telltale blue mushroom cap sticking up out of the fallen oak leaves we were walking through. It was a blewit. Down on our hands and knees, pulling away the pile of fallen leaves, we found more, and then more blewits. Within an hour we had collected more than a hundred.

Poisonous Mushrooms

These are not the only poisonous mushrooms, just the most common and commonly reported ones. There are others, but they either rarely show up in cases of reported poisonings or the poisoning is rarely more serious than vomiting and diarrhea. Curiously, the most common cases of reported mushroom poisoning among adults are from well-known edible mushrooms, such as morels, chanterelles, and king boletes. Partly this is because more people eat these mushrooms than any other wild mushrooms. Some people are allergic to some mushrooms, and some people eat too much or eat undercooked mushrooms or eat something decaying or infested. Small children and household pets are grazers, and they eat whatever they find raw. Sometimes this leads to serious consequences, especially when the child is very young, even if the mushroom when cooked is safe for adults to eat.

That said, there is still an aura of mystery surrounding mushrooms that makes them seem somehow different than plants, and thus poisonings are harder to understand. Various mushrooms have been known to cause liver failure; kidney failure; profuse sweating, tearing, and salivation; delirium, hallucinations, and even death.

There is even a mushroom that contains a toxic hydrazine similar to a component used in rocket fuel, and this mushroom in Europe is a popular edible but only if properly prepared; otherwise, it can be deadly.

The point is that all of these strange poisonings come from mushrooms that do not look all that different from edible mushrooms, making the whole venture of picking your own wild mushrooms seem too hazardous even to contemplate.

Nevertheless, very few people are seriously poisoned by mushrooms, and none need be poisoned if these guidelines are followed.

The Major Poisonous Look-Alikes

The following list represents those poisonous mushrooms that can be found in most parts of the world and that have been or could be gathered by mistake for edible mushrooms. Not every poisonous mushroom is listed here, nor are several that are too geographically restricted for a general chart on the world's major poisonous mushrooms. See Appendix II on page 186 for an essential guide to major poisonous mushrooms, symptoms of poisoning, and treatment.

- Destroying angels (*Amanita virosa* complex)
- Death cap (*Amanita phalloides*)
- Deadly galerina (*Galerina autumnalis*)
- Deadly cort (*Cortinarius orellanus* complex)
- False morels (*Gyromitra* spp.)
- Sweater (*Clitocybe dealbata*)
- Fiber heads (*Inocybe* spp.)
- Panther (*Amanita pantherina*)
- Fly-agaric (*Amanita muscaria*)
- Magic mushrooms (*Psilocybe* spp.)
- Big-laughing gym (*Gymnopilus spectabilis* complex)
- Alcohol inky cap (*Coprinus atramentarius*)
- Jack-o'-lantern (*Omphalotus* spp.)
- Green-spored lepiota (*Chlorophyllum molybdites*)
- Phenolic Agaricus species (*Agaricus xanthodermus* complex)
- Satan's bolete (*Boletus satanus* complex)
- False king bolete (*Boletus huronensis*)
- Blue staining bolete (*Boletus sensibilis*)

Alcohol inky-cap (*Coprinus atramentarius*)

Death cap (*Amanita phalloides*)

Seasonal Guide to Poisonous Mushrooms

Mushroom seasons and growing location for the poisonous mushroom groups are presented here. For definitions of the nine major regions of the world listed here, see page 19. Use extra caution when consulting local or regional mushroom guides to pinpoint precise growing seasons. See Appendix II, page 186, for information on the symptoms of poisoning and treatment of major poisonous mushrooms.

Mushroom	1. NA	2. RM	3. CAPNW	4. SA
DESTROYING ANGELS (*Amanita virosa* complex)	under oaks, summer and autumn	under gambol oak, summer	under liveoak, winter–spring	N/A
DEATH CAP (*Amanita phalloides*)	under oaks and pines, autumn	N/A	under oaks, Nov–Feb	under introduced pines
DEADLY GALERINA (*Galerina autumnalis*)	on rotting conifer logs, autumn and spring	on rotting conifer logs, summer and autumn	on rotting wood, autumn and winter	N/A
DEADLY CORTS (*Cortinarius orellanus* complex)	under hardwoods, summer–autumn	N/A	under conifers, summer–autumn	N/A
FALSE MORELS (*Gyromitra* spp.)	under conifers, spring and autumn	under conifers, spring–summer	under conifers, spring–summer	N/A
THE SWEATER (*Clitocybe dealbata* complex)	grassy areas, summer–autumn	roadsides, summer	grassy areas, autumn–mid-winter	N/A
FIBER HEADS (*Inocybe* spp.)	under hardwoods and conifers, summer–autumn	under hardwoods and conifers, summer	under hardwoods and conifers, autumn–winter	under hardwoods, Feb–April
PANTHER (*Amanita pantherina*)	under hardwoods, summer	under conifers, summer	under conifers, autumn–spring	N/A
FLY-AGARIC (*Amanita muscaria*)	under hardwoods and conifers, summer–autumn	under conifers, summer	under conifers, autumn–early winter	N/A
MAGIC MUSHROOMS (*Psilocybe* spp.)	in pastures, on wood, in wood mulch, autumn	N/A	in pastures and wood mulch, autumn	in pastures, Feb–Apr
BIG LAUGHING GYM (*Gymnopilus spectabilis* complex)	on wood, summer–autumn	N/A	on wood, Oct–Feb	N/A
ALCOHOL INKY-CAP (*Coprinus atramentarius*)	in grassy areas, spring and autumn	near rotting wood, spring and autumn	in grass near rotting wood, Oct–Apr	near rotting wood, Jan–Mar
JACK-O'-LANTERN (*Omphalotus* spp.)	on hardwoods, autumn	N/A	on hardwoods, autumn–mid-winter	N/A
GREEN-SPORED LEPIOTA (*Chlorophyllum molybdites*)	in grassy areas: late summer–autumn, often in fairy rings	in grass, in parks, summer	in grass, in parks, summer	in grassy areas, autumn
PHENOLIC AGARICUS (*Agaricus xanthodermus* complex)	in grassy areas, summer–autumn	in grass in parks, late spring–early autumn	in grass and under trees, Oct–Feb	N/A
FALSE PUFFBALLS (*Scleroderma* spp.)	under hardwoods (oaks), summer–autumn	on ground near rotting wood, summer	under hardwoods (oaks), autumn	on ground near trees, Feb–Apr
SATAN'S BOLETE (*Boletus satanus* complex)	under hardwoods, summer	N/A	under hardwoods and conifers, Nov–Feb	N/A
FALSE KING BOLETE (*Boletus huronensis*)	under hemlocks, autumn	N/A	N/A	N/A
BLUE-STAINING BOLETES (*Boletus sensibilis* complex)	under hardwoods, summer–autumn	N/A	under hardwoods and conifers, spring and autumn	N/A

N/A= not reported or not yet found
1. (NA) Eastern and Central North America from Canada to Mexico and through Central America
2. (RM) Rocky Mountains of North America
3. (CAPNW) California and the Pacific Northwest of North America
4. (SA) South America
5. (EUR) Europe (including western, central, and eastern Europe)
6. (MED) Mediterranean (including southern Europe, North Africa, and parts of the Middle East)
7. (AFR) Southern Africa
8. (ASIA) Asia (from India to Japan)
9. (ANZ) Australia and New Zealand

5. EUR	6. MED	7. AFR	8. ASIA	9. ANZ
hardwoods, but under conifers in mountains, summer–autumn	under oaks, autumn–winter	under hardwoods and conifers, Dec and March	under oaks and conifers, summer and autumn	in east Aus woods, Sept–Oct
under hardwoods, autumn	under hardwoods and conifers, autumn–winter	under hardwoods and conifers, Dec and March	N/A	under oaks, March–Apr
on decaying conifer wood, autumn	on rotting wood, autumn–winter	N/A	on rotting wood, autumn	on rotting wood, June and August
under hardwoods and conifers, summer–autumn	N/A	N/A	N/A	N/A
under conifers, spring–summer	under conifers, spring	N/A	on ground in woods, spring	on the ground, Nov–Dec
grassy areas, summer–autumn	in grassy areas, autumn	N/A	toxic lookalike in Japan, autumn	grassy areas, Nov–Dec
under hardwoods and conifers, summer–autumn	under hardwoods and conifers, autumn–winter	under introduced pines, Mar–June	under hardwoods and conifers, summer–autumn	under hardwoods, Apr–June
under hardwoods, summer–autumn	under oaks, autumn–winter	under introduced hardwoods and conifers, Jan–June	under hardwoods and conifers, autumn	N/A
under hardwoods and conifers, summer–autumn	under hardwoods, autumn–winter	under introduced pines and oaks, Jan–June	under hardwoods and conifers, autumn	under introduced pines, Feb–Apr
in pastures and woods, autumn	on wood debris, autumn	in garden mulch near trees, June	on dung and wood debris, autumn	in pastures and garden mulch, Apr–May
on wood, autumn	on wood, autumn–winter	on wood, June	on wood, autumn	on wood, Feb–Apr
in pastures, parks, mulch, autumn	on wood, in mulch, Nov–Dec	in wood mulch, June	on dung, in mulch, Sept–Oct	in parks, wood mulch, Feb–Apr
on hardwoods, Southern Europe, autumn	on hardwoods, like olive, autumn–winter	N/A	on wood or buried wood, summer–autumn	on wood or in grass on buried wood, Feb–Apr
in parks, Southern Europe, spring–autumn	in grassy areas, Nov–Jan	N/A	in grassy areas, southern Japan, autumn	in grassy areas in NSW and Queens-land, Mar–Apr
woods and grasslands, summer–autumn	in grassy areas, Nov–Feb	in grassy areas, Jan–Apr	in grassy areas, spring–summer	in grassy areas in Queensland, March
common in parks under hardwood trees, autumn	in grassy areas, near hardwoods, autumn and winter	under hardwoods, such as acacias, Mar–July	in parks and woods under trees, autumn	in grassy areas and under shrubs and trees, Apr–June
under hardwoods, summer	under hardwoods, autumn	N/A	under hardwoods, summer	N/A
N/A	N/A	N/A	N/A	N/A
under hardwoods, summer–autumn	under hardwoods, summer–autumn	N/A	under hardwoods, summer–autumn	N/A

Death cap (*Amanita phalloides*)

Destroying angel (*Amanita virosa* complex)

ANGEL OF LOVE

It was a sparklingly clear autumn day, and I met a couple walking through the woods holding hands. In the man's free hand he held a large white mushroom, which I could easily tell was a destroying angel. I told the couple that they had one of the most beautiful mushrooms in the woods, but it was such a shame it was so poisonous. The man asked me what I meant—it was pure white, unmarked, and very fresh, clear signs to them that it must be good to eat. I told them he was holding the destroying angel. He was unfazed by the name. He challenged me by saying that nothing that beautiful could be that dangerous. The woman said I was right about the "angel" part. I replied that eating this one mushroom could provide a sufficiently lethal dose of poison for both of them. The man, still affronted, resented my intrusion on their privacy and claimed that I wanted the mushroom for myself. I assured them that I didn't, that they should throw the mushroom away in the woods somewhere where I couldn't find it, and that if they ate it I would read about it in the newspaper within two days.

They walked past me, still clutching the destroying angel. I checked the papers for the next week but never saw any mention of a mushroom poisoning in the area.

Destroying Angels and Death Caps

The genus *Amanita* contains hundreds of species throughout the world. A very few (the destroying angel and the death cap) are known to be deadly, but a single mushroom of one of these species can be lethal. Nearly all known mushroom fatalities in the world are caused by these few mushrooms. Because the genus *Amanita* is relatively easy to recognize and the species are often very difficult to tell apart, it is common practice to avoid these mushrooms that can be common in the yards, parks, woods, and forests of the world.

It can get confusing when one of these species shows up for sale in a local market. In Italy, for example, the egg stage of the Caesar's mushroom, *Amanita caesarea*, is a favorite edible mushroom. In parts of Asia, Europe, and Mexico, species of Amanita, usually those very similar to the European Caesar's mushroom, are often brought to market. It can give the impression that the genus is not all that dangerous. Some species of *Amanita* besides those known to be deadly are known to cause serious poisoning, some others cause delirium, and still others cause digestive upset.

Given the risk of misidentifying the species, and the likelihood that you may find one about whose edibility nothing is known, there is nothing to be gained by experimenting with mushrooms in the genus *Amanita*. Besides, if these mushrooms are common in the woods, then so are many others that are easier to identify correctly and known to be safe and choice edibles.

Destroying angel (*Amanita virosa* complex)

Destroying angel (*Amanita virosa* complex)

Cross-section of an *Amanita* "egg"

Amanitas

COMMON NAMES:
Destroying angel, death cap

SCIENTIFIC NAMES:
Amanita virosa, A. bisporigera, A. ocreata,
A. phalloides

FIELD DESCRIPTION:

⊙ Grows on the ground, singly or several but not clustered, under oaks and conifers in parks and woods.

⊙ *Amanita* is a large gilled mushroom with white or gray-green cap, white gills unattached to stem (free), white spore print.

⊙ Veil covers immature gills, leaving a skirtlike ring on upper stem.

⊙ Saclike cup encloses base of stem.

⊙ The whole arises out of an egglike membrane.

SYMPTOMS:
There are no symptoms for eight to twelve hours, then severe cramping, nausea, vomiting, and diarrhea for twenty-four hours. Symptoms abate, but then signs of liver damage appear, leading, if untreated, to liver failure, coma, and death.

TREATMENT:
Liver enzyme levels can indicate the severity of the poisoning. Good hospital care is sometimes all that is needed, but milk thistle extract is now being used to protect the liver. In extreme cases, liver transplants have been performed with good results.

A few other mushrooms are known to cause this same kind of poisoning. There are some small, relatively fragile mushrooms in the genera *Lepiota* and *Conocybe* that contain toxic amounts of the same compounds as these *Amanitas*. There is also the deadly galerina, which has become a problem because it can look like one of our popular edible mushrooms, the honey mushroom (page 114).

CALL YOUR LOCAL POISON CONTROL IN CASE OF EMERGENCY

Deadly Galerina

COMMON NAME:
Deadly galerina

SCIENTIFIC NAME:
Galerina autumnalis

FIELD DESCRIPTION:
- Grows singly or many, but not clustered, on rotting logs.

- Appear as small, brown-capped gilled mushrooms, caps fading quickly on picking and on aging to yellowish.

- Gills are yellowish, becoming rusty brown on maturity.

- Veil covers young gills, leaving a small brownish (from dropped spores) ring on upper stem.

COMPARISON WITH HONEY MUSHROOMS:
The edible honey mushroom is typically a large mushroom that grows in clusters on wood and has a white spore print, while the deadly galerina is a smaller, thinner stemmed mushroom that grows singly to scattered on rotting logs and has a rusty brown spore print.

SYMPTOMS:
As above, with destroying angel poisoning.

TREATMENT:
As above, with destroying angel poisoning.

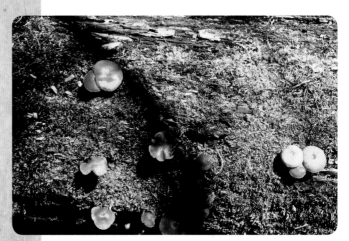

Deadly galerina (*Galerina autumnalis*)

Deadly Galerina: LBM Death

The rule of thumb is to avoid LBMs—Little Brown Mushrooms. There are a great many different kinds of LBMs, and most are very difficult to identify to species without a microscope. Nothing is known about the edibility of most of them and, though a few are known to be edible, a few are also known to be quite deadly. Deadly galerina (*Galerina autumnalis*) is one of the deadly LBMs. *Galerina autumnalis* is a small brown mushroom with brownish gills that will produce a brown spore print. The mushroom grows on wood, sometimes in quantity, but usually scattered along a log, not growing in clusters. It is conspicuous, especially late in the autumn and early in the spring, when there are few other mushrooms about. Because it has been confused with the honey mushroom, a comparison of the two is offered here.

Deadly galerina
(*Galerina autumnalis*)

Honey mushroom
(*Armillaria mellea* complex)

UNHAPPY TREAT

In addition to the destroying angels, the death cap, and the deadly galerina, there are other deadly mushrooms in the parks and woods of the world. Although they are not likely to be mistaken for the edible gilled mushrooms included in this book, a few people have, for whatever reason, picked and eaten them. One that has caused a few high-profile fatalities recently is the small inconspicuous deadly lepiota, *Lepiota josserandii* complex. Another, which is scattered across the northern tier of the northern hemisphere is the deadly conocybe, *Conocybe filaris*. Because there will always be poisonous mushrooms out there that are not described or illustrated in books, it's of the utmost importance to be 100 percent certain of your identification of any mushroom you think is a choice edible.

It was the Sunday after Halloween. There had been a frost or two and the woods were almost leafless and seemed bare of mushrooms. Our group dispersed over a wide area as we searched for any mushrooms at all. At our midday lunch break, one person showed up with the bottom of his large paper shopping bag filled with mushrooms. "Honeys," he said, smiling. He was the only person to find anything fresh that day. The rest of us had to content ourselves with half-frozen or rotten mushrooms.

That evening, he cooked and ate these mushrooms with his wife. About eight hours later they both awoke to severe cramps, diarrhea, and vomiting. He called to report that they had eaten the honey mushrooms he gathered on Sunday and now they were both very sick. He wondered whether they were suffering from food poisoning, whether the mushrooms he had gathered had been somehow decayed. It didn't seem like the symptoms of any kind of normal stomach upset from eating bad mushrooms.

Because they had eaten all the mushrooms he'd gathered, it seemed advisable to drive him back to the woods to see whether he could find more of

Deadly galerina (*Galerina autumnalis*)

the same thing. This was the surest way we could correctly identify what they had eaten. The journey was harrowing. He threw up on the drive to the woods, and he passed out briefly once or twice while ambling around the area where he thought he had picked the honey mushrooms.

After a few hours of searching, he cried out that he had found them. When we joined him, he was standing over a fallen, moss-covered tree dotted with a number of small brown mushrooms. We knew immediately they weren't honey mushrooms. It took a look through several books to discover that what he had found, and what they had eaten, was the deadly galerina, something up to that time we didn't even know we had in the nearby woods. On searching through the woods later we discovered it was one of the most common mushrooms appearing on wood in the late autumn. It was conspicuous mostly by the absence of most other mushrooms that couldn't survive cold autumn weather.

Although they had to spend ten days in the hospital, they both survived the ordeal. Afterward, he said he had thought there weren't any deadly mushrooms that grew on wood. Live and learn.

CALL YOUR LOCAL POISON CONTROL IN CASE OF EMERGENCY

Deadly Corts

COMMON NAME:
Deadly cort

SCIENTIFIC NAMES:
Cortinarius orellanus and several still undetermined species in this group

FIELD DESCRIPTION:
- Grows on the ground under conifers and hardwoods (oaks).
- Appear as small to medium, orange to orange-brown or reddish brown gilled mushrooms with a cobweblike veil covering the immature gills and leaving a hairlike ring on the upper stem.
- Spore print is rusty brown.

COMPARISON WITH THE CHANTERELLES:
Chanterelles have wavy-shaped caps and clearly thick-edged, forked gill-like folds that descend the stem somewhat. There is no veil covering the young gills or ring on the stem. Chanterelles have a fruity odor and produce a white spore print.

SYMPTOMS:
Symptoms don't occur until several days to two weeks after the mushrooms have been eaten, usually in sequential meals, leading to renal dysfunction or failure.

TREATMENT:
Symptomatic but kidney dialysis, if needed.

Deadly Corts

There could be a thousand species of *Cortinarius* in the forests. They are all associated with conifers and hardwood trees, such as oaks. Late summer and autumn the woods can be carpeted with great numbers of these mushrooms. They vary in size and color, but all grow on the ground and have a cobweblike veil covering the young gills, and all produce a rusty brown spore print. They are very difficult to identify to species and none is known to be a choice edible, although a few species are said to be safe. Mushroom hunters may admire and photograph them, but they don't bring them home to eat.

The essential problem with the corts is at least one group of species is known to contain toxins that cause kidney failure, and there have been reports, especially in Europe, of people picking these corts having mistaken them for chanterelles! A recent, high-profile case involved Nicholas Evans, the author of *The Horse Whisperer*, who accidentally poisoned his whole family with these mushrooms while on vacation in Scotland. Several members of his family were put on kidney dialysis machines for months. The first known case in the United States occurred in 2008, where a woman ate some mushrooms she found in her backyard. A year later she remained on dialysis.

Unrelated to the poisoning in the genus *Cortinarius*, but also causing kidney failure, is Smith's Amanita (*Amanita smithiana*), a Pacific Northwest poisonous look-alike for the widely sough-after matsutake *Tricholoma magnivelare*.

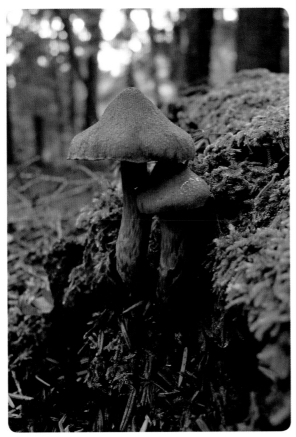

A deadly cort, *Cortinarius rubellus*, in the *Cortinarius orellanus* complex

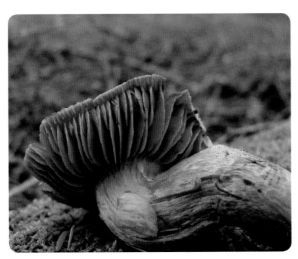

A deadly cort, *Cortinarius rubellus*, showing the gills

MUSHROOM DETECTIVE

Sometimes mushroom poisoning requires the expertise of a Sherlock Holmes. Just such a case occurred in Poland many years ago. A statistically significant number of people, and far more men than women, had come down with kidney failure. A doctor examining the evidence asked the right questions and discovered the cause. What connected all these people was that they had all been collecting mushrooms under a particular bridge. They had been eating these mushrooms believing them to be edible and were suffering no noticeable poisoning symptoms. One of the mushrooms that they all were eating was an orange-brown mushroom that had a cobweblike veil over the immature gills, and produced a rusty brown spore print. It was a species of *Cortinarius*, a genus that until that time was believed to be harmless.

It turns out that *Cortinarius orellanus* is one of a group of species in this genus that can cause kidney failure. The symptoms sometimes don't appear until a week or more after eating the mushrooms, and because the mushrooms taste good and there is no reason to fear poisoning, the mushrooms are eaten several days in a row, as long as they can be collected. It turned out that men were eating many times more mushrooms than women purely because they were eating larger volumes of food, which is why they were exhibiting many more cases of kidney failure than their wives, who were sharing the same meals.

CALL YOUR LOCAL POISON CONTROL IN CASE OF EMERGENCY

False Morels

COMMON NAME:
False morel

SCIENTIFIC NAMES:
Gyromitra esculenta complex, *G. brunnea*

FIELD DESCRIPTION:
- Found on ground under trees and shrubs, in spring and autumn.
- Appear brownish to reddish brown, brain-shaped, saddle-shaped, or draping cap with folds.
- Have a simple to compound stem.
- When sliced in half, chambered or stuffed with tissue.

COMPARISON WITH MORELS:
Morels are off-white to cream or yellowish to almost black, with a honeycomb-like head on a stem; when cut in half, the interior is hollow.

SYMPTOMS:
Six to twelve hours after ingestion (sometimes sooner), bloating, vomiting, diarrhea (sometimes bloody), cramping, and weakness; in severe cases, leading to convulsions, coma, and death.

TREATMENT:
Prompt and competent medical care.

False Morels

False morels mostly look like brains; some look like drapes; a few look like saddles on a stalk. They don't really look like morels, but because they often occur at the same time and look more like morels than anything else does in the spring, they are called "false morels." The primary species in Europe is known as *Gyromitra esculenta*, and it is sold in markets there and consumed by many people. It is also quite poisonous and requires special care in processing it safely, something that some people don't know or forget.

In North America, there are several species of *Gyromitra*, almost all of which fruit in the spring. Some species are popular edibles in localities where they occur and no poisonous species of false morels also occur. In the St. Louis, Missouri, area, for example, big red is a popular false morel spring edible. In the eastern United States, however, there are several known species, and a few of these are known to be poisonous, even life threatening. There are also several species of false morels in the western United States, and although a few species are eaten, the rest are left alone.

In Europe and in other regions where traditional mushroom hunting and preparation is still actively passed down the generations, false morels are safely eaten because the preparers have learned over time how to prepare them.

False morels are best identified by cutting them in half lengthwise. Whereas morels are hollow, false morels are either chambered or stuffed with tissue.

A false morel, *Gyromitra korfii*

POT LUCK

The fear of mushroom poisoning is so ingrained that people who appear to be perfectly rational can become inflexible in an instant.

False morels are known to be poisonous, even deadly, yet some people eat some kinds that appear to be perfectly safe to eat. A friend came east from California and, among other gifts, brought with him a false morel dip. Although leery of eating a mushroom with so checkered a reputation, we trusted his judgment that the ones he had gathered in California were safe to eat.

We went out to a mushroom club event where people were invited to bring a mushroom dish to share. He brought along his false morel dip. As we were proceeding to put out the various things we had brought for others to taste, word got around that a false morel dip was being put on the table. This led to a ferocious war of words between my friend and some of the officers of the club, who refused to let him put his false morel dip on the table. They didn't care that it was very tasty or even edible, or that he knew it well and had eaten it safely for years. They said the club had a rule that certain mushrooms could not be served at their gatherings, and one of those mushrooms was the false morel. It didn't matter that this one came from California, that nobody would be poisoned by tasting it. They said the rule was the rule; there were no exceptions.

CALL YOUR LOCAL POISON CONTROL IN CASE OF EMERGENCY

Left: edible fairy ring mushroom (*Marasmius oreades*), **Right:** the sweater (*Clitocybe dealbata*)

Muscarine Poisoning

COMMON NAME:
Fiber heads

SCIENTIFIC NAME:
Inocybe (various species)

FIELD DESCRIPTION:
- Very commonly found on the ground under conifers and hardwood trees, such as oaks, and can be found in almost every city and suburban park, and along every woodland trail.

- Appear as small to medium-sized, gilled mushrooms with brownish conical caps that have distinct fibrils or scales running from the center to the edge.

- Gills are gray-brown to brown.

- Leaves a brownish spore print.

COMMON NAME:
The sweater

SCIENTIFIC NAME:
Clitocybe dealbata

FIELD DESCRIPTION:
- Occurs in lawns, sometimes in fairy rings.

- Have a small white to gray capped gilled mushroom, with white gills attached to and running somewhat down a short stem.

- Leaves a white spore print.

SYMPTOMS:
Profuse, intermittent perspiration, salivation, and lacrimation, abdominal cramps, diarrhea, blurred vision, pinpoint pupils, and slowing of pulse.

TREATMENT:
Symptomatic hospital care in severe cases. Atropine sulfate sometimes employed as an antidote.

Besides the mushrooms listed above, other mushrooms have been reported to contain toxic amounts of muscarine. One or more of the red-pored blue-staining boletes is reported to cause muscarine symptoms.

Fiber cap (*Inocybe* sp.)

Muscarine Poisoning

There are two common groups of mushrooms that are known to cause a syndrome called *muscarine poisoning*. The syndrome is recognized by waves of perspiration, salivation, and lacrimation (tearing), sometimes along with vomiting, diarrhea, and abdominal cramps, as well as blurred vision. One of these groups is the genus *Inocybe*, a genus of LBMs (Little Brown Mushrooms); the other is an often common, white-spored, gilled mushroom, known as the sweater, *Clitocybe dealbata*. Other mushrooms known to cause muscarine poisoning symptoms include the fly agaric (*Amanita muscaria*) and, in Australia, a bolete that recently caused a muscarine poisoning fatality. Normally, muscarine poisoning is treatable with atropine sulfate, and fatalities are rare.

SWEATER...UNRAVELED

An artist friend of mine goes mushroom hunting to clear his mind. His favorite mushroom is the fairy ring mushroom (*Marasmius oreades*). He always finds it growing in lawns, frequently in arcs or rings, called fairy rings. He gathered a basketful one day, took them home, used them in making dinner that night, and within an hour began to feel distinctly unwell. He started sweating profusely, soaking through his clothes, which he changed, but continued to sweat. He was also salivating, with saliva running down his chin. His eyes were tearing and he found it getting harder to see clearly. He knew he had been poisoned by some kind of mushroom, but he had no idea what it was or what would happen to him next. His wife was beside herself with fear and wanted him to go to the hospital immediately. Instead, he went to his bookshelf and started reading about mushroom poisoning in all the books he had about mushrooms.

He found his symptoms were those of muscarine poisoning, and he discovered the mushroom he must have collected inadvertently with the fairy ring mushroom was a poisonous look-alike called *Clitocybe dealbata*, known as the sweater. One book said that the symptoms would not get any worse than he was experiencing and that they would last for about five hours or so. With that piece of information, he assured his wife that he wasn't going to die, and he sat down to wait out the duration of the poisoning.

CALL YOUR LOCAL POISON CONTROL IN CASE OF EMERGENCY

The panther (*Amanita pantherina*)

Panther Amanita

COMMON NAME:
Panther amanita

SCIENTIFIC NAME:
Amanita pantherina

FIELD DESCRIPTION:
- The panther amanita is a medium-sized gilled mushroom with a brownish cap adorned with off-white patches from the universal veil (egg), a veil covering the immature white gills that are free (not attached to stem), leaving a skirtlike ring of tissue on the upper stem.

- Stem base shows tissue remnants, sometimes ring-like, from the egg out of which the mushroom arises.

- Spore print is white.

SYMPTOMS:
Delirium, raving, repetitive behavior.

TREATMENT:
Symptomatic; self-limiting, twenty-four-hour duration.

Panther Amanita

The panther amanita doesn't pounce; it just sits there and waits. A mushroom hunter comes along, sees it, thinks it's something else, something edible, and plops it in his basket. Later, over a cocktail or two, he cooks and seasons the mushrooms and serves them with dinner. They taste fine. Unless the mushroom is identified correctly in the beginning, the poisonous nature of this mushroom is not likely to be noticed until the symptoms appear, thirty minutes to an hour after eating it. Delirium is one of the most noticeable features, a raving that will likely need to be tranquilized in a hospital setting. The panther amanita is not a deadly mushroom, but an accidental poisoning is scary for both the victim and those around him. Usually the patient is his or her "old self" within twenty-four hours, but those twenty-four hours are experienced, as has been described, as though living through a horror movie in which it is all happening to you.

BEWARE OF THE PANTHER

The panther amanita (*Amanita pantherina*) is sometimes eaten by people who have mistaken it for an edible species of *Agaricus*. The resulting poisoning can be described as a twenty-four-hour-long deliriousness. The victim sometimes sees insects coming out of his body or crawling over his skin, and may misidentify doctors in white lab coats as angels. People who have read that you can get high from eating this mushroom will try it and discover that it's nothing they are prepared to experience.

A common symptom of the delirium following ingestion of the panther is for the victim to fall into a repetitive feedback loop; that is, whatever he does, he does again and again. One person sitting on a low bridge fell into the water and was observed getting up, returning to the bridge, sitting down, and falling off again.

Alcohol Inky Caps

There are a few mushrooms, the alcohol inky cap (*Coprinus atramentarius*) and a common autumn white-spored gilled mushroom (*Clitocybe clavipes*), that are known to cause a strange and transient poisoning when eaten before consuming an alcoholic beverage. The mushrooms contain a compound that inhibits a liver enzyme that detoxifies alcohol. If they have been ingested and alcohol is then consumed, usually a day to three days later, within thirty minutes of drinking a beer or even taking an alcohol-based cough medicine, a swift but brief and violent vomiting is likely to occur. The alcoholic beverage is usually blamed because it's the most recent thing the person had before the sudden nausea and vomiting.

Despite the startling nature of this poisoning, it doesn't afflict everyone, but it puts us all on notice to avoid certain mushrooms if we consume alcohol. In Sweden, it was thought to be a natural alternative to Antabuse, something that is given in pill form to alcoholics in the morning so that if they drink during the day they will get sick. Unfortunately, it was learned in the testing procedures prior to patent approval that coprine, the active ingredient in the alcohol inky cap, also interferes with sperm count. This alarmed the authorities, who feared lawsuits, and the project was dropped.

Alcohol inky-cap (*Coprinus atramentarius*)

Alcohol Inky Cap

COMMON NAME:
Alcohol inky cap

SCIENTIFIC NAME:
Coprinus atramentarius

FIELD DESCRIPTION:
- Often grows clustered, in lawns and on wood debris.
- Appears as a medium-sized, fleshy, grayish, cylindrical-shaped mushroom with embedded (not shaggy) scales about the top of the cylindrical cap.
- Has off-white gills, covered with a veil at first, leave a ring at base of stem, that then turn black and dissolve on maturity into an inky mass.

COMMON NAME:
Fat-footed clitocybe

SCIENTIFIC NAME:
Clitocybe clavipes

FIELD DESCRIPTION:
- Grows on the ground in woods.
- Appears as a small to medium-sized, gilled mushroom.
- Cap and stem are often tan to light brown.
- Gills are white, decurrent, or running somewhat down the stem.
- Stem enlarges downward to spongy base.
- Spore print white

SYMPTOMS:
Vomiting within thirty minutes of consuming an alcoholic beverage with or after a meal of the alcohol inky cap or fat-footed clitocybe.

TREATMENT:
Symptomatic; self-limiting, soon after initial vomiting.

CALL YOUR LOCAL POISON CONTROL IN CASE OF EMERGENCY

Jack-o'-lantern (*Omphalotus illudens*)

Jack-o'-Lanterns

COMMON NAMES:
Jack-o'-lantern, false chanterelle

SCIENTIFIC NAMES:
Omphalotus olearius, O. illudens, O. olivascens

FIELD DESCRIPTION:
- Appear as large, typically clustered gilled mushrooms on wood or buried wood.

- Have bright orange caps, gills, and stems.

- Gills are thin, close, knife-edge-like, and decurrent, running somewhat down the stem.

- Leaves a white spore print.

COMPARISON WITH CHANTERELLES
Chanterelles grow singly; have a wavy cap and thick-edged, forked, gill-like folds; and have a fruity odor.

SYMPTOMS:
Nausea, vomiting, abdominal cramping, diarrhea.

TREATMENT:
Symptomatic; self-limiting, twenty-four-hour duration.

Jack-o'-Lantern

One of the most beautiful mushrooms is the jack-o'-lantern. It can grow in large bouquets of hundreds of fruiting bodies, with individual caps measuring up to 4 inches (10 cm) or more across. The bright orange caps, gills, and stems almost glow against the brown backdrop of a tree or the surrounding green grass. When fresh, these mushrooms glow in the dark. The light can be so bright that you can read a newspaper by the eerie yellowish green light given off by fresh jack-o'-lanterns. The mushrooms are also poisonous.

Not only are they notable for their attractiveness, but as a look-alike for chanterelles, the jack-o'-lanterns are one of the most common cause of mushroom poisoning. The symptoms, though violent and sometimes prolonged, are not life threatening, but it's not something you'd ever want to repeat.

All species of jack-o'-lantern mushrooms (*Omphalotus*) are poisonous and cause the same basic kind of poisoning. You don't die, but you feel at times that death would be better than suffering the agony of abdominal cramps, nausea, and vomiting.

Jack-o'-lanterns also occur in southern Europe and the Middle East, wherever olive trees are found. It grows in clusters at the base of these trees. In Israel, after the rainy season begins in December, olive orchards are awash with clusters of jack-o'-lanterns at the base of the gnarled trees. Presumably, the olive orchards glow in the dark! Once, a group of Czech tourists (from a country where jack-o'-lanterns do not occur) while traveling in Yugoslavia found what they thought were chanterelles, and twenty-five of them spent the night in a local hospital.

Jack-o'-lanterns occur across much of North America, usually on oaks, and in California in particular there are at least two distinct species.

Eastern United States jack-o'-lantern
(*Omphalotus illudens*)

California jack-o'-lantern (*Omphalotus olivascens*)

California jack-o'-lantern (*Omphalotus olivascens*)

Why Do Some Mushrooms Glow in the Dark?

It is believed that glow-in-the-dark mushrooms glow to attract nocturnal animals to visit them and disperse their spores. Although they are apparently fine for animal consumption, none is known to be edible for humans, and several cause severe gastro-intestinal distress.

Mushrooms exist as the primary way for the fungus to disperse its spores. Most spores are airborne and are dispersed by the wind. Truffles and other under-ground mushrooms are strongly fragrant to attract animals to eat them and disperse their spores. There are also mushrooms that glow in the dark. Most of these produce a pale to bright yellowish green light. They live mostly on wood, and different kinds can be found throughout the world. Two com-mon ones are the large, clustered, orange gilled mushroom jack-o'-lantern (*Omphalotus illudens*) (shown at left) and the much smaller, often densely overlapping on logs, gilled mushroom *Panellus stipticus*.

GLOWING IN THE DARK

Once on a camping foray we found a fruiting of about 300 jack-o'-lanterns. We collected them by the armful and placed them in the woods along a trail leading to our tent sites. That night, after a bonfire party, we headed back to our various tents in the dark. There, glowing along the trail were dim lights that lit up the darkness and showed us the path to our tents. Jack-o'-lanterns may be poisonous mushrooms, but that doesn't mean they're not useful.

CALL YOUR LOCAL POISON CONTROL IN CASE OF EMERGENCY

Green-spored lepiota (*Chlorophyllum molybdites*)

Green-Spored Lepiota

COMMON NAME:
Green-spored lepiota

SCIENTIFIC NAME:
Chlorophyllum molybdites

FIELD DESCRIPTION:

⊙ Appear as large (up to 12 inches [30.5 cm]
across, but mostly 4 to 6 inches [10 to 15 cm]),
white-capped gilled mushroom, with some
beige scales over the cap center.

⊙ Closed at first, then expand to flat, with
white gills (at first) becoming grayish green
on maturity.

⊙ Occur free from (unattached to) the stout stem,
with a veil covering the immature gills, leaving an
often movable ring of tissue on upper stem.

⊙ Spore print is green or grayish green.

SYMPTOMS:
Severe vomiting, cramps, diarrhea.

TREATMENT:
Symptomatic; self-limiting, twenty-four-hour
duration.

Green-spored lepiota showing its mature green gills

Green-Spored Lepiota

In pantropical regions after a summer rain, dinner plate–size white caps of green-spored lepiota come up. Wherever summer temperatures rise upward of 90°F (32°C), this mushroom can appear suddenly and unexpectedly. In more temperate regions, several years can go by without seeing any, and then they seem to turn up everywhere, in lawns, in mulch, in parks. When young, when the gills are still white or whitish, it can be mistaken for edible mushrooms, such as the parasol (*Macrolepiota procera*) or even an *Agaricus*, such as *A. arvensis*. If a spore print is made, or if mature mushrooms are examined, the gills (and spore print) will appear gray-green, rather than white, like the parasol, or chocolate brown, like the *Agaricus*. A hasty (mis)identification can lead to a couple of days in the bathroom.

Some people claim that boiling the mushroom renders it edible. Although it can be abundant and looks clean and "eatable," if it's fruiting, there's every reason to look for other mushrooms, safe ones, and choice edibles, that should also be fruiting at the same time, if not quite so abundantly or so conspicuously.

A SPORE OF A DIFFERENT COLOR

The mushrooms found growing on a lush summer lawn had caps the size of dinner plates. Some were growing in a fairy ring. Others were scattered over a wide area. We had been gathering the horse mushroom, *Agaricus arvensis*, up in a cooler region earlier in the month, and these looked like giant specimens of the horse mushroom. When we turned one over, it had a ring on the stem like an *Agaricus*, and its gills were white to off-white. We assumed the mature gills would be dark brown from the ripening spores. If we were wrong, then the spore print we would make would be white and it would be some kind of parasol mushroom, just not one that we knew. We picked some of the mushrooms, took them inside, and made spore prints. Some hours later when we checked, we were amazed to see greenish gray spore prints. We had found the green-spored lepiota (*Chlorophyllum molybdites*), a poisonous look-alike for edible *Agaricus* and *Lepiota* species.

Without making a spore print, we wouldn't have known that the spores would be green, the color of the mature gills, and, if we had eaten the mushrooms, we would have gotten sick. Never underestimate the value of making spore prints.

CALL YOUR LOCAL POISON CONTROL IN CASE OF EMERGENCY

Agaricus xanthodermus complex

Because the white button mushroom is known around the world, it's no wonder that people who pick wild mushrooms would look for wild species of the cultivated *Agaricus*. In fact, there are several good edible species, but there are others that will cause digestive upset, and these occur in the group known as the "*xanthodermus* group," the ones that, when cut in half lengthwise, show a yellow coloration in the base of the stem, and that have a distinct medicinal or metallic odor, which sometimes is only present during cooking. These poisonous species of *Agaricus* occur everywhere, and they are much more abundant than the edible species of *Agaricus*.

Agaricus xanthodermus complex

COMMON NAME:
Yellow-foot agaricus

SCIENTIFIC NAME:
Agaricus xanthodermus and related species

FIELD DESCRIPTION:
- Occurs as a large white mushroom with free gills (unattached to stem), whitish at first, then dingy pink and finally chocolate brown.

- A veil covers the immature gills breaking as the cap expands, leaving skirtlike ring of tissue on upper stem.

- Base of stem shows bright yellow when cut.

- Gills typically smell medicinal or metallic.

- Leaves a dark brown spore print.

SYMPTOMS:
Nausea, vomiting, and diarrhea.

TREATMENT:
Symptomatic; self-limiting, twenty-four-hour duration.

LOST IN TRANSLATION

It was the last day of our mushroom-hunting trip to Spain. We had planned a farewell dinner to have with our host mycologists. A woman in our group arrived with a basket full of mushrooms. She had just found a huge fairy ring of very fresh *Agaricus* near the Madrid zoo. She said they would make a perfect appetizer and she would clean and cook them for us in just a couple of minutes. It was clear from looking at the mushrooms that although she had, indeed, found *Agaricus* mushrooms, what she had found was the toxic species *Agaricus xanthodermus*. We pointed this out to her and she was enraged. Did we doubt her identification skills? Were we simply going to throw away all her time and effort collecting these beautiful mushrooms?

The typically reliable clue for recognizing the poisonous species of *Agaricus* is to cut the mushroom in half lengthwise. The inside base of the stem turns a bright yellow when exposed to air. We showed her this, and she still insisted that she knew these mushrooms and that they were good. We had to have a local Spanish mycologist convince her that the mushrooms were not good to eat. Only then did she relent, but she never forgave us.

Boletus huronensis and Other Boletes

As a whole, boletes are a benign group of mushrooms. There are several hundred kinds of boletes associated with the roots of trees in parks and forests around the world. A few, such as the king bolete complex, are choice edibles. Many others are very good edibles. Many more are edible without comment. A very few are too bitter to eat but are not poisonous. A few others cause mild to severe stomach upset. One or two have been claimed to be the cause of a fatality. Avoiding the bitter boletes, such as *Tylopilus felleus*, is fairly simple.

Avoiding an upset stomach from one group of boletes is also fairly simple: don't eat boletes that have red or orange pores and that, when cut in half lengthwise, stain blue instantly. Satan's bolete, *Boletus satanus*, is notorious in this regard. Other red- and orange-pored boletes that bruise blue and are known or suspected to cause severe stomach upset include *Boletus pulcherrimus* (in California) and *Boletus subvelutipes* (in eastern North America). One European bolete, *Boletus erythropus*, is a popular edible, but as a group these boletes should not be eaten by beginners. None of these, in any case, even remotely resembles the king bolete group, the only group I recommend for the table for beginning mushroom hunters.

Boletus sensibilis, a common bolete in eastern North America, has yellow pores that stain blue instantly on cutting; it is known to cause stomach upset. Some boletes can cause stomach upset if not well cooked. Often the bolete stem, as with the genus *Leccinum*, is fibrous and tough, whereas the cap is quite soft, and cooking the mushrooms until the caps are done leaves you with uncooked and indigestible stems, unless you remove them before cooking. In Australia, a recent report of a mushroom-caused fatality cited a bolete that produced muscarine symptoms and led to death in just ten hours.

A BOLETE BY ANY OTHER NAME

Boletes are one of the safest groups of mushrooms for beginners to eat. Not only does the group include the fabled king bolete, also called porcini or cèpe (*Boletus edulis*), but it also includes more than 100 other species. Some are good edibles, a few are too bitter to eat, and a few can cause digestive upset.

One poisonous bolete recently discovered in the United States is known as *Boletus huronensis*. It's a dead ringer for the king bolete. If you do not know the differences between these boletes, *Boletus huronensis* may easily and unfortunately be confused with the king bolete. One person ate a small amount of this mushroom, declared it excellent, and an hour or so later proceeded to retch the entire night. Another person ate just a very small piece and then vomited for hours.

Boletus subvelutipes

CALL YOUR LOCAL POISON CONTROL IN CASE OF EMERGENCY

Boletus huronensis

COMMON NAME:
False king bolete

SCIENTIFIC NAME:
Boletus huronensis

FIELD DESCRIPTION:
- Appears as a large, fleshy, stout mushroom with bunlike brown cap.

- Has a white spongy layer of pores beneath cap.

- Has a somewhat yellowish fleshy-solid stem devoid of any fishnetlike cross-hatching near stem apex.

- Flesh is yellowish and bruises blue, sometimes slowly.

SYMPTOMS:
Vomiting, diarrhea, abdominal cramping.

TREATMENT:
Symptomatic; self-limiting, twenty-four-hour duration.

LOOK-ALIKES:
For boletivores (those who eat boletes) in northeastern North America, there is a new worrisome bolete look-alike for the king bolete. It's called *Boletus huronensis*. As little as a single bite of the mushroom can cause a night of agony, even a day or two of cramps, vomiting, and prostration. This bolete favors eastern hemlock trees, but it can grow in mixed woods. It has the size and meaty solidity of the king bolete, even the shape at times. It does differ, though, in several important respects. The king bolete has a conspicuous white netlike reticulation near the top of the stem; *Boletus huronensis* does not. The king bolete does

Poisonous king bolete look-alikes (*Boletes huronensis*)

not turn blue on cutting the mushroom in half; *Boletus huronensis* has cap flesh that slowly stains blue. The flesh of the king bolete is white and unchanging; the flesh of *Boletus huronensis* is yellow, slowly staining blue.

There are other differences, but these are readily observable. Only the excitement at thinking you have found a king bolete could blind you to these differences. The cause of the resulting stomach upset, when other mushrooms or foods are also eaten at the same time as *Boletus huronensis*, will even be misunderstood if you believe you couldn't have misidentified a king bolete. Even drying and storing *Boletus huronensis* doesn't render it any less toxic. It retains its ability to cause a severe stomach upset after several years of storage.

Psychedelic and Psychotherapeutic Mushrooms

Mushrooms generally referred to as "magic mushrooms" can be very different in their effects, depending on which ones are eaten, how many, the setting in which they are eaten, and the expectations of those who eat them. In general, there is a more physical and outgoing response from eating the fly agaric; a more passive, introspective response from the magic mushrooms; and a somewhat insightful response, often interrupted by fits of unprovoked hilarity, from the big laughing gym.

The fly agaric is used traditionally by ethnic minorities in the Russian Far East, by shamans or healers, and more so by average villagers. Magic mushrooms are used traditionally by Native Americans in Mexico, primarily by shamans and *curanderas* to diagnose illness and treat the spiritual needs of the community. Magic mushrooms are currently proving to be very useful psychotherapeutic tools for treating alcoholism and behavioral disorders, and even to ease the often paralyzing anxiety of end-of-life cancer patients. The big laughing gym has no recorded use, except recently as the result of a mistaken identification or an intentional ingestion by people who have read about its reputed effects.

Tatiana, a Koryak shaman, with a Siberian fly-agaric

Psychedelic and Psychotherapeutic Mushrooms

- Fly agaric amanita
- Magic mushrooms: the psilocybin mushrooms
- Big laughing gym

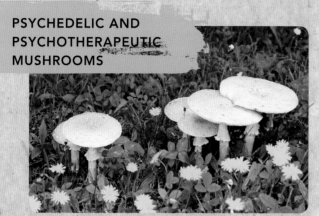

Eastern United States fly agaric (*Amanita muscaria*)

Fly Agaric

COMMON NAME:
Fly agaric

SCIENTIFIC NAME:
Amanita muscaria

FIELD DESCRIPTION:

◉ Appears as a medium-sized gilled mushroom with blood-red to orange-red to yellowish cap adorned with white to yellowish patches.

◉ White gills are free from (unattached to) the stem, leaving a skirtlike ring of tissue on upper stem.

◉ Stem base is adorned with rows of white rings of tissue from the universal veil (egg) out of which the mushroom arose.

◉ Spore print is white.

SYMPTOMS:
Forty-five minutes or so after eating a dried cap or two of the fly agaric the person becomes very tired, sleeps soundly, and wakes some hours later with a burst of energy, sometimes yelling or singing, and becomes very active, moving things about, eager to take on all the labors of Hercules. The experience can be extended by consuming urine that contains the unchanged compounds in the mushroom (this has been cited in the literature and experimentally confirmed recently).

DURATION:
Six to twelve hours.

Fly Agaric Amanita

The fly agaric is the most photogenic mushroom in the world. It graces the covers and pages of many children's books and is often on greeting cards and bric-a-brac about the house. It has been used to kill flies, hence its name. The mushroom is cut into pieces and placed in a bowl of milk. Flies are attracted to the milk and, after drinking some, become very sleepy or disoriented. The mushroom doesn't kill the flies, but it slows them down so they can be swatted.

The fly agaric is still used in Siberia by ethnic minorities to help celebrate the annual harvest. Under the influence of this mushroom, the Koryak and Chukchi minorities in Kamchatka and the Chukchi Peninsula in northeastern Russia claim that they can fly, descend into the earth to visit with dead, rise up into the heavens to connect to the spirit world, and communicate with rocks, trees, water, and animals. The mushroom even allows reindeer herders to transform into reindeer during an annual ceremony, thereby dissolving any distance between the herder and the herd. In general, under the influence of the fly agaric, a person loses all fear of danger and assumes the strength and powers of a god, or so it is believed.

The fly agaric is listed as poisonous in every field guide, and in some European guides it is considered one of the most poisonous mushrooms. Nevertheless, when properly prepared, it is known to be eaten as a food. It has been reported that some Scandinavian farming communities have cooked and canned the peeled caps.

People who inadvertently eat the fly agaric, mistaking it for a good edible mushroom, and therefore just sauté it, still get sick from it, although the symptoms, unlike most gastrointestinal irritants, are mostly a kind of intense but transient delirium rather than a stomach upset.

Magic Mushrooms and the Law

There is a law prohibiting the possession of psilocybin, the active compound in many species in the genus *Psilocybe* and some other genera, but its en-

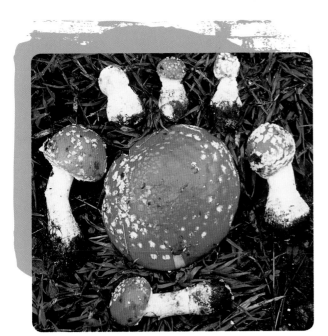

Siberian fly-agaric (*Amanita muscaria*)

SOME MUSHROOMS JUST SEEM TO BE CULTURE-BOUND

There are two basic levels for experiencing the fly agaric mushroom (*Amanita muscaria*). One level is physical. The mushroom makes you feel inebriated, so you move, dance, sing, yell, and run around. You are said to have a song inside you that the mushroom allows to come out. The song is the mushroom speaking. The other level, often called the shamanic level, is more internal or spiritual; it allows you to believe you can fly, see dead people, transform into animals, and communicate with all of nature. The experience varies according to factors such as expectation, setting, prior experience, and the mix of compounds in any given population of mushrooms.

While on a trip to Kamchatka, we met with dozens of Koryak villagers, a local ethnic minority, who told us about their use of this mushroom. We decided to try it for ourselves. Seven of us took the mushroom and seven others served as "watchers," just in case we needed help. We ate dried caps of *Amanita muscaria* and sat quietly for an hour. Nothing happened except that we got very sleepy and slept the afternoon away. We got up for dinner. I stood up at the dinner table to offer a toast to our host. I pushed my chair back, and it slammed against the wall and broke into pieces. People said I was shouting as I made the toast. After dinner I felt like I could push down a standing tree or flip over a car.

Two days later, on my flight home, trying to buckle my seatbelt, I pulled the strap out of its unit. It took a week to return to normal.

forcement is quixotic at best. There is no law prohibiting the possession or use of the fly agaric, *Amanita muscaria*, although its use, while fascinating to read about, is less than desirable to experience. The big laughing gym, *Gymnopilus spectabilis*, contains hispidin, a compound about which no laws have been written to date regarding its possession or use. None of these mushrooms is known to be dangerous if used within the guidelines established by the primary cultures that use them.

Caveat: Although some people have taken to eating the fly agaric as food, parboiled, and some have used it, dried, as a recreational drug, side-effects including muscarine-like symptoms have been reported in the U.S. and Europe. This is not a safe edible mushroom.

Magic Mushrooms

COMMON NAMES:
Magic mushrooms, blue stainers

SCIENTIFIC NAMES:
Psilocybe cubensis, P. cyanescens, P. semilanceata, P. caerulipes

FIELD DESCRIPTION:
- Different species grow in pastures, on wood mulch, on logs, in manure.
- Appear as small- to medium-sized gilled mushrooms with smooth, somewhat sticky brownish caps.
- Gills are brown, becoming darker on maturity, and attached to the stem. Some species have a veil covering the immature gills, leaving a skirt-like ring on the upper stem.
- Stem turns blue on bruising, as the cap and flesh may do as well.
- Spore print is purple-brown.

LOOK-ALIKES:
There are many LBMs (Little Brown Mushrooms) in our lawns, parks, and woods. Identifying magic mushrooms correctly is critical, especially because there are many poisonous LBMs growing in the same places, and the deadly galerina is the same size and shape as many of the magic mushrooms.

SYMPTOMS:
About 45 minutes after ingesting a small amount of mushrooms a number of symptoms manifest themselves. Shapes become geometrical and move. Colors become fluorescent and intense. A sense of silliness can prevail. A larger dose can produce a transient out-of-body experience or lead to introspective ruminations. A very large dose can produce what has been described as a mystical experience, a sense of oneness with the world.

DURATION:
Regardless of the dose, about four hours

Magic Mushrooms: The Psilocybin Mushrooms

Magic mushrooms got their reputation in the 1960s when music stars trekked to Oaxaca, Mexico, to take these mushrooms from a spiritual healer, Maria Sabina. She was profiled in a 1957 *Life* magazine article written by R. Gordon Wasson, now regarded as the "father of ethnomycology," the science of the use of mushrooms among different cultures.

It is believed that magic mushrooms have been used in Mesoamerica among native peoples for thousands of years. When the Spanish conquistadors encountered native peoples in the Americas, the priests with them wrote books describing the various cultures they conquered. They described native peoples sitting on the ground in a circle, some laughing, some crying, some looking ecstatic, some appearing terrified and gripped with fear, but all experiencing the mushroom they had just ingested. Magic mushrooms played a big part in their religious lives. Under the influence of magic mushrooms, they were able to visit with their dead relatives, learn how to solve problems in their daily lives, and see what the future had in store for them. In today's Mexico, shamans still perform an ancient ceremony in which they eat the mushrooms to learn how to help people who come to them with problems.

Profoundly Therapeutic

Johns Hopkins medical school is now pioneering a study using magic mushrooms to help people find a life-affirming alternative to alcoholism and certain behavioral disorders. Dr. Roland Griffiths, the head researcher of the study, has discovered that a significant number of the people participating in the study have reported that, under the influence of the mushroom, they have had a profound and intense mystical experience, and when interviewed, most of them said that taking the mushroom was one of the most meaningful experiences in their lives. Another study is using magic mushrooms to lessen anxiety and depression among end-of-life cancer patients. The use of magic mushrooms as a psychotherapeutic

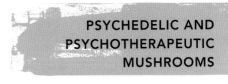

Magic mushroom (*Psilocybe cyanescens*)

tool is in its infancy in Western medicine, but it is heir to an ancient tradition of similar uses among native peoples in the Americas.

Magic mushrooms are usually those found in the genus *Psilocybe*, but the compound responsible for the psychedelic effects, psilocybin, is known to be in a number of unrelated gilled mushrooms, including species of *Conocybe*, *Copelandia*, and *Pluteus*. Psilocybin is a compound that it is illegal to possess in the United States and many European countries. Growing psilocybin-containing mushrooms, or selling them, for example, is against the law. For a number of reasons, not the least of which is the unusual nature of the forbidden item—a mushroom, after all—few cases have been brought to trial.

Psilocybe mushrooms occur worldwide. Although they are most diverse and numerous in Mexico, they are plentiful along the North and South American coasts, as well as along the Amazon River and its tributaries. Various species occur across Europe from the U.K. to the Russian Far East. Other species fruit in North and South Africa.

Magic mushrooms pop up in the hill stations, high above the heat in southern India. Thailand is famous for its magic mushrooms, which can be found on elephant dung, and Bali attracts "mushroom tourists." Magic mushrooms grow in the pastures of Papua New Guinea and the mountains of Japan. Species still unknown to science occur in New Zealand and Australia, especially Tasmania.

SLOW RIDE

There are two levels of experiencing magic mushrooms. One is bodily or sensory, sometimes referred to as psychedelic; the other is out-of-body, sometimes referred to as spiritual or psychotherapeutic.

Walking through Stribling Arboretum in Golden Gate Park in San Francisco many years ago, we encountered a young man carrying a handful of small mushrooms. We asked him what he had, and he said "magic mushrooms." A glance told us that he had a mix of several different kinds of mushrooms. When I pointed this out to him, he said it didn't matter. He said he always ate them all and got high.

We continued walking along the paths and saw a squirrel holding a thin, small-capped mushroom in the midst of a mushroom patch. We walked over and saw a number of mushrooms growing in the wood chip mulch. One was a blue-staining species of *Psilocybe*, *P. cyanescens*, one of the magic mushrooms. The others were just various decomposers, probably edible but of no culinary interest. We decided to eat the *Psilocybe cyanescens* right there.

We found a bench to sit on while waiting to see what would happen. It started to rain. It didn't bother us at all. We couldn't have left if we wanted to because our legs felt like jelly. The sidewalk in front of us started to move and change shape, the blocks of cement morphing into geometrical patterns. The grass acquired fluorescent yellow tips. The tall trees in the distance, moving gently in the wind, looked like gigantic prehistoric birds flapping their wings, staring at us but not approaching. We sat for more than an hour transfixed by the "magic" of the moment.

Big Laughing Gym

COMMON NAME:
Big laughing gym

SCIENTIFIC NAMES:
Gymnopilus spectabilis, G. luteus, G. junonius

FIELD DESCRIPTION:

◉ Often grows in massive clusters at the base of hardwood trees, sometimes found in grass on buried wood.

◉ Appears as a large orange to orange-yellow capped gilled mushroom; the individual caps in a cluster are very small, but several rising up out of the cluster to grow into large mushrooms.

◉ Gills are orange, as is the stem, and the gills are covered at first by a veil that breaks to leave a brown (from the spore) skirtlike ring of tissue about the upper part of the stem.

◉ Spore print is orange brown.

◉ Intensely bitter taste

SYMPTOMS:
Forty-five minutes or so after ingestion of a 2- to 3-inch (5 to 7.5 cm) dried cap (which is extremely bitter), anything that is seen or heard appears to be hilarious. This can continue for a couple of hours. In addition, you can follow lines of thought that appear at the time to be profound insights into life, but on later reflection are seen as impossible or ridiculous. Nevertheless, the impression you get is that you are really capable of reexperiencing past events but with different outcomes, that you can "see" evolution take place before your very eyes—at the speed of millions of years a minute. All of life is perceived as plastic, pliable, and changeable, and your response to this is laughter. You are uninhibited, and socially suppressed behaviors can experience a transient public airing.

DURATION:
Several hours.

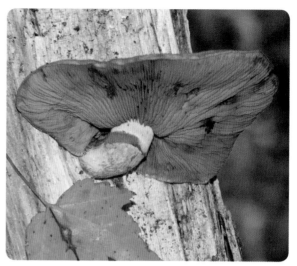

Big laughing gym (*Gymnopilus spectabilis*)

Big Laughing Gym

Unlike fly agaric and magic mushrooms, there is no known history of the use of the big laughing gym. Its effects came to light not very long ago in Japan, where, at a very formal dinner party, the hostess, dressed in a kimono, got up and started dancing about and laughing gaily. One of the invited guests joined her. The host of the dinner ran out to find a doctor, fearing food poisoning. When he arrived back at the house with the doctor, they were greeted by his wife, who was by now partially undressed, delighted with herself, and laughingly teasing the other dinner guests. After a study of this case it was determined that the cause of the disruption was a mushroom that had been misidentified and cooked and served by mistake. The mushroom was identified as *Gymnopilus aeruginosus*, the first of what we now know to be a group of mushrooms commonly referred to as big laughing gyms.

Caveat: Despite its name and often-reported *Alice in Wonderland* effects, this is not a food mushroom; it's much too bitter to eat. It's still unbelievably bitter even when dried. While its consumption (dried) has not resulted in any reported poisonings, the possibility exists that harm could come from its ingestion.

Big laughing gym (*Gymnopilus spectabilis*)

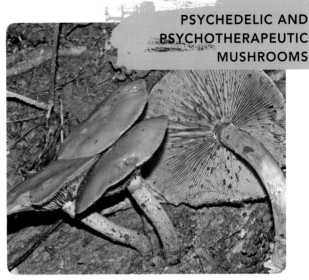

Big laughing gym (*Gymnopilus spectabilis*)

EVOLUTION OF A TRIP, EVOLUTION IN ACTION

There are two levels, known so far, for experiencing big laughing gyms. One is the level of laughter: uninhibited or goofy behavior, where everything is funny or terribly important for no apparent reason, whether it's a sunbeam, a PTA meeting, or someone tying his shoe. It is hard not to blurt out whatever is on your mind at any given moment. Whatever discomfort this causes other people, the feeling you have is cathartic. You feel great. The other level is one of insight: a feeling of profound insight into the nature of things, and of life itself. This stems from seeing something and interpreting it in terms of some kind of archetype or historical or metaphysical construct. The reaction varies depending on how much is eaten, how active the compounds are in a given mushroom population, the person's expectations, the setting in which it's taken, and the people with whom it's taken. It works much better in a group setting than if taken while alone.

One time, a group of us, including two physicians, dried a number of these intensely bitter mushrooms, then ate them like crackers we covered with jelly to conceal the bitter taste. After an hour, one person in our group was observed walking around a tree, one hand always in contact with the tree. He did this for almost an hour. When asked later why he did this, he answered simply that it made him feel good. Someone else sat near a swimming pool, staring into it. He later told us that he was mesmerized watching the dolphins swim about. A third person stood on her head for two hours, saying when asked that she felt just fine, thank you. I watched people in the distance mounting horses and riding them, and I interpreted this as witnessing arboreal primates standing up for the first time and becoming bipedal before my very eyes, then putting on clothes and domesticating animals, as if evolution happened just this quickly. We had all eaten the same amount of mushrooms, but our experiences were very different, some seemingly much more profound than others.

CHAPTER 4:

Medicinal Mushrooms

Reishi (*Ganoderma lucidum*)
on buried wood overgrown with ivy

Although mushrooms have been used as medicines in Asia for centuries, it is only since the turn of this century that people in the West have taken seriously the idea that mushrooms can have medicinal value. Although everyone recognizes the value of penicillin as a fungal antibiotic, except for ergot, a fungus that parasitizes grasses, which has been used successfully to treat migraines and cluster headaches, mushrooms—or more generally, fungi— have been overlooked by Western medical science.

There are about 500 different mushrooms found around the world that are now being referred to as medicinal mushrooms. Many are restricted to certain localities or cultures. Some have been given inflated importance because of culturally transmitted myths, but many others are now being shown to have recognized medicinal value because of extensive controlled experiments in labs worldwide.

A dozen or so of these medicinal mushrooms are both widely distributed and highly regarded as providing protection against or treating a variety of ailments. The most important of the medicinal mushrooms are polypores, a group of shelf or bracket fungi that grows on living or dead trees, logs, or stumps. These polypores, and all but the gilled shiitake mushroom and the Chinese caterpillar fungus (both native to Asia), occur throughout much of North America and Europe.

Medicinal mushrooms are not just, or even especially, for people who are sick, although much of current research is focused on the tumor-inhibiting qualities of these fungi. Rather, medicinal mushrooms are for healthy people who want to maintain their good health. They are also for people suffering from a variety of ailments that conventional drugs can treat, but often with undesirable side effects, which are absent in medicinal mushrooms. Because many medicinal mushrooms contain orally active compounds and can be cooked and eaten as food, we place these in a category we call medicinal foods. Another category exists for mushrooms that are valuable as medicinal teas but are too leathery or woody to eat as food.

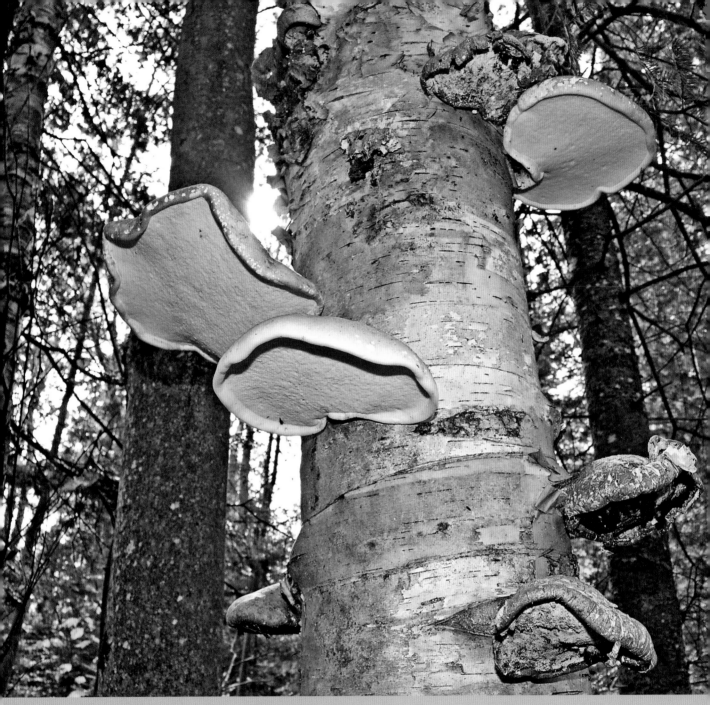

Birch polypore (*Piptoporus betulinus*)

Guide to Medicinal Mushrooms

Unlike plants, mushrooms known to be poisonous are not used by people in any form for anything of a medicinal nature. Researchers, on the other hand, have discovered that some of our most poisonous mushrooms, such as the death cap, offer very useful compounds for learning how cancer cell replication can be inhibited or stopped.

Hunting for medicinal mushrooms is the same as hunting for edible mushrooms. You can hunt for them online, in health food stores, in farmers' markets, and at upscale food stores, as well as in your own backyard, local parks, and woods. Some are so common you will be embarrassed not to have noticed them before. If they are leathery or woody bracket fungi, you will be surprised to learn that despite their apparent inedible nature, they can be dried and powdered or chipped and used as a medicinal tea, a daily tonic to help maintain a healthy and active lifestyle into old age.

Maitake, Hen-of-the-Woods
(*Grifola frondosa*)

Mushroom hunters have been quick to incorporate maitake, also called hen-of-the-woods, into their autumn collecting pattern. People with little knowledge of the great diversity of mushrooms in the woods feel safe with this one. Although it has long been used as a medicinal in Asia, maitake has become popular everywhere among a younger generation for its reported medicinal value. It's available in health food stores in pill form as an immune enhancer and reputed energy booster. The more widely it's becoming known, the more we are learning about new ways to use this common autumn mushroom.

FIELD DESCRIPTION: See page 97.

USES: Fruiting bodies have antitumor properties (against breast and colorectal cancers), enhance immune response, and lower glucose levels. The fruiting bodies can be eaten cooked as a food.

Birch polypore (*Piptoporus betulinus*)

COMMERCIAL AVAILABILITY: Sold fresh in farmers' markets. Sold fresh and loose or packaged in upscale food markets. Marketed online.

A MOTHER'S SOUP IS THE BEST MEDICINE

Shortly after moving to the suburbs, a couple noticed that their teenage daughter had developed chronic sinus infections. Recurrent bouts of sinusitis and bronchitis followed all winter. The illnesses, plus antibiotics and steroids taken to treat her symptoms, left her completely exhausted. They consulted Dr. Andrew Weil, the leading authority in integrative medicine in the world, and he recommended a daily dose of 10 grams of dried maitake pieces rehydrated in boiling water. She was given this in a daily vegetable soup, and when she tired of it after awhile, it was marinated and turned into a pickle. It was even mixed into pastries. When she took her daily "medicine" each winter, her energy and appetite would slowly return. She would discontinue its use when the debilitating symptoms disappeared each summer, but come autumn the symptoms would return, and only a daily dose of maitake would hold them in check. Nothing else seemed to do the trick, and this mushroom allowed her to live a normal life.

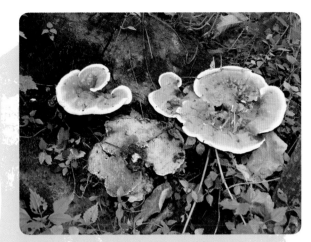
Reishi (*Ganoderma lucidum*)

Reishi, Shellac Polypore, Ling-Zhi
(*Ganoderma lucidum*)

Until very recently, this large, shiny, red-capped bracket fungus was ignored by many. Even though Chinese and Japanese cultures treated this mushroom with reverence, elsewhere it was believed that this had more to do with tradition than science.

FIELD DESCRIPTION: Soft to corky-fleshed shelf fungus with flat, red-varnished cap and white to brown pores.

HABITAT: At base and lower trunk of many deciduous hardwood trees, especially maples, oaks, elms, and willows. Often ubiquitous about the base of street trees, such as oaks.

DISTRIBUTION: On hardwood trees throughout the northern hemisphere, during the growing season (i.e., not a perennial like the Artist's Conk, *Ganoderma applanatum*)

SEASON: May to November. An annual species that may overwinter but then decays.

LOOK-ALIKES: Hemlock varnish shelf (*Ganoderma tsugae*) grows on dead conifers, especially hemlocks.

USES: Fruiting bodies have significant antitumor, immune-enhancing, cholesterol-reducing properties. The dried fruiting bodies can be pulverized and consumed as a tea.

COMMERCIAL AVAILABILITY: Sold in Chinese medicinal herb stores and also readily available online.

A MUSHROOM TEA FOR ALL AGES

On a trip to Japan, we met an eighty-year-old Japanese mycologist who looked all of sixty-five. When he stood next to his American counterpart, also eighty, the physical difference between them was striking. One had jet black hair, the other gray; one had an erect posture, the other stooped a bit; and one seemed to have endless energy and good humor, while the other was somewhat dour. Our Japanese host attributed these differences to his daily consumption of reishi tea. He also told us that he couldn't remember the last time he had a cold. He said as young as he looked he felt even younger. We took that, respectfully, with a grain of salt.

Later, while out hunting mushrooms in the hills outside of Kyoto, we came across a group of teenage girls on a day hike up the mountain. We had our picnic lunch at the same spot and talked with them about what they had brought for lunch. We were shocked to discover that each had a thermos of reishi tea, not like American teens, who would have brought along a soft drink or an energy drink. When we asked them about this, they said matter-of-factly that by drinking reishi tea they expected to be able to climb mountains like their parents and grandparents still do, well into their eighties. We were doubly shocked to hear teens so openly admire their elders and talk about a distant future that American teens seem unaware exists.

Turkey tail (*Trametes versicolor*)

Turkey Tail, Yun Zhi
(*Trametes versicolor*)

In Asia, the turkey tail polypore has held a position as one of the most important medicinal fungi. If this could just be ascribed to a tradition passed down from one generation to another, it could be dismissed as a curious use of a leathery polypore. After all, it's too tough to eat, even cooked a long time.

However, tests on this mushroom found that it contained several important anticancer compounds, one of which, krestin (or PSK), is a protein-bound polysaccharide that inhibits tumor formation. Moreover, it has little or no toxicity and produces few if any side effects.

FIELD DESCRIPTION: Often overlapping, small, leathery, thin-fleshed, stalkless caps with alternating hairy and smooth multicolored zones and white pores below.

HABITAT: In wounds on dead deciduous and sometimes conifer trees. Often common along fences used to mark the border between a parking lot and the woods beyond.

DISTRIBUTION: Cosmopolitan on dead wood, during the growing season.

SEASON: May through December in eastern North America; through February in California and Pacific Northwest. An annual species that sometimes revives and persists a while.

LOOK-ALIKES: Other species of *Trametes* lack the multicolored zones. Other similar small, flat, shelf fungi on wood include the smooth-undersided *Stereum ostrea* and the gill-like undersided *Lenzites betulina*.

USES: Fruiting bodies offer immune-enhancing, antitumor, antiviral, antibacterial, and antioxidant properties. The dried fruiting bodies can be pulverized and consumed as a tea.

COMMERCIAL AVAILABILITY: Readily available online.

SOMETIMES WHAT WE SEEK IS HIDDEN IN PLAIN SIGHT

On a mushroom-hunting trip to Indonesia, we met a villager in Bali who was carrying with both hands a large green leaf in which he had placed a great number of turkey tail polypores. We stopped to talk with him and discovered that he was taking them home to make a medicinal tea.

Later, when I was invited to attend a medicinal mushroom seminar at a large pharmaceutical company, I was asked which mushroom, of all the mushrooms in all the remote corners of the world, they should select to work with to develop a new drug. I answered, "The turkey tail," and went on to say that it was something right under their collective nose, that it grew along the wooden fence that surrounded the company's parking lot. I think they were hoping to hear about something in some exotic locale, like Papua New Guinea. They were unimpressed that something so conspicuous, common, and abundant could possibly be as valuable as it was reported to be in China. The Chinese enthusiasm over the medicinal properties of the turkey tail was dismissed as so much local lore rather than the result of experimental double-blind scientific studies. Unfortunately, this pharmaceutical company wasn't ready to see that.

Umbrella Polypore, Zhu Ling (*Polyporus umbellatus*)

The Chinese name for this mushroom is *zhu ling*, which refers to the mushroom's sclerotia, or underground growth. It's this sclerotia that the Chinese value, well above the edibility of the mushroom growing up out of it.

On a mushroom study tour of China, we learned that a tea made from the sclerotia of this mushroom, when given to lung cancer patients after radiation therapy, resulted in a significantly higher recovery rate and a dramatically improved quality of life. That this traditionally used (as a tea) medicinal mushroom is orally active against the spread of lung cancer is something that should become known and explored more widely.

FIELD DESCRIPTION: Large bouquetlike, soft-fleshy mushroom with a large cluster of small, circular whitish to tan caps, with whitish pores underneath, rising from short white stalks attached to a single basal stalk, and arising from an underground blackish tuberlike structure.

HABITAT: On the ground near deciduous trees. Common some years in eastern North American summers, often some distance from any tree base.

DISTRIBUTION: On the ground on or near the base of hardwood trees, especially oaks, in wooded parks and forests across much of North America, Europe, and Japan.

SEASON: Summer and autumn

LOOK-ALIKES: Maitake (*Grifola frondosa*) occurs in the autumn at the base of oak trees and lacks any tuberlike underground structure.

USES: The sclerotia (underground black, tuberlike growths) have antitumor (lung, bladder, liver), immune-enhancing, antibiotic, and anti-inflammatory properties. The aboveground fruiting bodies can be eaten as a cooked food.

COMMERCIAL AVAILABILITY: Available online.

Umbrella polypore (*Polyporus umbrellatus*)

A DOUBLE-WHAMMY MUSHROOM: EDIBLE ABOVE, MEDICINAL BELOW

I got a call from a friend one July morning saying that she just found some hen-of-the-woods in a park near her home. I told her that it was too early for that mushroom to appear, that it had to be something else. She invited me to come out to have a look for myself. Two hours later we were standing beside it in a wooded park. It was as large as hen-of-the-woods, a little bit lighter in color, but the main difference seemed to be that it was growing out of the ground. There was no tree, oak or otherwise, beside it, or very near to it. Until then, I didn't think the hen-of-the-woods had any conceivable look-alike besides the harmless, though not as good an edible, black-staining polypore (*Meripilus sumstinei*). Here was clearly something else.

It proved to be the umbrella polypore, *Polyporus umbellatus*. Instead of growing up out of a tree root, like hen-of-the-woods does, it was growing up out of a hard, tuberlike, black sclerotial mass.

Chaga (*Inonotus obliquus*)

Chaga, Clinker Polypore
(*Inonotus obliquus*)

In his novel *Cancer Ward*, the Russian writer Aleksandr Solzhenitsyn writes about this mushroom as something that can be found in the woods, broken off, boiled, and drunk as a tea to keep a person healthy and vigorous. It has a long list of reputed benefits, including curing various cancers, and confers specific healing effects in some people.

One woman, for example, nearly crippled with arthritis, says that taking chaga tea every morning has nearly cured her. When she is unable to use it for any extended period, the pain returns. Although anecdotal, it speaks volumes to those of us who know her as someone who would never stretch the truth to make a point.

FIELD DESCRIPTION: Large, black, stalkless, cracked, very hard "canker" looking like burned charcoal.

HABITAT: Common in autumn northeastern birch woods. Easily seen against white-barked birches.

DISTRIBUTION: On birch throughout its range in the northern hemisphere.

SEASON: Year-round.

LOOK-ALIKES: None.

USES: The powdered fruiting bodies have anti-inflammatory properties and are being seen as effective against arthritis pain. They also have antitumor, antibacterial, antiviral, and cholesterol-reducing properties. Used powdered as a tea.

COMMERCIAL AVAILABILITY: Available online.

Birch Polypore
(*Piptoporus betulinus*)

The birch polypore has a compound in it that is effective against intestinal parasites. It is known as a traditional or folk treatment of wounds and to stanch the flow of blood. The mushroom has antibacterial, antiviral, and anti-inflammatory properties. It also contains medicinal compounds absorbed from its birch tree host. By digging out strips of the flesh just beneath the pore surface of the mushroom, the birch polypore can be used as a safe, clean, blood-stanching, anti-inflammatory bandage or wrap over cuts sustained while hiking in the woods.

FIELD DESCRIPTION: Tough-fleshed, semicircular to kidney-shaped white to gray caps with inrolled margins and white to brownish pores.

HABITAT: On living and especially dead birch trees. Abundant and easily spotted by the distinctively shaped caps on standing and downed birch trees.

DISTRIBUTION: On birch throughout its northern hemishpere range, during the growing season.

SEASON: Summer to autumn. An annual species that stays on overwinter.

LOOK-ALIKES: None.

USES: The fruiting bodies have antibacterial, antiviral, anti-inflammatory, and immune-enhancing properties. The mushroom is not eaten but is used as an extract or a bandage.

COMMERCIAL AVAILABILITY: Available online.

Shiitake, Dongu (*Lentinula edodes*)

Known as shiitake and as *dongu* in China, this is the second most commonly cultivated mushroom in the world. It appears now in many mainstream grocery stores, both dried and fresh. Its meaty quality makes it a good substitute for meat in some dishes. Like meat, it excites our taste buds for the savory, something known as umami. If it were just another cultivated edible mushroom, even a very tasty one, it wouldn't be so important a food as it has become, and the reason is because in Asia it's a medicinal food, not just a flavor and a texture.

Shiitake has at least two demonstrated orally active antitumor compounds, as well as other attributes giving it the patina of a panacea. As a result, it is eaten as a regular part of the daily diet, with the orally active dose being a little less than ¼ pound (115 g) a day, and it is prepared in many, many ways.

FIELD DESCRIPTION: Tough-fleshy, 2-inch-wide (5 cm), scaly, reddish brown caps, with white gills, yellowing on age, and short, thickish, tough-fleshy stems growing along deciduous hardwood logs.

HABITAT: On deciduous wood.

DISTRIBUTION: Southeast Asia. Collected in the wild in Japan and Indonesia.

Shiitake (*Lentinula edodest*)

SEASON: Autumn

LOOK-ALIKES: Other species of *Lentinula* are hard to differentiate, but all commercial mushrooms are this species.

USES: The fruiting bodies have immune-modulating, cholesterol-reducing, antiviral, and liver-fortifying properties. Used as an injectable anticancer drug in Asia. The fruiting bodies are cooked as a food.

COMMERCIAL AVAILABILITY: Sold fresh and dried in grocery stores and online.

THE ICEMAN AND HIS MUSHROOMS

Ötzi is the name given to the body recently found buried in ice near the border between Austria and Italy. Ötzi was a man who lived some 5,000 years ago, was murdered, and subsequently covered by snow and ice so effectively that his body, his clothes, and all that he was carrying at the time survived intact. One extraordinary element of all this is that he had in a leather satchel two mushrooms. One was the tinder polypore, *Fomes fomentarius*. The other was the birch polypore, *Piptoporus betulinus*.

Since neither of these is an edible mushroom, what were they for? The answers are not hard to find. The tinder polypore was a reliable source of quick-acting tinder to start a fire. The birch polypore could have served as a form of tinder as well, but it is more likely to have been used as a first aid kit.

Enoki (*Flammulina velutipes*)

LOOK-ALIKES: The deadly galerina grows singly but in numbers on wood and has a smooth stem with a ring; it gives a rusty brown spore print.

USES: The fruiting bodies have orally active anticancer properties and are commonly cooked as a food.

COMMERCIAL AVAILABILITY: Fresh enoki mushrooms are available in specialty food stores.

Enoki, Winter Mushroom
(*Flammulina velutipes*)

In the markets you can find little plastic packages of enoki mushrooms. These look like clusters of long, thin white stems with tiny white caps on top. This is the cultivated form of a wild mushroom known as the winter mushroom or velvet foot, *Flammulina velutipes*. It's a late autumn to winter mushroom in the wild, and this rather small, relatively short-stemmed mushroom has a somewhat tacky golden brown cap and dark brown velvety stem. In cultivation, however, these surface colors and qualities disappear completely, and the result, from a culinary point of view, is somewhat disappointing. The point missed, however, by the gourmands of the world, is that the importance of this mushroom is as a medicinal food, not a taste treat.

FIELD DESCRIPTION: Clustered, small sticky, tawny caps, white gills, and short, dark brown velvety stems (wild). Clustered in long-stemmed bunches, with very small white caps and long, slender white stems (cultivated). White spore print.

HABITAT: On deciduous wood. Wild enoki can be common in autumn on wounds on trees, especially aspens, elms, and maples, and in holes in tree trunks overwinter.

DISTRIBUTION: On hardwood trees across the northern hemisphere.

Oyster Mushroom, Hiratake
(*Pleurotus ostreatus*)

It could be argued that this is the most valuable mushroom in the world. It is not only effective in cleaning up some polluted sites in the environment but is also an important edible mushroom in some countries and a medicinal mushroom of growing significance. That it is easy to grow and available in many stores makes it even more appealing.

The common oyster mushroom (*Pleurotus ostreatus*), the one found on trees and stumps in parks and woods, contains compounds that can significantly

SOME MEDICINES TASTE MUCH BETTER THAN OTHERS

In the prefecture of Nagano, Japan, where most of the enoki is cultivated, there is a significantly reduced incidence of cancers of all kinds compared with the rest of Japan. It turns out that the people living in the Nagano prefecture are great consumers of this mushroom. Although it lacks a flavor and texture that would have wide appeal, it is known to be an orally active tumor-inhibiting mushroom that is easy to consume in a variety of ways. The inhabitants of Nagano add it to their soups or stews of mixed vegetables. It is also steamed in foil and eaten with dipping sauces. If eaten at all outside Japan, it is as a condiment or conversation piece. Fortunately, its popularity has nowhere to go but up.

reduce cholesterol and promote general well-being. The growing popularity of the king oyster (*Pleurotus eryngii*), which grows wild in Mediterranean countries and is now widely cultivated, has more to do with its flavor and texture than any medicinal value. In the market, the king oyster looks like a foot-long (30.5 cm) daikon, or white radish, with a very small cap and tiny gills at the very top of the thick, fleshy stem. Another exotic oyster mushroom, one that grows in the Levant on a giant fennel, is renowned for promoting sexual energy, a benefit it reportedly acquires from its fennel host.

FIELD DESCRIPTION: See page 112.

HABITAT: The oyster mushroom is one of the most common, conspicuous, and year-round mushrooms in much of the Northern Hemisphere.

USES: The fruiting bodies have cardiovascular, antibacterial, antiviral, anti-inflammatory, cholesterol-reducing, and immune-enhancing properties. The fruiting bodies are cooked and eaten as a food.

COMMERCIAL AVAILABILITY: Sold in upscale food markets and some large chain grocery stores.

Lion's Mane, Yamabushitake
(*Hericium erinaceus*)

The Chinese have traditionally used lion's mane as a tonic, to help digestion, ameliorate gastritis, and promote bodily vigor. Elsewhere, it is collected by mushroom hunters for food because it is hard to confuse with anything poisonous, and it offers a satisfying, meaty meal, with a flavor and texture reminiscent of crabmeat.

Recent research has found that it has antibacterial, anti-inflammatory, and tumor-inhibiting properties. That it can now be found in upscale grocery stores, often marketed as pom-pom, and is also featured on menus in some pricey restaurants is all to the good. Because it is easy to grow, its price will drop and it will become more widely available as people discover its culinary and medicinal delights and demand for it increases.

Oyster (*Pleurotus ostreatus*)

FIELD DESCRIPTION: See page 77.

HABITAT: Lion's mane is often missed by mushroom hunters who only look down. This mushroom complex typically occurs in the autumn, fruiting on trees just above one's head.

USES: The fruiting bodies have anti-inflammatory, antitumor, and antibacterial properties. The fruiting bodies are cooked and eaten as a food.

COMMERCIAL AVAILABILITY: Sold in some upscale food markets.

A HOTEL LOBBY DISPLAYING MEDICINAL MUSHROOMS?

In the lobby of a major tourist hotel in Beijing we saw an exhibit unlike any other ever seen in a hotel lobby anywhere. It was a display of natural medicinals, of plants, animals, and mushrooms. Among the exhibits was a large monkey head mushroom, the mushroom also called bear's head or lion's mane. All these animal names refer to the same mushroom genus, *Hericium*. It was in the display case because in China, where this mushroom grows wild and is also cultivated, it is a well-known medicinal food.

Cultivated caterpillar fungus (*Cordyceps militaris*)

COMMERCIAL AVAILABILITY: Available fresh and dried in Chinese markets and in an increasing number of upscale food stores

WHAT THE EAST HAS ALWAYS KNOWN THE WEST IS JUST LEARNING

While involved in a study at a major hospital complex, one of the participants occasionally showed an unexpected lengthening of the clotting time of his blood. When his diet was investigated, researchers learned that sometimes before coming in for morning testing he had dinner the previous night at a Chinese restaurant. By testing all the foods he ate, they discovered that one, the wood-ear mushroom (*Auricularia polytricha*), was responsible for the observed anticoagulant effect. Further research demonstrated that this mushroom could be helpful as a blood thinner, that platelets were less likely to clump, thus, perhaps, forestalling a thrombosis or life-threatening blood clot.

Wood-Ear, Mu-ehr
(*Auricularia auricula* and *A. polytricha*)

Traditional Chinese medicine has used the wood-ear mushroom for millennia as a tonic, as a food for convalescents, and for debilities of all kinds. It is now thought to be a natural and safe substitute for some of the benefits of aspirin. It is so much a part of the Chinese diet that the wood-ear mushroom, which has no noticeable flavor and a texture that could best be described as reminiscent of seaweed, is a component of nearly every Chinese meal. When working abroad, the Chinese take their wood-ear mushrooms with them, and small farms are set up to grow it solely for the Chinese market in countries where nobody else recognizes it as even edible.

FIELD DESCRIPTION: See page 102.

USES: The fruiting bodies have anticoagulant properties, inhibiting platelet aggregation perhaps similar to aspirin, and are believed to be helpful in reducing the risk of stroke. The fruiting bodies are cooked and eaten as a food, usually in soup.

Chinese Caterpillar Fungus; Summer Grass, Winter Worm; Vegetable Caterpillar
(*Cordyceps sinensis*)

In Asia, especially China, but also Japan, the knowledge and use of the caterpillar fungus preceded its awareness elsewhere by millennia. Although the genus *Cordyceps* and allied forms grow worldwide, and there are hundreds of known species, its medicinal value has only recently become known outside Asia. When three mid-level Chinese athletes in an international meet in the early 1990s not only won their races but also broke world records, it was assumed they had taken illegal performance-enhancing drugs. It turned out that the only compound they had taken was made from the caterpillar fungus, *Cordyceps sinensis*. There was nothing illegal about it, but it raised a host of questions about whether this compound made the difference and, if so, why.

Subsequent research discovered that the answer might be as simple as increased blood flow to the heart. This increased blood flow might also explain its popularity among aging Chinese men who are concerned about erectile dysfunction, although local mythology might also be involved. This mushroom is traditionally known as "summer grass, winter worm" and is believed to be part vegetable, part animal. What is hoped for by the male consumers of this mushroom might be a similar transformation of one of their body parts.

FIELD DESCRIPTION: Small, dark, fingerlike fruiting bodies rising up out of insect larvae.

HABITAT: Open grasslands.

DISTRIBUTION: Himalayas. Much of the harvest of these fungi comes from Tibet and is used in China and exported to the West.

SEASON: Spring and summer.

LOOK-ALIKES: Other species of *Cordyceps* can appear similar to the untrained eye.

USES: The fruiting bodies have antitumor, immune-stimulating, cholesterol-reducing, and cardiotonic properties. Used in Asia to treat lymphoma and other cancers. Increases blood flow, enhancing endurance and improving sexual performance. The fruiting bodies are cooked and eaten in soup or with other foods, or taken as an extract.

COMMERCIAL AVAILABILITY: Sold dried in Chinese markets specializing in medicinal herbs; also available online.

Another species, *Cordyceps militaris*, found throughout the northern hemispere, is being cultivated on silk worm larvae, and a relatively inexpensive mushroom, minus its insect host but with much the same reputed medicinal benefits, is now available in Chinese markets everywhere.

TIP: How Does This Fungus Grow?

The spores of the fungus invade the body cavity of an insect, usually in the overwintering larval stage, and, feeding on it, grows through it until only the shell of the insect remains. The fungus then puts up fruiting bodies to disperse its spores, and this appears as a "plant" attached to an "animal."

A CATERPILLAR MUSHROOM SOUP IS NOT FOR EVERY TASTE OR EYE

A Chinese woman came to a large mushroom gathering in Telluride, Colorado, and offered to make caterpillar fungus soup. When the soup was served, some people dropped their soup and a few even screamed. The Chinese woman made the soup as it is made in China—with the dried caterpillar still attached to the fungus. As she explained, the medicinal value is as much in the caterpillar as in the fungus, and both were essential parts of the soup. Unfortunately, when she put the dried bundle in the soup stock, it absorbed water and expanded so that a spoonful of the soup included a fat, 3-inch (7.5 cm) caterpillar dangling off the end of the spoon. The participants were shocked to see this. She was insulted that they behaved like children. It was a teaching moment, a rare opportunity to learn firsthand how another culture uses medicinal fungi. Unfortunately, the lesson was lost in the overexcited reaction to seeing a "worm" in the soup.

CHAPTER 5:

Bringing Home the Harvest: Mushroom Recipes

Preparing chanterelles

What Julia Child did for home cooking in 1965, with her groundbreaking *Mastering the Art of French Cooking*, that is, giving it a new identity, a taste, a texture, a passionate presence in the kitchen and at the dinner table, Jane Grigson did for mushrooms a decade later. Her 1975 *The Mushroom Feast* began an awakening love affair with all kinds of mushrooms cooked and used in all kinds of ways. That was even before wild mushrooms and exotic cultivated mushrooms began showing up in stores.

Today, there are more than thirty kinds of mushrooms, both wild and cultivated, available in some stores, and there's a long shelf of books devoted just to mushroom cookery. Almost every mushroom club has at some point put out its own mushroom cookbook. Some of the recipes are intriguing, and some are much more elaborate than others. Still, Jane Grigson concluded her book by saying, "There is nothing better than meadow mushrooms (*Agaricus campestris*) that you have gathered yourself, on toast, for breakfast."

Because mushroom enthusiasts want mushrooms in many of their dishes, I present here a miscellany of recipes, from black trumpet omelet for breakfast, to mushroom soup, to a few delicious mushroom-based desserts, and every course in between. Although many mushrooms need not be improved by the addition of anything but a simple sauté and light seasoning, and some mushrooms in Japan are even more simply prepared by steaming and serving with dipping sauces, I offer here a range of recipes that involve cooking mushrooms with some basic staples, such as wheat, rice, corn, barley, potatoes, and tofu. No recipes include any meat or fish, except as stock, because I want the mushroom to be the principal ingredient, not an accompaniment.

The only thing all these mushrooms have in common is that none is eaten raw; they are either cooked first or pickled or processed in some way. Because raw mushrooms have cell walls that are too tough to digest, cooking guarantees that they are not only digestible but also that we benefit from the food value they contain. The following recipes exhibit the range and depth of what wild and cultivated mushrooms have to offer us.

Rules to Follow for Eating Wild Mushrooms Safely

RULE #1:   **TRIPLE-CHECK YOUR IDENTIFICATION.**
"Falsify" your answer if possible. That is, challenge yourself by trying to see whether your identification fits any of the look-alikes. If it does, reexamine the description and photos of the mushroom.

RULE #2:   **CHECK THE CONDITION OF THE MUSHROOMS.**
Even if identified correctly (or bought in a store), make sure the mushrooms are fresh, not buggy, wormy, too soft, or moldy.

RULE #3:   **KEEP MUSHROOMS REFRIGERATED UNTIL USED.**
Edible, fresh mushrooms left outside can decompose overnight and cause a stomach upset.

RULE #4:   **ALWAYS LEAVE AT LEAST ONE UNCOOKED MUSHROOM IN THE REFRIGERATOR WHEN COOKING AND EATING WILD MUSHROOMS . . . JUST IN CASE!**
Just in case you need it for reference in a medical situation, that is. And always keep your local Poison Control number on hand.

RULE #5:   **COOK ALL MUSHROOMS, AND COOK THEM THOROUGHLY.**

RULE #6:   **COOK ALL MUSHROOMS FOR THE FIRST TIME THE SAME WAY.**
Sauté in a butter and oil mixture, cook for 5 to 10 minutes, and season lightly. This is not the ideal way to cook some mushrooms, but it works for most, and it helps you determine the mushroom's digestibility.

RULE #7:   **DON'T MIX MUSHROOMS UNTIL YOU KNOW HOW YOU RESPOND TO EACH KIND YOU COOK.**

RULE #8:   **EAT A MODERATE AMOUNT.**

RULE #9:   **IF DRINKING ALCOHOL, DRINK MODERATELY.**

RULE #10:   **AVOID GIVING MUSHROOMS, EVEN WELL COOKED, TO THE VERY YOUNG OR VERY OLD.**
Both groups have shown an inability to digest mushrooms as well as does the general population.

RULE #11:   **DO NOT FORCE MUSHROOMS ON THE UNWILLING.**
Even superb edibles, well cooked, can cause a psychosomatic stomach upset in people who are reluctant to eat them.

RULE #12:   **THERE ARE NO RULES, ONLY GUIDELINES.**
People once believed that poisonous mushrooms could be detected if silver coins thrown in the cooking pot tarnished or onions blackened. Some believed that nothing deadly grew on wood. The hardest guideline, closest to a rule, to follow is: when in doubt, throw it out. For true believers, however, it can't hurt to carry along a copy of the 23rd Psalm.

Recipe Type and Suitable Mushrooms

For quick reference when planning your mushroom menu, here is a chart that sorts types of recipes by types of mushrooms.

Recipe Type	Mushroom(s)
PICKLES	Hen-of-the-woods, orange milk cap
DIPS	Black trumpet
BUTTER	Black truffle
DUXELLES	*Agaricus*
SOUP	Mushroom barley: Morel, king bolete; bisque: lobster mushroom; hot and sour: wood-ear; noodle soup: shaggy mane, matsutake
OMELET	Black trumpet
PASTA	White truffle, chicken mushroom, shrimp russula
RICE	Matsutake
RISOTTO	Chanterelle
WILD RICE	Hen-of-the-woods
POLENTA	King bolete
POTATO	Black trumpet
KASHA	Cauliflower mushroom
Cooking Style	**Mushroom(s)**
SAUTÉ	*Hericium*, chicken mushroom, honey mushroom, fish milk cap
GRILLED	Stuffed *Agaricus* cap, King bolete
BROILED	Oyster mushroom
BAKED	Roasted blewit
TEMPURA	Giant puffball
Desserts	**Mushroom(s)**
ICED DESSERT	Chanterelle
TEMPURA	Sweet coral club
COOKIES	Candy cap

Maitake Pickles

A refreshing hors d'oeuvre, picked up with toothpicks. Crunchy and sparkling.

YIELDS: 1 PINT (270 G)

Marinade

1 cup (235 ml) dry white wine
⅓ cup (80 ml) olive oil
Juice of 1 lemon
A few slices of onion
A few sprigs of parsley and dill
A few cloves of garlic
Pinch of salt
6 peppercorns
1 pound (455 g) maitake mushrooms
Olive oil, for preserving

Bring a pot of salted water to a boil.

To make the marinade, combine the marinade ingredients.

Clean and separate the "leaves" of the maitake, and cut into bite-size pieces. Boil for 2 minutes, drain, and let cool on paper towels.

Bring the marinade to a boil and cook the mushrooms in the marinade until done to taste (crunchy to soft). Remove the mushrooms. Discard the solids from the marinade. Store the mushrooms, covered with marinade, in glass jars, with a thin layer of olive oil on top to help preserve. Store in the refrigerator.

Orange Milk Cap Pickles

A classic Eastern European way to preserve milk caps, which remain crunchy and flavorful.

YIELDS: 5 CUPS (675 G)

1 pound (455 g) *Lactarius deliciosus* or other orange, red, or blue latex *Lactarius*
4 cups (940 ml) cider vinegar
2 cups (470 ml) water
1 small onion, sliced
1 tablespoon (18 g) salt
1 teaspoon caraway seeds
6 peppercorns
3 bay leaves

Clean the mushrooms and separate the caps from the stems. Use only the caps. In a 4-quart (3.8 L) saucepan, combine the vinegar, water, onion, salt, caraway seeds, peppercorns, and bay leaves and bring to a boil. Add the mushrooms. Reduce the heat and boil gently for 20 minutes. Transfer the mushrooms to a glass jar. Pour the pickling liquid over the mushrooms. Let cool. Refrigerate covered. These mushrooms will keep for up to 3 days. Longer storage requires sterilizing the jars and implements.

(Adapted from Amy Farges's The Mushroom Lover's Mushroom Cookbook.*)*

Black Trumpet Dip

A delicious hors d'oeuvre spread on crackers, but be sure to make enough dip and have enough crackers on hand.

YIELDS: 1 CUP (225 G)

> 1 tablespoon butter
> 6 black trumpet mushrooms, diced
> 1 scallion, diced
> 4 ounces (115 g) cream cheese, softened
> ¼ cup (60 g) sour cream
> Salt

Heat the butter in a skillet over medium heat. Add the mushrooms and sauté for 5 minutes. Combine the cooked mushrooms, diced scallion, softened cream cheese, and sour cream in a bowl. Add salt to taste. Refrigerate to chill and harden. Serve on crackers or cut vegetables.

Black Truffle Butter

Like an herb butter, but better. Use as a spread on crackers or as topping or stuffing in omelets or fish dishes.

YIELDS: ¼ (112 G) POUND

> ½ ounce (15 g) black truffle (1 small truffle)
> 8 tablespoons (112 g) butter, softened

Pulverize the truffle in a mortar and pestle. Add the butter and mix. Let stand for 1 hour. Place in a container and refrigerate. Use as you would butter to spread, melt, or brush over other foods. Freeze to preserve.

Butter a slice of bread and partially toast in a toaster oven. Remove and place a few thin slices of truffle in the warm butter and return to the toaster. When done, the buttered toast will have a truffle smell and taste.

Agaricus Duxelles

These sautéed mushrooms are especially good on top of bruschetta or any crusty, toasted bread, or as a stuffing.

YIELDS: 2 CUPS (250 G)

> 1 pound (455 g) *Agaricus* (cultivated or edible wild)
> ½ cup (112 g) butter
> Salt and pepper

Clean and dice the mushrooms. Heat the butter in a large saucepan. Add the mushrooms a little at a time. Cook slowly until all the liquid has disappeared, 20 to 30 minutes. Season with salt and pepper. Cool and store in the refrigerator or freeze for later use.

Cream of Morel Soup

For purists, a cream of morel soup would be a three-ingredient dish: morels, cream, and butter. A pinch of salt and ground nutmeg adds sparkle to this already tasty dish. This also makes a morel cream sauce for pasta. (Note: Fresh morels do not work as well, and yellow morels are more flavorful than blacks, at least in some regions.) Use 4 dried morels (8 halves) per 1 cup (235 ml) of cream.

YIELDS: SERVES 4 (1 CUP [235 ML] EACH)

> 1 quart (946 ml) cream or half-and-half
> 16 dried morels, halved
> 2 tablespoons (28 g) butter
> Salt
> A pinch of nutmeg (optional)
> Chives or ramps, minced (optional)

In a stockpot, warm the cream on the stove top over low heat. Add the morels to the warm cream and allow them to soak for at least 1 hour. Remove the morels from the cream, and snip some into small pieces with kitchen shears (leave some intact).

(continued on page 172)

In a saucepan, warm the butter and sauté the morels for several minutes. Add the cooked morels to the cream and heat thoroughly (but do not bring to a boil).

Season with salt to taste. If desired, add a pinch of freshly ground nutmeg (which is best stored in the freezer) or chives for color; their flavor won't compromise the morel flavor.

This soup can be used as a sauce over pasta (it is particularly good over fusilli). Add finely chopped sautéed red pepper and scallions. One cup (235 ml) of cream of morel soup is enough sauce for ½ pound (225 g) of pasta. (If more morels are available, add more. If fresh morels are available, add them, cooked well first, to the dried and rehydrated morel soup sauce. Remember, this is a pasta dish with morels, not a morel dish with pasta.)

Lobster Mushroom Bisque

A lobster bisque without lobster! This is an easy-to-make, flavorful way to prepare the fleshy, meaty lobster mushroom.

YIELDS: SERVES 2

- 4 tablespoons (60 ml) extra-virgin olive oil
- 1 shallot, diced
- 1 stalk celery, diced
- 1 leek, cleaned and diced
- 1 lobster mushroom, diced
- 1 tomato, diced
- A pinch of chopped fresh thyme
- ½ cup (120 ml) heavy cream
- Salt and pepper
- Finely chopped chives, for garnish

Heat the oil in a skillet and add the shallot. Sauté until soft. Add the celery and leek and cook until soft, about 5 minutes. Add the mushroom and cook until tender, about 10 minutes. Add the tomato, thyme, and cream. Heat through. Season with salt and pepper. Using an immersion blender or a countertop blender, purée some of the soup, then return to the pot and stir to combine. Ladle into bowls, garnish the chives, and serve.

Shaggy Mane Soup

A great soup for a crowd, a party pleaser. Easy to freeze and bring out to heat on a cold winter day.

YIELDS: SERVES 4

- 4 tablespoons (62 g) butter
- 1 clove garlic, minced
- ¾ cup (75 g) chopped scallions
- 2 cups (140 g) chopped shaggy mane mushrooms
- 2 tablespoons (15 g) all-purpose flour
- 1 cup (235 ml) milk
- 1 cup (235 ml) chicken or vegetable stock

Heat the butter in a skillet over medium heat and sauté the garlic, then add the scallions. Cook over low heat for 5 minutes. Add the mushrooms and cook for 3 minutes longer. Add the flour and cook for 3 more minutes. Add the milk and stock, cover, and cook over low heat for 20 minutes, or until heated through.

Matsutake Noodle Soup

A little matsutake goes a long way, and this noodle soup spreads the flavor no matter how few matsutakes are available.

YIELDS: SERVES 4 TO 8

- 10 matsutake mushrooms
- Soy sauce, for brushing
- 1 tablespoon (15 ml) oil
- 1 tablespoon (14 g) butter
- 1 clove garlic, minced
- 1 red onion, diced
- 2 quarts (2 L) soup stock
- ½ pound (225 g) soba noodles
- 5 scallions, finely chopped
- Salt and pepper
- 2 tablespoons (30 ml) fish sauce

Preheat a grill.

Clean the mushrooms and separate the caps from the stems. Dice the stems and set aside. Brush the caps with the soy sauce and grill for 6 to 7 minutes. Cut into quarters or eighths.

In a skillet, heat the oil and butter and sauté the garlic and onion. Add the diced matsutake stems and cook for 10 minutes, or until soft. Bring the soup stock to a boil in a large pot and cook the pasta until tender, following the package directions. Add the scallions and grilled matsutake caps and sautéed stems. Season with salt and pepper and add the fish sauce to taste.

Hot and Sour Soup with Wood-Ear Mushrooms

The classic Chinese hot and sour soup includes wood-ear mushrooms, and this variation highlights them.

YIELDS: SERVES 6

- 6 cups (1.4 L) vegetable or chicken stock
- 12 wood-ear mushrooms
- 2 tablespoons (28 g) garlic and chile paste
- 2 tablespoons (30 ml) soy sauce
- Freshly ground black pepper
- ¼ cup (60 ml) rice vinegar
- ½ pound (225 g) soft tofu, sliced into small cubes
- 5 tablespoons (40 g) cornstarch
- 3 eggs, lightly beaten
- 1 teaspoon sesame oil
- 2 scallions, chopped
- 1 sprig cilantro, chopped

In large pot, bring the stock to a simmer. Add the wood-ears, chile paste, and soy sauce. Simmer for 10 minutes. Add the pepper, rice vinegar, and tofu. Simmer for 10 minutes longer, then bring to a boil.

In a bowl, combine the cornstarch and 5 tablespoons (75 ml) of the boiling water, and then add to the soup while stirring. Bring the soup back to a simmer.

Pour the beaten eggs in a thin stream into the soup. Let stand for 10 seconds, and then stir in the sesame oil. Serve, garnished with the scallions and cilantro.

King Bolete Mushroom Barley Soup

The classic Eastern European soup. Great for cold winter nights.

YIELDS: SERVES 6

- 1 oz. (28 g) dried king boletes (porcinis, cèpes)
- 1 cup (200 g) barley
- 8 cups (1.9 L) water
- 2 cloves garlic, minced
- ½ red onion, diced
- 2 tablespoons (30 ml) olive oil
- Salt and pepper

- ½ pint (230 g) sour cream (optional)
- Parsley for color (optional)

Break mushrooms into small pieces and soak in one cup (240 ml) of water. Let sit for one hour.

Bring one cup of barley to a boil in 7 cups (1.7 L) of water, then let simmer, covered, for 45 minutes, until soft. Heat olive oil in skillet and add minced garlic. Cook two minutes or until garlic starts to turn dark. Add diced onion and cook two minutes or until onion becomes translucent. Then add rehydrated boletes. Saute 5 minutes, adding the rehydrating liquid bit by bit. Season with salt and pepper. Add the contents of the skillet to the barley, and cook together for 15 minutes. Serve in bowls with a dollop of sour cream in each.

Black Trumpet Omelet

A perfect match to bring out the fragrance of the black trumpet.

YIELDS: 1 SERVING

- 1 tablespoon (14 g) butter
- 6 black trumpet mushrooms, cut into bite-size pieces
- 2 eggs, lightly beaten
- Salt and pepper

Melt the butter in a skillet over medium heat and sauté the mushrooms for 5 minutes. Add the eggs, cook until the eggs are dry, season with salt and pepper, and serve.

White Truffled Pasta

Use a truffle grater, if available; otherwise, use the fine screen on a vegetable grater. The amounts listed are per person.

YIELDS: 1 SERVING

- 1 medium-size white truffle
- 4 ounces (115 g) cooked pasta

Grate the white truffle over a steaming bowl of pasta. The aroma rising up out of the pasta is almost overwhelming, as will be the taste.

Chicken Mushroom Pasta

The orange mushroom pieces in the pasta are as colorful as they are tasty. A great way to eat chicken mushroom without overeating it.

YIELDS: SERVES 2 TO 4

- 1 pound (453 g) chicken mushrooms
- ¾ cup (176 ml) oil
- 1 onion, chopped
- 4 cups (940 ml) chicken or vegetable stock
- Salt and pepper
- 8 ounces (225 g) fusilli pasta (multicolored, if available)
- ½ cup (75 g) fresh peas (blanched for 30 seconds)
- Parsley, for garnish

Bring a pot of salted water to a boil.

Clean the mushrooms by cutting into bite-size pieces and wash, if necessary. Let stand on paper towels to dry somewhat. Heat the oil in a skillet over medium heat and sauté the onion until translucent. Add the mushrooms and stock to cover. Cook, covered, for at least 10 minutes, or until completely tender. Season with salt and pepper.

Cook the fusilli pasta according to the package directions, and then drain. Toss with the mushrooms and peas. Garnish with the parsley and serve.

Shrimp Russula Pasta

A seafood pasta without seafood? Nothing beats the shrimp russula, and there's no fear of shellfish poisoning.

YIELDS: SERVES 4

- 12 or more shrimp russula mushrooms
- 3 tablespoons (42 g) butter
- 3 tablespoons (45 ml) oil
- 1 clove garlic, minced
- 1 red onion, diced
- Salt and pepper
- 4 quarts (3.8 L) water
- 8 ounces (225 g) fusilli pasta
- Lemon juice, for drizzling
- 1 sprig parsley, chopped

Clean and slice the mushrooms. Heat the butter and oil in a skillet. Sauté the garlic briefly, then add the onion and sauté until translucent. Add the mushrooms and cook for 10 minutes over medium heat. Season with salt and pepper and set aside.

Bring the water to a boil in a large pot. Add the pasta and cook until al dente, following the package directions. Add the mushrooms, drizzle a little lemon juice over the top, garnish with the parsley, and serve.

Cauliflower Mushroom Kasha Varnishkas

A mushroom variation on the classic Eastern European kasha and bow-tie noodle dish. Great for a light lunch.

YIELDS: SERVES 2 TO 4

- 1 cauliflower mushroom (about 12 inches [30.5 cm] across)
- ¼ cup (60 ml) olive oil
- 1 cup (150 g) buckwheat groats (kasha)
- 1 egg
- 1 onion, minced
- 1 teaspoon salt
- 3 cups (705 ml) boiling water
- ½ cup (115 g) sour cream (optional)

Preheat the oven to 350°F (180°C or gas mark 4).

Pull apart the leaves of the cauliflower mushroom, keeping only those that are good looking, crisp, and tender (not discolored or limp); discard the mushroom base. Wash to remove any debris and drain. Measure 2 cups (140 g) of cleaned mushrooms.

Heat the olive oil in a skillet over medium heat and sauté the mushrooms for 10 minutes.

Place the groats, egg, onion, and salt in a baking pan and stir until the groats are covered. Roast in the oven, stirring occasionally, for 10 minutes, or until the groats are brown. Add the boiling water and cover. Cook until the water is absorbed, about 7–10 minutes.

Pour the cooked groats into bowl, and top with the sautéed cauliflower mushroom. Stir to combine. Add salt to taste. Top with sour cream, if desired, and serve.

Giant Puffball Panko Parmesan

Crunchy and sparkly on the outside, creamy on the inside, this is the best way to cook giant puffballs.

YIELDS: SERVES 2

1 giant puffball, cleaned and thinly sliced
1 egg, lightly beaten
1 cup (235 ml) Panko bread crumbs
½ cup (120 ml) canola oil

Dip a slice of mushroom into the beaten egg, then dredge in the bread crumbs. Repeat for each slice. Heat the oil in a skillet and sauté the mushrooms in batches until golden brown on one side, about 2 minutes. Flip and cook the other side until golden brown. Drain on paper towels, then serve.

Matsutake Rice

A classic Japanese preparation of this meaty, fragrant mushroom; it flavors everything around it.

YIELDS: SERVES 4

Pinch of salt
2 cups (470 ml) water
1 cup (195 g) uncooked rice
1 matsutake mushroom, thinly sliced

Add the salt to the water and bring to a boil in a pot. Add the rice. Top with 2 or 3 very thin slices of matsutake. Cover and steam until the water is gone. The rice should be soft and flavored with matsutake.

Chanterelle Risotto

An ideal complement for chanterelles, and an excellent lunch or dinner entrée.

YIELDS: SERVES 4

3 cups (705 ml) vegetable or chicken stock
2 tablespoons (28 g) butter
1 onion, chopped
1 cup (195 g) uncooked Arborio rice
1 cup (235 ml) white wine
Salt and pepper
1 tablespoon (15 ml) olive oil
8 ounces (225 g) chanterelles
2 shallots, minced

2 teaspoons minced garlic
1 sprig parsley, leaves snipped

Heat the stock in a stockpot over medium-high heat. Melt 1 tablespoon (14 g) of the butter in saucepan and add the onion. Cook for 2 minutes. Add the rice and stir to combine. Add the wine and cook for 1 minute. Reduce the heat and add the stock, 1 large spoonful at a time, until absorbed by the rice. Cook, stirring, for 20 minutes. Season to taste with salt and pepper, turn off the heat, and cover.

Heat the remaining 1 tablespoon (14 g) butter and the oil in a skillet, then add the mushrooms and sauté until tender, about 5 minutes. Add the shallots and garlic. Cook until the shallots are translucent. Season to taste with salt and pepper.

Ladle the risotto into soup plates. Top with the chanterelles. Garnish with the parsley.

(Adapted from Amy Farges's The Mushroom Lover's Mushroom Cookbook.*)*

Maitake (Hen-of-the-Woods) Wild Rice

Two autumn foods come together for a marriage made in the kitchen.

YIELDS: SERVES 4

1 pound (455 g) maitake mushrooms
2 tablespoons (28 g) butter
3 tablespoons (45 ml) oil
¼ cup (25 g) chopped walnuts
4 cups (940 ml) water
1 cup (160 g) uncooked wild rice
1 sprig parsley, minced
Salt and pepper

Clean the mushrooms and separate into bite-size pieces. Melt the butter and oil in a skillet over medium heat and sauté the mushrooms for 5 minutes. Add the chopped walnuts and sauté for 5 minutes longer.

Bring the water to a boil. Add the wild rice and cook for 45 minutes, checking to see that the grains do not open. When soft but still unopened, add the maitake-walnut mixture and the parsley, season with salt and pepper, and serve.

King Bolete Polenta

A popular Italian autumn dish, using polenta as a base to set off the king bolete's flavor and texture.

YIELDS: SERVES 6 TO 8

> 2 cups (275 g) cornmeal
> 2 cups (470 ml) cold water
> 6 cups (1.4 L) boiling water
> 1 tablespoon (15 g) salt
> 4 tablespoons (55 g) butter
> 4 cups (280 g) king bolete mushrooms, chopped
> ½ cup (80 g) diced onion
> 1 clove garlic, minced
> 2 teaspoons lemon juice
> ⅛ teaspoon freshly ground pepper
> ⅓ cup (80 ml) light cream
> ¾ cup (75 g) grated Parmesan cheese
> 6 caps king bolete mushrooms

Combine the cornmeal and cold water. Pour into the saucepan containing the boiling water and add 2 teaspoons of the salt, stirring constantly. Cook until thickened, about 10 minutes, stirring. Cover and cook over low heat for 10 minutes longer. Spoon into a loaf pan and let stand until cold and firm.

Preheat the oven to 350°F (180°C or gas mark 4).

Melt 3 tablespoons (41 g) of the butter in skillet over medium heat. Add the mushrooms, onion, garlic, lemon juice, the remaining 1 teaspoon of salt, and the pepper. Sauté for 5 minutes.

Remove the cold cornmeal mush from the pan. Split it in half lengthwise. Return the lower half to the pan. Spoon the sautéed mushroom mixture over the cornmeal and pour the light cream over all. Sprinkle with the grated cheese. Top with the remaining cornmeal layer.

Bake for 20 minutes. Melt the remaining 1 tablespoon (14 g) butter in a small skillet. Dip the mushroom caps into the melted butter, arrange over the top of the polenta, and bake for 10 minutes longer. Let cool, then slice and serve.

(Adapted from Craig Claiborne's The New York Times Menu Cookbook.*)*

Black Trumpet Potato

A lot cheaper than truffled potatoes but no less memorable.

YIELDS: 1 SERVING

> 1 baking potato
> 1 tablespoon (15 ml) oil
> 2 black trumpet mushrooms, minced
> Salt

Preheat the oven to 400°F (200°C or gas mark 6). Bake the potato until a fork sticks in easily, about 50 minutes. Warm the oil in a skillet and sauté the mushrooms. Season with salt. Cut the potato in half. Scoop out the potato flesh and combine in a bowl with the sautéed mushrooms. Replace in the potato skins and return to the oven for another 5 to 10 minutes, until warmed through.

Chicken Mushroom Sauté

A classic standard preparation for this favorite choice wild edible. Best served as a lunch dish or a side dish at dinner.

YIELDS: SERVES 4

> 1 pound (455 g) chicken mushrooms
> 2 tablespoons (28 g) butter
> 2 tablespoons (30 ml) oil
> ½ cup (75 g) fresh peas (optional, for color contrast)
> Salt and pepper

Clean the mushrooms carefully. Wash if necessary. Choose only soft edges; the closer to the tree, the woodier the texture. Sliver or cut into bite-size pieces.

Bring a pot of salted water to a boil and prepare an ice bath.

Combine the butter and oil in a skillet and melt over medium heat. Add the mushrooms and sauté for at least 10 minutes. If the mushrooms are very fresh, they will exude a certain amount of water so that it, in effect, stews in its own juices. While the mushrooms are cooking, blanch the peas in the boiling water for 30 seconds, then shock in the ice bath.

When the mushrooms are cooked through and tender, they usually turn a brighter orange. Some people prefer it cooked dry, so that it is like finger food; others prefer a juicier mushroom dish, so cook to your preference. Season with salt and pepper, toss with the peas, and serve.

Fish Milk Cap Sauté

The simplest, most satisfying way to prepare this abundant northeast North American summer mushroom. Its fishiness disappears, and it serves as a good, savory meat substitute.

YIELDS: SERVES 4

6 fish milk cap mushrooms
1 tablespoon (14 g) butter
2 tablespoons (30 ml) oil
1 clove garlic, minced
1 red onion, diced
Salt and pepper

Clean the mushrooms and cut into bite-size pieces. Heat the butter and oil, add the garlic, and sauté briefly. Add the onion and sauté until translucent. Add the chopped mushrooms and cook for about 10 minutes. Season with salt and pepper to taste.

Hericium (Bear's Head) Crab Flakes

This crablike texture demands a crablike preparation, and no shells. Note: Some people boil the hericium, if it's bitter, and throw off the water, then proceed with the recipe.

YIELDS: SERVES 2 TO 4

1 *Hericium*, cleaned of any old or discolored parts and its tough base
1 tablespoon (15 ml) oil
2 shallots, chopped
Salt and pepper
1 to 2 tablespoons (15 to 30 ml) lemon juice

Pull apart the *Hericium* and clean it carefully. Taste it raw to be certain it is not bitter. (If it is bitter, discard it.) Cut into a medium dice. Heat the oil in a skillet and sauté the shallots until translucent. Add the *Hericium* and sauté for 10 minutes. Season to taste with salt and pepper. Add the lemon juice to taste and serve.

Honey Mushrooms with Spinach

Honey mushrooms are great with pasta because they cling to the noodles, but here's a refreshing way to eat them with a tasty green.

YIELDS: SERVES 2

½ pound (225 g) honey mushrooms
1 tablespoon (14 g) butter
1½ teaspoons oil
Salt and pepper
1 cup (30 g) small spinach leaves

Clean the mushrooms. Chop the stems but leave the caps whole. Heat ½ tablespoon of the butter and the oil in a skillet over medium heat. Add the mushrooms, season with salt and pepper, and cook, covered, for about 5 minutes, shaking the pan often.

Uncover and continue cooking until the mushrooms are glazed and cooked through, 5 to 10 minutes longer. Add the spinach leaves and toss for about 30 seconds. Remove from the heat and add the remaining ½ tablespoon butter. Stir to combine and serve.

(Adapted from Elizabeth Schneider's Vegetables from Amaranth to Zucchini.*)*

Simply Grilled King Bolete

The no-fuss, no-muss approach to mushroom cookery. This simple preparation brings to the forefront this mushroom's meaty flavor.

YIELDS: AS DESIRED

King bolete mushrooms
Olive oil, for brushing
Salt and pepper

Heat a grill to medium.

Slice the mushrooms lengthwise. Brush with olive oil and grill for 1 minute on each side. Season with salt and pepper and serve.

Stuffed Grilled *Agaricus* Caps

The shape and size of *agaricus* caps beg to be stuffed and grilled, and this is a crowd-pleaser. Great served with salad greens for lunch or dinner.

YIELDS: SERVES 4 TO 6

12 agaricus (cultivated or edible wild)
½ cup (112 g) butter
¼ cup (60 ml) oil, plus extra for brushing
1 clove garlic, minced
1 red onion, diced

Preheat the grill.

Clean and separate the caps from the stems and dice the stems. Scoop out the gills and add to the diced stems. Heat the butter and oil in a skillet and sauté the garlic. Add the onion and cook until translucent, 3 to 4 minutes. Add the mushroom stems and gills. Sauté for 5 minutes. Place the cooked mushroom stems inside the mushroom caps. Lightly brush the caps with oil and place on the grill. Grill until soft, 5 minutes, then serve.

Broiled Crisped Oyster Mushrooms

One of the best ways to prepare oyster mushrooms, which would just soak up the oil in a simple sauté. This crisped, fleshy preparation brings out their best flavor and texture.

YIELDS: SERVES 6

12 oyster mushrooms with large caps
1 clove garlic, minced
1 teaspoon thyme
1 tablespoon (15 ml) lemon juice
Salt and pepper
2 tablespoons (30 ml) oil
1 sprig parsley, minced

Preheat the oven to 450°F (230°C or gas mark 8), line a baking sheet with foil, and place it in the oven.

Clean the mushrooms. Discard the stems and use only the caps (the stems, if present, are too tough). In a bowl, combine the garlic, thyme, lemon juice, and salt and pepper to taste. Add the oil and blend. Brush the mushroom caps with the mixture.

Place the mushrooms, gillside down, on the hot baking sheet, and cook until the tops are crisp, 3 to 4 minutes. Turn with tongs and continue roasting until browned and crisp all over, 3 to 5 minutes longer. Remove from the oven, garnish with the parsley, and serve.

(Adapted from Elizabeth Schneider's Vegetables from Amaranth to Zucchini.*)*

Roasted Blewits with Salad Greens

Crisped, fleshy caps of blewits are a great way to enhance an arugula-endive autumn salad.

YIELDS: SERVES 4

12 blewits
4 sprigs parsley
1 shallot, halved
¼ cup (60 ml) white wine
¼ cup (60 ml) water
Salt and freshly ground pepper
1 bunch arugula
2 Belgian endives
3 tablespoons (45 ml) olive oil
4 teaspoons (22 ml) sherry vinegar
1½ teaspoons soy sauce

Clean the mushrooms. Separate the caps from the stems. Set the caps aside. Chop the stems, parsley, and half the shallot and combine with the wine and water in a saucepan. Season with salt and pepper. Cover and simmer for 30 minutes.

Preheat the oven to 450°F (230°C or gas mark 8). Cover a baking dish with foil and set on the top shelf.

Rinse and trim the arugula and endives.

Combine 1 tablespoon (15 ml) of the olive oil, 1½ teaspoons of the vinegar, and the soy sauce and pour over the reserved mushroom caps.

Mince the remaining half shallot and combine with the remaining 2½ teaspoons vinegar and the remaining 2 tablespoons (30 ml) oil.

When the mushroom stems are cooked, press and drain the juices and return to the saucepan. Reduce to 2 tablespoons, about 5 minutes. Add to the shallot and vinegar mixture.

Spread the mushroom caps on the heated baking sheet, gillside up. Bake until tender throughout and crisp on the edges, 4 to 5 minutes. When cooked, toss the dressing with the greens. Arrange the greens on plates and arrange the caps on top. Grind fresh pepper over the top and serve.

(Adapted from Elizabeth Schneider's Vegetables from Amaranth to Zucchini.*)*

Sweet Coral Club Dessert

A delightful light tempura dessert with great texture and sweetness.

YIELDS: SERVES 2 TO 4

8 sweet coral club mushrooms, sliced
2 eggs, lightly beaten
Flour, for coating mushrooms
Cooking oil
Confectioners' sugar
Orange juice

Clean the mushrooms and dredge in the egg and then the flour batter. Pour the cooking oil to a depth of 1½ inches (3.8 cm) and heat to 350°F (180°C or gas mark 4) or until a drop of water sizzles. Deep-fry until golden brown, about 1 minute or so. Drain on paper towels. Sprinkle with the confectioners' sugar and drizzle with the orange juice. Serve hot.

Chanterelle Iced Desert

Chanterelles are so fragrant that they beg to be used in desserts, especially sorbets and ice creams.

YIELDS: SERVES 4

1 cup (70 g) chopped chanterelles
4 cups (940 ml) water
1 cup (235 g) sugar
1 tablespoon (15 ml) lemon juice

Place the chanterelles in a pot, cover with water, and bring to a boil. Drain and discard the water, which may smell like chanterelles but can be bitter.

Combine the 4 cups (940 ml) water and the sugar in a pot and boil for 5 minutes. Add the chanterelles and bring back to a boil. Let cool. Puree the chanterelles in a blender with the cooled sugar water and add the lemon juice. Pour into a container and

place in the freezer. Remove when firm and reblend to put air into the iced mixture. The texture will be like a snow cone.

Alternatively, add 1 cup (235 ml) cream to the container before placing in the freezer. Reblend after freezing. The texture will be like a frappuccino.

Candy Cap Cookies

Mushroom cookies with a hint of maple syrup? You can't make enough to keep them in the house.

YIELDS: 6 DOZEN COOKIES

1 cup (100 g) dried candy cap mushrooms
½ cup (120 ml) warm water
1 cup (225 g) butter, softened
1 cup (200 g) sugar
1 egg
½ teaspoon vanilla extract
2½ cups (275 g) flour

Crumble the dried mushrooms into a bowl and soak in the warm water for 15 minutes. Drain. Heat 1 tablespoon (14 g) of the butter and sauté the mushrooms until dry. Cream the remaining butter and the sugar in a large bowl. Beat in the egg and vanilla. Stir in the flour, then add the sautéed candy caps.

Form into a roll 1½ inches (3.7 cm) in diameter. Wrap in waxed paper and chill overnight.

Preheat the oven to 350°F (180°C or gas mark 4). Remove the dough from the refrigerator. Cut into thin slices and place on an ungreased cookie sheet. Bake for 8 to 10 minutes, or lightly browned at the edges. Transfer to a cooling rack and let cool before serving.

APPENDIX I:

Mushroom
Arts & Crafts

People who hunt for edible wild mushrooms are often so passionate about their pursuit that they want to surround themselves with images of mushrooms. Mushroom bric-a-brac, in the form of salt and pepper shakers, dish designs, placemats, wall posters, postage stamps, even clothing, are expressions of this passion. Some people at mushroom forays, such as the world-famous Telluride Mushroom Festival, even dress up like mushrooms and parade down the main street at the close of the event.

While many people still draw or paint pictures of mushrooms, mushroom photography has become a major part of the mushroom hunting pastime. Mushroom photography contests are held each year by mushroom clubs, both to celebrate this art form and encourage others to participate.

Some people want to use mushrooms as art, rather than use other materials to represent mushrooms. For example:

◉ While making spore prints is part of the process involved in identifying mushrooms, using spore prints in creative ways has provided some people with a means of turning a pedestrian product into a work of art.

◉ The artist's conk fungus is a hard bracket fungus with a soft underside that can be drawn on to make pictures.

◉ Inky-cap mushrooms can be soaked in water, where they will deliquesce (or auto-digest) and turn into a black inky mess, which can then be used to paint pictures or even write letters.

◉ Paper can be made from mushrooms, as crafts people share information about just how to turn hard, woody bracket fungi into pliable sheets of paper.

"Spore Print" by Samuel Stephen Ristich, Ph.D

⊙ One woody bracket fungus found in Eastern Europe has been worked into a felt-like waterproof hat.

⊙ Other mushrooms, such as small, colorful leathery bracket fungi, have been turned into necklaces, earrings, and brooches.

⊙ Fiber artists use many natural materials to dye wool, and several mushrooms have a wealth of color potential. International mushroom dye conferences are held almost every year now to allow crafts people the opportunity to get together, see what's new in the field, and talk shop with their fellow mycophiles.

A "Mastodon" spore print

Opposite page: "Spore Prints" by Samuel Stephen Ristich, Ph.D

Mushroom necklace by
Rhoda Roper

Mushroom jewelry by
Rhoda Roper

Spore Print Art

To create a spore print, first remove the cap from a gilled mushroom and place it gillside down on a piece of card stock paper. Cover it with a bowl and leave it for a few hours. Afterwards, a circular pattern of a particular color will be left on the paper. This spore print is as fine as powder and can be smudged by just touching it. Use a fixative spray to glue it in place so you can use the print in any number of art forms. A unique greeting card, for example, can be made from overlapping spore prints of the same or different colors. Using a small hand fan set up beside the mushroom as it drops its spores produces beautiful swirls and patterns in the print, which can then be sprayed and preserved.

Mushroom Jewelry

Mushrooms may not seem an ideal medium for jewelry, but there are certain kinds, primarily small flat polypores, that lend themselves to home crafting. The two most common kinds, as shown here, are the ubiquitous turkey-tail (*Trametes versicolor*) and the relatively common and conspicuous cinnabar-red polypore (*Pycnoporus cinnabarinus*) and its sub-tropical and tropical sister species, *Pycnoporus sanquineus*. These are easily collected and transported home.

Although they may appear to be dry, they should be dehydrated (in the oven or a food dehydrator) to ensure that no insect eggs survive to hatch and eat through the polypores. These polypores can then be glued together and made into necklaces, earrings, and pendants.

Artist's Conk

Of all the bracket fungi found on trees, one stands out as a common, large, perennial shelf fungus that has an underside that stains readily. Just touching it with your thumb leaves a thumbprint that is permanent. Collect it carefully so as not to mark it, and use a sharp pointed tool to draw an image on it. Place out of harm's way while it dries. Once dried the surface cannot be further marked, and the drawing is permanent. Artist's conks make popular bric-a-brac on fireplace mantles, book shelves, and desks.

Paper from Mushrooms

Different colors and textures of paper can be made from different woody or leathery conks. Turkey-tail (*Trametes versicolor*), for example, makes a very pliable white paper. The artist's conk (*Ganoderma applanatum*) makes a dark brown paper. Indian paint fungus (*Echinodontium tinctorium*) makes orange, and the rosy polypore (*Fomitopsis cajanderi*) makes a mauve paper. The mushrooms are soaked in water (1), then broken into small pieces and blended in an industrial grade blender (2). The mix is poured into a

Artist's conk by David Work

Artist's conk by David Work

Artist's conk by David Work

Paper from mushrooms, step by step

①

②

③

④

flat-bottomed container into which small wood-framed screens are dipped, lifted out, drained, and the material in the screen flipped onto a drying surface (3). There is a pectin-like substance in these mushrooms that glues the material into long-lasting paper-like sheets, some of which, for example, the turkey-tail, can even be folded without cracking (4).

Mushroom Dyes and Fiber Art

Some mushrooms can be used to dye wool and other materials, offering a rainbow of color possibilities. When mixed with mordants, these dyes can be made color-fast so that the colors won't fade on washing. While many mushrooms that give a dye, such as several of the polypores, produce yellow colors, a few, such as some species of *Cortinarius* (*Dermocybe*) give bright red colors. A few others, such as the tooth fungus *Hydnellum*, create green and at least one mushroom, a polypore (*Hapalopilus nidulans*), creates purple.

Artisans are so enamored of the red and purple dyes that there is a dyer's market for barter and sale of these mushrooms.

Amanita muscaria tapestry by Jytte Albertson. The red cap is wool dyed with *Cortinarius sanguineus*. Photo by Dorothy Smullen

A rainbow of colors—samples of mushroom and lichen dyed wool made at the International Fungi Fiber Symposium (IFFS) in Denmark. Photo by Dorothy Smullen

A rack of drying mushroom dyed wool made from *Phaeolus schweinitzii* (yellows), *Hydnellum* (green), and *Inonotus hispidus* (orange). Photo by Dorothy Smullen

Felted slippers made from *Cortinarius semisanguineus*-dyed fleece by Melanie Spock. Photo by Dorothy Smullen

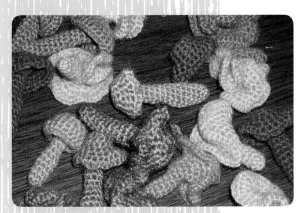

Mushroom-dyed wool made into crocheted mushrooms by Susan Hopkins. Photo by Dorothy Smullen

Fabric art moth and leaves made by Dorothy Smullen. All silks and wools are mushroom- or lichen-dyed.

Essential Guide to Major Poisonous Mushrooms, Symptoms of Poisoning, and Treatment

Poisonous Mushrooms	Onset of Symptoms	Symptoms	Treatment	Scientific Name	Edible Look-alike
DESTROYING ANGELS	8–12+ hrs	n, v, d, cr for 24 hrs monitor liver enzyme levels	false recovery followed by symptomatic kidney &/or liver failure; IV milk thistle used with success in Europe; recovery within 2 wks	*Amanita virosa, A. bisporigera, A. ocreata*	*Agaricus* spp., Parasol lepiota
DEATH CAP	8–12+ hrs	as above	as above	*Amanita phalloides*	*Agaricus* spp., Green Russula
DEADLY GALERINA	8–12+ hrs	as above	as above	*Galerina autumnalis*	Honey mushroom, magic mushroom
DEADLY LEPIOTA	8–12+ hrs	as above	as above	*Lepiota* spp. (small mushrooms)	Parasol lepiota
DEADLY CONOCYBE	8–12+ hrs	as above	as above	*Conocybe filaris* (small, easily overlooked)	Magic mushrooms
DEADLY CORTS	2 days–2 wks	n, v, progressive	symptomatic care; kidney failure may require dialysis recovery prolonged in severe cases	*Cortinarius* spp.	Chanterelles
FALSE MOREL	2–24 hrs	n, v, d, cr, int. bleeding	symptomatic care	*Gyromitra esculenta*	Morels
SWEATER	30+ min; usually 4–8 hrs	profuse sweating; tearing, salivating, visual distortion, irreg. pulse, shortness of breath	symptomatic care; atropine sulfate used if necessary	*Clitocybe dealbata*	*Marasmius oreades*
FIBER CAPS	30+ min	as above	as above	*Inocybe* spp.	*Marasmius oreades*
PANTHER	30 min–2 hrs	confusion, visual distortion; deep sleep; delusions; acting out	supportive care; recovery overnight	*Amanita pantherina*	*Agaricus* spp., Honey Mushroom
FLY AGARIC	30 min–2 hrs	as above	as above	*Amanita muscaria*	Caesar's mushroom (*Amanita caesarea* complex)
MAGIC MUSHROOMS	45–60 min	heightened sensory, awareness, hallucinations, anxiety, delusions	supportive care; recovery in 4 hrs	*Psilocybe* spp.	*Agaricus* spp., Marasmius oreades
BIG LAUGHING GYM	45–60 min	giddiness, hilarity, delusions, sense of profound insights	recovery in 4+ hrs	*Gymnopilus spectabilis*	Honey mushroom

Abbreviations used above: n (nausea), v (vomiting), d (diarrhea), cr (cramps)

Poisonous Mushrooms	Onset of Symptoms	Symptoms	Treatment	Scientific Name	Edible Look-alike
ALCOHOL INKY CAP	30+ minutes after drinking alcohol, even a few days after eating the mushroom	racing heart, tingling in the extremities after eating the mushroom, flushing, sometimes rash, headache	recovery rapid	*Coprinus atramentarius*	Shaggy mane
JACK-O'-LANTERN	30 min–2 hrs	n, v, cr, d	supportive care; recovery after 24 hrs	*Omphalotus* spp.	Chanterelles
GREEN–SPORED LEPIOTA	30 min–2 hrs	n, v, cr, d	as above	*Chlorophyllum molybdites*	Parasol lepiota, *Agaricus* spp.
PHENOLIC AGARICUS SPP.	30 min–2 hrs	n, v, cr, d	as above	*Agaricus xanthodermus* complex	*Agaricus* (edible species)
BOLETES (RED-PORED SPECIES) E.G., SATAN'S BOLETUS (*BOLETUS SATANUS* COMPLEX)	30–60 min	n, v, cr, d	recovery within 24 hrs	*Boletus* spp. (red-pored species), *Boletus satanus* complex	*Boletus edulis* (porcini)
FALSE KING BOLETE	30–60 min	severe v, d, cr	recovery overnight	*Boletus huronensis*	*Boletus edulis* (porcini)
FALSE BICOLOR	30–60 min	severe v, d, cr	recovery overnight	*Boletus sensibilis*	*Boletus bicolor*

Abbreviations used above: n (nausea), v (vomiting), d (diarrhea), cr (cramps)

Photo credits

The images in this book are courtesy of the following photographers.

Gary Lincoff: 3 (right), 4 (all), 5 (top), 8, 10, 11, 13 (both), 14 (all), 15 (all), 16 (all), 17 (left), 17 (right), 18 (both), 20, 21, 22 (bottom), 23 (top), 24, 25 (top left), 25 (top right), 26 (top left), 26 (top right), 27 (top left), 27 (bottom row), 28 (top), 29 (all), 31 (all), 34, 36 (all), 37 (all), 38 (all), 40, 42, 44, 45, 46, 52 (right), 56, 58, 60, 62, 63 (all), 68 (center), 68 (right), 70, 71 (both), 73, 74, 78 (all), 80 (both), 82, 84 (bottom), 99, 103, 109, 119 (both), 120, 122 (both), 127 (bottom), 131 (bottom), 132 (top), 133, 137, 138, 139, 140, 141, 143 (center), 143 (bottom), 144, 145, 146, 147, 148 (top), 149, 151, 153, 164, 165, 166, 191

Samuel Stephen Ristich, Ph.D.: 180, 181 (both)

Christie P. Robertson: 3 (left), 135 (both)

Rhoda Roper: 182 (top), 182 (bottom)

Naomi Salzman: 183 (right column)

Mary E. Smiley: 67 (top), 75 (right)

Dianna Smith: 9, 17 (center), 22 (top), 26 (bottom), 27 (top center), 27 (top right), 28 (bottom), 48, 52 (left), 52 (center), 81 (both), 90, 98, 101, 105, 113 (all), 114, 115, 116, 121 (both), 125, 127 (top), 130 (both), 131 (top), 132 (bottom row), 142, 148 (bottom), 150, 154, 155 (both), 157, 158, 159, 161 (both), 162

Dorothy Smullen: 184 (all), 185 (all)

Jaume Soler-Bertrolich: 156

Nancy Ward: 3 (center), 5 (center), 5 (bottom), 33, 41, 43, 57, 61, 64, 65, 168

Michael Wood: 6, 72, 86 (both), 87, 89, 110, 123 (both)

David Work: 23 (bottom), 25 (bottom), 28 (center), 67 (bottom), 68 (left), 75 (left), 76, 77, 84 (top), 84 (center), 91, 93, 95, 96, 100, 108, 111, 112 (both), 117, 131 (center), 143 (top), 160, 163, 183 (top), 183 (left column)

Resources

Mushroom Clubs

There are hundreds of mushroom clubs around the world. Most of these have websites that post their schedules, programs, and parties. The average club has between fifty and one hundred members and has scheduled mushroom hunts throughout the season, lectures and workshops off-season, and a banquet. Club members come from all walks of life and hunt mushrooms as a hobby. Membership fees are low. Online searches for your local region will often procure several options.

The National Mushroom Society

www.namyco.org
The North American Mycological Association (NAMA) is the U.S. and Canadian national mushroom club. It has members from across North America, publishes a newsletter and journal, holds an annual mushroom foray in a different part of North America each year, and has a very useful website. The website includes contact information for all affiliated clubs in North America, an excellent section on mushroom poisoning, information about speakers who are available to give talks on mushrooms, and a list of video programs about mushrooms available for home and club use.

Three websites for information on identifying wild mushrooms are:

The Northeast Mycological Federation,
www.nemf.org

The Fungi of California,
www.mykoweb.com/CAF

Mushroom Expert,
www.mushroomexpert.com

The best book available on mushroom dyes is:

Rice, Miriam, and Dorothy Beebee. *Mushrooms for Dyes, Paper, Pigments, Myco Stix.* Mushrooms for Color Press, 2007.

Note on truffles: While Europeans are inundated with books and booklets about their famous truffles, it has only been in the past year or two that information about North American truffles has been generally available. In 2007 *Field Guide to North American Truffles* by Matt Trappe, Frank Evans, and James Trappe was published. In 2009, the USDA published *Diversity, Ecology & Conservation of Truffle Fungi in Forests of the Pacific Northwest*, by James Trappe, et al., an invaluable and free guide to the many truffles and truffle-like fungi found in the Pacific Northwest, with excellent photos.

Index

Acknowledgments

Writing a book about mushroom hunting, like mushroom hunting itself, is a collective enterprise. You learn so much from others over the years that sometimes you forget how indebted you are to the knowledge and experience of your teachers and peers, and to your students, who still ask questions that keep you on your toes.

I could never have begun to learn about mushrooms without the encouragement of the members of the New York Mycological Society, especially its founder Guy Nearing, as well as Emil Lang, John Bergman, Giorgio Cavallon, Ursula Hoffmann, and Bill Williams, with all of whom I hunted mushrooms every weekend for years.

Sam Ristich, the beloved mushroom guru of northeastern North America, was the most enthusiastic naturalist I have ever encountered, and it was my great pleasure and privilege to spend years in the woods with him discovering the marvels of nature, while assimilating his knowledge and passion for all things mushroom.

If it weren't for NAMA (The North American Mycological Association), I could never have met so many avid mushroom hunters or been able to share with them the best locations for some of our most beloved edibles.

At a time when I had never been west of the Ohio River, Emanuel Salzman, M.D., invited me to attend the Aspen Mushroom Conference. Our friendship over the past decades included our 30-year running of the Telluride Mushroom Festival

I still might never have ventured outside my country's borders, were it not for Manny and Joanne Salzman's suggestion that we lead a mushroom hunting group to China in 1983. Along with Andrew Weil, M.D., we created Fungophile, Inc., and co-led mushroom study tours to more than 30 countries, on every continent except Antarctica. Without the experience gained over the decades, I would never have been able to write a book about mushroom hunting as a worldwide activity.

I owe thanks to the more than 100 mushroom clubs around the world. When you visit a new place, where perhaps you don't speak the local language, these groups of mushroom hunters are welcoming ambassadors who speak the universal language of mushrooms.

Having taught mushroom identification courses at the New York Botanical Garden since the mid-1970s, I owe a debt of gratitude to a full generation of students. Beginners make you see through their eyes the kinds of mistakes you may no longer make, but which they'll make until they acquire the field skills necessary for accurate identification.

I am particularly grateful for the help I received in writing this book, and acquiring many of its photos, from my editors Rochelle Bourgault and Tiffany Hill, and my mushroom photographer friends Dianna Smith, Nancy Ward, Mike Wood, and David Work, who were wonderfully generous with their photos, as were Rhoda Roper, Naomi Salzman, Mary Smiley, and Dorothy Smullen. Finally, I want to thank my mushroom-loving, long-suffering wife, Irene, who has accompanied me on many of these mushroom-hunting adventures, and who has helped me prepare and test many of the mushroom recipes included in this book.

About the Author

Gary Lincoff is the author, co-author, or editor of several books and articles on mushrooms, including *The Audubon Society Field Guide to North American Mushrooms*. He teaches courses on mushroom identification and use at the New York Botanical Garden. He has led mushroom study trips and forays to 30 countries across Asia, Africa, Europe, and South, Central, and North America. Lincoff cofounded and helped organize the Telluride Mushroom Festival for 25 years (1980–2004), and still participates as its principal speaker. Gary Lincoff is also a featured "myco visionary" in the award-winning documentary *Know Your Mushrooms*, by Ron Mann.